Caveat Emptor!

An Introductory Analysis
of Consumer Problems

Caveat Emptor!

An Introductory Analysis
of Consumer Problems

ROGER M. SWAGLER
Drake University

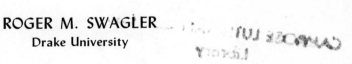

D. C. HEATH AND COMPANY
Lexington, Massachusetts Toronto London

To Carol Anne

Preface

Definitions of economics always stress the satisfaction of human wants. Thus, consumption is marked as the goal of economic activity. Extending this thought, it is only logical to apply the *basic* principles of economic *analysis* to the *actual* problems consumers face in the *marketplace*. That is the supposition on which this book is based.

The italicized words in the previous paragraph establish the approach that is taken in this textbook.

Basic—No elaborate theoretical procedures are needed to investigate consumer problems; fundamental economic principles are sufficient. This means that students who lack a background in economics can still follow the analysis.

Analysis—Describing problems is important, but it is also necessary to place them within an overall framework. This approach provides students with the means for penetrating the surface and exploring the causes of problems. It also provides cohesion, so that problems are seen to be part of an overall pattern instead of random developments.

Actual—Consumers face a variety of problems in their daily lives. These must be covered in any treatment of economics. Abstraction is necessary, but so is application to real-world problems.

Marketplace—This is the key to the analysis that follows. Consumers must operate in a large, impersonal marketplace that has the capacity to overpower them. Therefore, understanding the market forces that work on the consumer is the key to understanding consumer problems.

One more word is necessary to complete this summary—*affluence*. It is affluence that has changed the market, consumers, and consumption. The specialization that makes affluence possible requires a large and complex marketplace, within which the consumer is isolated. It is because of this isolation that consumer problems arise.

My own recent experiences have provided renewed support for that contention. I completed this book while serving as a Fulbright Professor in Liberia. The problems of affluence may seem far removed from the problems that confront an underdeveloped country, but the contrast provides an object lesson in what development does to the consumer.

Anyone who has had the opportunity of observing consumers in native markets of other countries knows how great these contrasts are. Consumers in such markets are thoroughly familiar with both the products available and the manner in which they are sold. A glance at a pile of cassava is all that is needed to estimate its value within a cent or two. As a result, buyers and sellers confront each other as equals.

These consumers are both literally and figuratively at home in their markets. They operate within them freely and easily. The problems that confound their fellow consumers in industrial countries are unknown to them. So, too, is the affluence that the latter enjoy. It is affluence that explains the difference between the friendly setting of an upcountry village on market day and the hostile marketplace in which most Western consumers operate.

Therefore, coming to grips with consumer problems requires that consumers be able to cope with the changes affluence has worked in the marketplace. Their guiding principle can be the universal *Caveat emptor,* or "Let the buyer beware." That is what this book is all about.

In recognition that consumer economics is still an emerging field, this book is designed to be used under a variety of circumstances. While it is intended as a primary text for consumer economics, it may also be used to complement other materials. Instructors with orientation towards personal finance should find it useful in providing a broad context for such matters. It could also be used in a course that surveys topics of current economic interest.

The questions and projects included at the end of the chapters are intended to be integral parts of the text.* They draw out important points, suggesting both applications and further lines of inquiry. Individual instructors can use the projects to whatever degree they see fit. The type of course and the size of the class will determine their appropriateness.

My experience has been that the projects are useful in providing students with concrete examples of the topics from the text. They furnish laboratory experience for students, who by this practical opportunity develop their understanding of economics. The Appendix contains a detailed discussion of the projects.

The annotated Bibliography and Suggested Readings included with each chapter serve a dual purpose. They are both reference for the footnotes and a list of additional readings. Some of the readings are elementary, while others are more difficult. Thus, students with differing backgrounds and interests are accommodated. The annotation is provided to inform students who want to read further on a particular question.

Full acknowledgement of the debt I owe to the many people who have helped with this project would require a volume in itself. I am pleased, however, to have the opportunity to say thank you to those who have made a

* No projects are included in Chapters 2 or 11. The material in those chapters does not lend itself to that approach.

special contribution. Professor David H. Ciscel of the Department of Economics, Memphis State University, deserves special thanks. As a former colleague and office-mate, he suffered through the development of the ideas that eventually took form in this book. Besides contributing to that development, he provided material on government regulation and read early drafts of the manuscript. I sincerely hope he never asks me to return the favor.

Thanks are also due my colleagues at Drake University. These include the chairman of the Department of Economics, Professor Dale A. Berry, who encouraged me to develop the course in consumer economics from which these ideas emerged. Professor Steven Gold, Department of Economics, and Professor Elliot Kline, Director of Programs in Public Administration, contributed significantly to the material on public consumption in Chapter 9. The students in my consumer economics courses at Drake University also deserve more than a passing acknowledgement for the stimulation they have provided.

All authors owe a debt to their editors, and in my case it is a special one. The editors at D. C. Heath have given continual help and understanding, and large measures of both were required when the preparation of the manuscript assumed intercontinental proportions. I want to thank the editors for providing the reviewers and the reviewers for their helpful comments.

Thanks go also to Cheryl Rohrsen Sypniewski and Helena Watson for their research and secretarial efforts. I must also apologize to two small Swaglers, Anne Renée and Tracy, for the months of shushing and silencing they had to endure while the manuscript was in preparation. No similar apology would be sufficient to acknowledge all that my wife has put up with these many months. This work is dedicated to her as a token of thanks for her patience, insight, and plain hard work, which contributed so much to its completion.

R. M. S.

Contents

Caveat Emptor!

**An Introductory Analysis
of Consumer Problems**

1

For Sale, One Island:
Our Price—$24

INTRODUCTION

A *Fact of Life*

In 1626, the quiet of the Manhattan Island wilderness was broken by a voice crying, "We've been taken by the Indians!" Had a group of frightened colonists been captured by savage natives? No, it turned out to be a case for Ralph Nader, not John Wayne. The occasion was the Dutch purchase of the island from the Indians, not the first instance of consumer fraud in America, but certainly one of the best-remembered.

As schoolchildren learn the story, it was the Dutchman Peter Minuit who bilked the Indians out of the land. But the Indian chief Manhasset knew what he was doing. His Canarsee tribe did not even own the island; they were just passing through when they happened on the Dutch. Manhattan was common hunting ground for *all* the tribes in the area. It is no surprise, then, that Manhasset was only too willing to unload the island on the unsuspecting white men, even if he only got $24 in junk jewelry for it.* We might reasonably assume that if the Brooklyn Bridge had been there at the time, the Dutch would have bought that too.

Nearly three and a half centuries have passed since that incident, taking with them the Dutch, the Indians, and the wilderness. Yet cries of "We've been taken!" still ring out, not just over Manhattan but over the entire United States. They are the cries of dissatisfied consumers, their voices blending into a chorus of dissent that marks one of the most significant developments in the American economy in recent years. The situation is such that should the combination of senseless hunting and DDT finally eliminate the bald eagle, as conservationists suggest they might, an

---

* There is evidence to support this version of the story, but the details of the incident are still a matter of debate. Perhaps it is best to say, as Winston Churchill did about the legend of King Arthur, "It is all true, or it ought to be."

angry consumer—fist raised in defiance—would make a fitting replacement as the national symbol.

American consumers are in revolt. That is a fact. Just a few years ago, when consumers were still being characterized as sheep, such a statement would have been ridiculed—but no more. Consumer organizations are proliferating, and some, borrowing from the civil rights movement, use boycotts, sit-down strikes, and demonstrations. Rent strikes, automobile recalls, and blasts against do-nothing government agencies have become daily features in the news. Senator Warren Magnuson, a congressional supporter of consumer protection, summarized these changes by noting:

> Consumer advocates, once considered "untouchables" by the media, now appear on the covers of national magazines. Businessmen, some of whom at first derided the consumer movement, now take it seriously and often exploit it in their advertising. Most importantly, the consumer's consciousness has been raised. . . . [5, pp. 1–2]

While these issues enjoy center stage, new heresies are building in the wings. There are ominous whisperings about the role of the consumer in a superaffluent society. The careful listener may even detect questions about the value of consumption itself. As leisure time becomes more important and attitudes towards work change, the word *consumption* is being reinterpreted. It is enough to send chills running up and down Madison Avenue—and it has [11]. Such chills, however, are not limited to Madison Avenue. The shock waves that originate with dissatisfied consumers radiate throughout the entire economy. The reason is fairly simple, but critically important. Consumption is such a fundamental part of both the economic and the social systems that changes in consumer behavior have implications for the whole society. It is hardly an exaggeration to say that consumers and consumption affect the very foundation of modern life.

The economic importance of consumption is obvious and can be illustrated by considering the impact of consumer expenditures on the economy. Consumption consistently accounts for about two-thirds of the gross national product. That means that consumer spending generates twice as much income as business investment, government expenditures, and exports combined. In 1971, consumers spent $662 billion out of a gross national product of $1,047 billion [1, p. 195].* In a country in which fractional changes in the level of income make front-page news, the impact of consumer expenditures cannot be overrated. If consumers decide to spend just a little less, as they did during 1970–1971, ulcers spread throughout the ranks of the business community. In this case, the change was only a small percentage, but it was enough to confound the experts in Washington and concern everyone from New York stockbrokers to Detroit automobile workers and San Francisco restaurateurs. They had reason to be concerned. When

---

* Includes income from unincorporated businesses with consumption.

consumers buy fewer stocks, cars, meals, or anything else, those businesses will sell less and will therefore hire fewer workers. Unemployment goes up and income goes down.

How consumer spending determines income is explained well in most introductory economics books and is not our main concern [3]. But while we are focusing on the consumer per se, we should be aware that what the consumer does has a tremendous impact on economic performance, and that any radical changes in consumption behavior would revolutionize our thinking on the economy itself. Even that does not tell the whole story, however, for consumption has a social dimension that must be taken into account.

Consumption is bound up in the American social structure in many ways. In other countries, the American is stereotyped as a big spender; we often look at ourselves that way, defining success in terms of material well-being. Indeed, many people equate mass consumption with that cherished abstraction, the American way of life. Behind the stereotype, however, there are more significant influences. The things that people buy are expressions of themselves. Consumption is a very personal thing, telling something about the personality of the individual. Thus, if we talk about changing buying habits or consumption patterns, we are talking about something basic to the individual. We are also speaking of fundamental institutions, for a great deal of consumption is carried out through the family. Any big reorganization of consumption would have an impact on the family unit; and as sociologists never tire of pointing out, anything that affects the family affects the very structure of society.

Consumption and society are related in other ways, too. Consumption is in part culturally determined. The individual's consumption is shaped by social pressures and community attitudes, so that consumption can be held up as a mirror of society. Archaeologists can reconstruct the cultures of ancient civilizations through the artifacts they uncover. Similarly, the things we consume—our artifacts—tell a lot about our culture. Our early reference to the consumer revolt as "one of the most significant developments in the American economy in recent years" is strong language, but hardly an overstatement. The consumer revolt has the potential for altering the whole structure of American society. The changes up to now, while significant, haven't gone that far; however, since both consumption and consumers are normally stable and predictable, *any* variation in their behavior is noteworthy. It is no wonder that consumers are being analyzed with increasing interest and apprehension.

The Starting Point

It is safe to say, then, that never has there been so much interest in consumer problems. Few people would disagree with that. But would there be the same unanimity if that statement were rewritten to read, "Never has there been so much interest in consumer *economics*"? Probably not, and yet the second statement follows directly from the first. In view of that connection, the proper place to look for the content of consumer economics is in the actual problems confronting consumers in the marketplace.

Such an approach requires that we face a whole new set of questions. What are these problems? Where do they originate? How can they be solved? The study of consumer economics should provide answers. It must do more, however, than provide just a handy set of tips for shoppers or a how-to guide for buying. It must go beyond the confines of personal finance, where the emphasis is on becoming a good shopper. Being a good shopper is important; it is not enough. The good consumer, in addition, understands the present-day marketplace and the consumer's role. *The ultimate goal of a study of consumer economics should be to familiarize students thoroughly with the environment in which they as consumers must operate.* This means not only enabling them to cope with the difficulties of the marketplace as it now exists, but also developing the means to bring about necessary improvement.

That is a lot to ask. When we look into the marketplace, it is not always easy to tell what is happening, let alone why. It is easy for the consumer to get lost among all the complex interrelations of the market. The study of consumer economics should enable us to make some sense out of it all. That is why we are going to deal with the everyday problems that confront all consumers, systematically analyzing what the problems are and what approaches can lead to their solution. The key word here is *systematic*. Merely discussing selected consumer problems, regardless of how important they are, is not enough. Unless we begin to see how the various problems fit together, we shall continue brushfire engagements without getting to the real cause of the conflagration. Any hope we have of victory lies in understanding the basic forces at work on the consumer in the market.

We shall be going through unfamiliar territory and must be prepared to confront philosophical as well as pragmatic questions. Thereby arises a recurring problem in economics, the division between "big thinkers" and "little thinkers." Big thinkers are prone to talk in cosmic terms about the ultimate significance of things, while little thinkers are more concerned with the way things work. Economists, as Robert Solow has noted, tend to be little thinkers, concentrating more on the particulars of a question than on its broad implications. He recognizes that there are risks involved in that approach. If we have a "single-minded focus on how the parts of the machine work," we might never think to ask "whether the machine itself is pointed in the right direction" [13, p. 108]. Nothing is to be gained by arguing over which aspect is more important; they are both important. We must accept that decision. Individuals going about their day-to-day tasks as consumers face both big questions and little questions; therefore we must deal with both here.

That underscores the challenge we face in investigating consumer problems. We may concentrate on particular aspects of market operations that cause the consumer trouble, but at the same time we have to consider the impact of such developments on the economic and social system as a whole.

If we limit ourselves to one approach or the other, we shall not be able to deal with either adequately. For analytical purposes, it is useful to distinguish between little questions and big questions, but the two cannot always be separated easily—each affects the other. We shall often find that in tracing the impact of some specific development, a little question, we shall uncover a problem with broader implications, a big question. If we are to understand the consumer problem fully, we must be willing to deal with a wide range of issues.

EXPLORING THE CONSUMER REVOLT

Belaboring the Obvious

It doesn't take a Solomon to see behind the consumer revolt. It is clearly grounded in consumer dissatisfaction and frustration, the immediate sources of which are equally clear. Things seem to cost too much, but the fancy price tags are no guarantee that the product will work when it is out of the store. Even formal guarantees may not help; pity the hapless buyer who returns a silent but supposedly guaranteed radio to find that the guarantee covered only the transistors and not the faulty tuner.

Services are even more of a problem. A call to a plumber or electrician places the homeowner's Dun and Bradstreet rating in jeopardy, while the only doctors who make house calls are in television shows (to emphasize that the stories are fictional, no doubt). If something breaks, the frustrations mount even faster. Who hasn't carried a wounded appliance from dealer to repairman to fix-it shop only to conclude that it is cheaper and easier to buy a new one?

Even sports fans are not exempt from these frustrations. They may be devoted to their favorite team, accepting inflated ticket prices and player strikes. Yet this loyalty will come to nothing if the grass (or Astro-turf) looks greener somewhere else. Owners move their franchises at the drop of a dollar sign, as fans in Boston, Milwaukee, Seattle, San Diego, Washington, and scores of other cities will attest.

The consumer has to contend with all these problems in day-to-day dealings with legitimate businessmen. With the introduction of the all-too-common prospect of consumer fraud, matters get even worse.* Magazine salesmen who promise *free* magazines ("if you pay just 67¢ a week postage"), automobile repairmen who advertise an oil change and a lubrication for $2 (and then proceed to run up a bill for $100 in needless and often worthless repairs), and loan companies that offer "low monthly payments" (at interest

---

* Communist countries, too, are vulnerable to consumer fraud. *Pravda* reports that a man showed up at a collective farm claiming to be a movie director in need of horses for a battle scene. The farm manager obliged, but never saw the horses again. Shortly thereafter, a nearby meat-packing plant reported record weekly production.

rates worthy of a loan shark) all prey on the unsuspecting consumer [5, Chap. 1].

Is anyone looking out for the consumer? It is logical that the government should be—it seems as though the government has been in the consumer protection business for generations. Somehow, though, consumer protection laws seldom make it to the books without a series of crippling amendments. And then, in their watered-down form they are enforced with a vigor that would do justice to a snail. What about the regulatory agencies charged with upholding the "public interest"? Too often they act as though they were not the least bit interested in the public, becoming instead the spokesmen for the very industries they are supposed to be regulating. The tail wags the dog, and while the agency may bark now and then, the bite is usually toothless.

As if all this were not bad enough, the poor, embattled consumer has come under fire from another quarter. Consumption itself is under attack. The phrase *consumer society* is used in a mocking and derisive manner. Radicals see it as the final stages of a sick society that must be swept away and replaced by a new order. Others simply look on the consumer as shallow and crass. The endless quest for material things becomes a point of jest, with today's consumer emerging as the grandson of Mencken's *Boobus americanus*.* This has come as quite a shock to the typical consumer, who has to give up his preoccupation with why his new lawnmower doesn't work to face the charge that he represents a repository of misplaced values.

Recently the environmentalists have also taken after the consumer. They maintain that the drive for ever greater consumption is reducing the country to a giant trash heap. A presidential committee on the environment reported:

> Each year we must dispose of 48 billion cans (250 per person), 26 billion bottles and jars (135 per person), 65 billion metal and plastic caps and crowns (338 per person), plus more than half a billion dollars worth of miscellaneous packaging material. . . . Only a small part of our solid wastes is salvaged and processed for reuse. . . . The unsalvaged remainder represents a vast potential for litter and pollution. [9]

With the energy crisis and new concern about wasted resources, such statistics have become even more alarming. As the alarm rises, the image of the consumer as greedy, selfish, and wasteful is drawn ever more boldly.

Under this onslaught, consumers cannot be blamed if they give in to the final temptation and listen to the voices of the dropouts. Their siren song beckons consumers to join them in their rejection of the system. In

---

* H. L. Mencken was a journalist and the editor of the *American Mercury*, whose vicious satire ridiculed the American lifestyle of the 1920s. Other writers of the period played on similar themes, as Sinclair Lewis did in *Babbitt*. This sort of characterization was not new, but it is no accident that it became increasingly common during the affluent 1920s.

the extreme case, the commune holds forth the promise of a better life and offers an escape from the frustrations of the marketplace. Few have gone that far, but many have taken "Simplify" as their motto: everything, from food to clothes, is billed as *natural* (including things like makeup, which are intrinsically unnatural). The new asceticism is springing up everywhere, embracing, to turn Veblen's phrase, conspicuous *nonconsumption.**

The poor consumer who has survived all of this might well ask: "Whatever happened to the American dream?" The scenario was simple enough: Work, save, get ahead; a car, a house, a second car, a better house, and so on. That's the way it was supposed to go. Now the consumer finds that when he gets those things, they do not work, and he is treated like a criminal for having—or even wanting—them. No wonder the consumer is in revolt!

The Paradox of Plenty

While the revolt of the consumer is not surprising, it is in one sense paradoxical. In what seems like a cruel jest, all this frustration is building at a time when American consumers are becoming increasingly affluent. More Americans have more money to buy more things today than any other people in history. Yet we can only nod our heads in resignation and mumble agreement when one of columnist Art Buchwald's characters, an economist, says: "I predict it will be a good enough year that people will be able to feel how miserable a healthy economy can be." If we're so rich, why aren't we happy?

This apparent paradox holds the key to the solution of consumer problems. Unraveling it shows that *the very developments that have brought our affluence have also brought us our problems as consumers.* Anyone who has survived an introductory course in economics knows that increased production (or income) follows from increases in specialization and the division of labor. As this process continues, the market becomes more and more important, since individuals become progressively less self-sufficient and more dependent on goods purchased from others:

Adam Smith is credited with first recognizing this point. He devoted the first four chapters of *The Wealth of Nations* to specialization and exchange. He noted that

> it is but a very small part of man's wants which the produce of his own labor can supply. He supplies the far greater part of them by exchanging . . . for parts of the produce of other men's labor. . . . Every man thus lives by exchanging. [12, p. 22]

---

* Thorstein Veblen was an American economist of the early part of this century. He was among the first to analyze the impact of mass consumption and recognize its relation to class and social status. In *The Theory of the Leisure Class* [14], he coined the phrase "conspicuous consumption" in reference to spending for the sake of impressing others. Despite recent changes, such traits are obviously still common.

Smith correctly hailed the process as the source of material progress. Since he was writing in 1776, he cannot be blamed for failing to see what a mess it would get us into two hundred years later. A retrospective glance should make this point clear.

Americans living on the frontier a century ago endured a bare, subsistence-level existence. They did not share our problems as consumers, because for them consumption equaled production. If the frontier family had food, clothing, and shelter, it was because members of the family had grown or killed the food, made the clothing, and built the cabin. They were self-sufficient, their consumption limited to what they themselves could produce. There were some exceptions, but contact with the outside world of the market economy was usually limited to buying salt and axe heads and selling a few agricultural products. It was a harsh life, in which the problem was production, not consumption.

As specialization increased and individuals were drawn into the market, living standards increased also. The situation changed, but most consumers could manage the changes. Americans of even a couple of generations ago did not face the consumer problems their grandchildren have had. In smalltown America, where everyone knew the butcher and the baker, market operations were personalized. The person on the other side of the counter was most likely a friend who could be relied on to guarantee the product. Those who were not reliable, like the butcher with his thumb on the scales, could be sure that the story would soon be all over town and that their competitors would thrive as a result. In short, markets were less complex and individuals could rightly feel that they maintained effective control over them.

This helps to explain an interesting and seemingly anachronistic aspect of the American character—our penchant for making folk heroes out of fast-talking, slightly shady rogues. Examples abound. The snake-oil salesman or medicine-show operator, generally portrayed sympathetically as an eccentric, became a fixture in all Westerns. Earlier, no one complained when P. T. Barnum hurried them to the "Egress," and even in the midst of a great depression, millions paid to see the antics of that consummate con man W. C. Fields. Ralph Nader would have had no chance against any of them. Notice, however, that each of these examples is set in the past, in that simpler, more personal America. Such characters are without modern counterparts. Enshrined in the past, they would be imprisoned today. This difference is a very telling illustration of the changes that have taken place. We can laugh at a stubbed toe, but serious illness is not funny; a grimace, not a grin, marks today's consumers. To understand this transformation, this "loss of innocence," as pundits like to call it, we need to understand the changes in the marketplace.

Love and War in the Marketplace

It was specialization that worked these fundamental changes. The virtue became a vice as it was extended throughout the economy. This is the ultimate paradox. The very process that lifted humanity out of centuries of poverty and enabled people for the first time to enjoy widespread material benefits has turned on them. The resulting problems are so serious that many people would happily return to a poorer but less complex life. The specifics of these changes can be easily identified. As the economy developed, the so-called roundabout method of production was refined. This featured increases in specialization, the application of capital, and the size of establishments. Its resulted in lower-cost production, which meant in turn higher incomes and living standards. It also meant, however, that individuals produced fewer and fewer of the things they used, until now it has reached the point where most of us do not produce any of the goods we consume directly.

To put it differently, individuals have become increasingly tied to the marketplace. This process is efficient to a fault, and the fault is clear. People are not just dependent on the market—they are at its mercy. Consumers have found that this is not the simple, personal marketplace of their grandparents, but a complex mechanism that overshadows the individual. Consumers no longer know the people with whom they do business. Instead of dealing with a friend when they have a complaint, they find themselves confronting a computer (which has become the symbol of modern business organization). Businesses are so large that the patronage of any one individual seems unimportant. The threat "I'll take my business elsewhere" is hollow, because that business doesn't really matter, and "elsewhere" is probably no better.

Thus, the heart of the consumer revolt, indeed the heart of all consumer problems, is that *consumers operate in a hostile environment.* Too often they are not equipped to protect themsleves. Purchasing decisions are complicated, requiring detailed technical information that most people lack. The array of products is confusing, a confusion heightened by the constant bombardment of advertisements. Under such circumstances, a gambler would never put money on the consumer. Wesley Clair Mitchell, one of this country's first great economists, identified this problem as early as 1912. Writing in the *American Economic Review,* Mitchell noted that while production was being revolutionized,

> as a unit for consuming goods, for spending money, the family . . . remained substantially where it was in colonial days. Division of labor in spending has not progressed beyond a rudimentary division between the adult men and women of the family. . . . No trade has made less progress than this, the most important of all trades. [6, p. 5]

The years that have passed since Mitchell wrote those words have only underscored his insight.

Anyone who doubts that should compare purchasing practices for a business and for a family. Businesses, even relatively small ones, have purchasing agents who specialize in buying for the company. Important purchases involve studying professional literature, setting specifications, and letting bids. Families buy a wider range of products, but no similar pattern of specialization is evident. While Professor Mitchell might be overwhelmed by today's giant multinational corporation, he would find the family, "as a unit for consuming goods," virtually unchanged from his time.

The final frustration, as if one were needed, is that consumers lack the power to control what is happening to them. They are at the mercy of forces over which they have no control. Consumers lack leverage because their individual purchases are small relative to the size of the market. As a result, they are reduced to a passive role—offered products on a take-it-or-leave-it basis. Their decision is without consequence to anyone else. In some consumers, the feeling of helplessness that comes from these conditions causes despair and may finally lead to bitterness, if not rejection of the whole idea. The alienated consumer can be found in suburbia just as easily as in the commune. In others, this helplessness generates dissatisfaction that can finally grow into militancy. Thus, those who are fighting back against the system and those who have given up on it are not so different as it might appear. Both consumer militancy and consumer alienation can be traced to *consumer impotence* in the marketplace.

The consumer revolt emerges as an outgrowth of our supercharged, superaffluent, postindustrial economy. A number of other recent developments in American life can be traced to the same source. Environmental problems, alienated workers (the blue-collar blues), and our growing uneasiness with dehumanization of society are all tied to our high level of development. We have mastered many of our traditional economic concerns—shelter, food, and clothing—only to discover that a new set of equally demanding concerns awaits us.

To illustrate the difference, contrast the type of problems we're discussing here with the consumer's traditional nemesis, inflation. Given the way in which prices have spiraled over the past few years, most consumers would probably list inflation as their major concern. In doing so, they would be following a well-established pattern, for inflation has been a concern of consumers for centuries. Economists have shared this concern and have developed an extensive analysis of inflation, although it has not always become translated effectively into policy. This familiarity hasn't exactly generated affection, but consumers have learned to live with inflation.

The consumer problems with which we are dealing were not common in earlier generations and therefore did not draw the attention of economists. Furthermore, these problems have taken consumers by surprise. Inflation, while unpleasant, is at least familiar. The new consumer problems are forbidding not just because they are new, but also because they are tarnishing the vision of the good life.

THE ANALYSIS OF CONSUMER PROBLEMS

Facing the Facts of Life

The new problems are difficult to deal with because we do not have very much experience with them. As we set out to overcome the difficulties, we should keep in mind that consumer problems are not an isolated development, but one of a series of difficulties that a highly developed economy must face. There is, in other words, nothing mysterious or demonic about them. Since they can be understood, they can be analyzed; and if they can be analyzed, they can be solved.

That point deserves emphasis because a number of people seem to have missed it. Some consumers would rather not acknowledge these problems; they either try to avoid them or vent their rage on the system itself. We can understand that reaction. People feel betrayed by a system that held out the promise of affluence, but then turned on them when affluence was achieved and compounded their problems. This feeling of betrayal has produced a number of unhealthy reactions in consumers, the worst of which is the what's-the-use syndrome. It amounts to unconditional surrender, accepting that consumer problems are so overpowering that there is nothing that can be done about them. The opposite reaction—the angry consumer—represents a more positive development. Too often, however, such anger lacks direction. As a result, it is wasted in outbursts that have no real impact. In either case, consumers emerge in the familiar role of their own worst enemies. In the words of the comicstrip character Pogo: "We have met the enemy, and he is us."

Before anything can be done about consumer problems, they must be squarely faced. The initial reaction of consumers has been immature, a tantrum or pout because someone spoiled their party. It is now time to abandon such reaction and recognize consumer problems for what they are. Once consumer problems have been identified and placed in perspective, developing a means of analysis will point the way towards solutions.

The Uses and Abuses of Theory

We have established that consumer problems follow from the inability of consumers to control their environment—consumer impotence. Medical science has unfortunately produced no magic drug to cure consumer impotence, but there is a means at hand to treat this condition. Since we are dealing with what is fundamentally a question of how the consumer operates in the marketplace, it is logical to use the best available analysis of that process. That conclusion suggests using economic theory—what we have so far called the economics of consumer problems. To be specific, we need to use the economic theory of consumer equilibrium.

Let us pause to recover from that statement. Anyone who has looked at chapters on consumer equilibrium and demand in an introductory economics textbook recalls assumptions, abstractions, and graph upon multicolored graph. But where is specific coverage of consumer problems? These problems simply do not receive textbook treatment. Since that is true, how can we use economic theory in this case? Many economists might ask the same question. Consumer economics has been shunted by economists, treated like a foster child worthy of only passing professional interest. There has been a general failure to recognize that consumer economics is the economics of consumer problems. Some economists have identified the interrelations, but their work has been at an advanced level and has not been effectively integrated into either consumer education or introductory economics [2]. There is no reason this integration must be lacking, however, since the analysis follows from elementary principles that do not involve the mystical elements often associated with the higher realms of economic theory.

It is useful to think of theory as a road map. The typical map does not identify every highway, intersection, hill, or cluster of houses. Yet it is tremendously valuable in getting from one place to another, because it gives enough information to guide you through unfamiliar territory, without burdening you with unnecessary detail. A road map that contained all possible information would only confuse the driver, assuming that it would be possible to fit such a map into the car. Theory should serve a similar function, abstracting key elements that allow making sense out of what would otherwise be a bewildering mass of detail. In short, it lets you see the forest as well as the trees. To that end, we shall use theory in our pursuits. We do not expect theory to fit every case or even that it will deal directly with the problems involved. We need the theory, however, to provide a framework.

By so using theory, we are running counter to a current fashion that holds economics to be outdated. In an era of affluence, so the argument runs, a science that deals with scarcity has little to say. We shall find out that it is those who put forth such arguments who have little to say. Obvious limits exist to applying economic theory, but it can nevertheless be a valuable tool in analyzing the new problems of affluence, just as it helps in analyzing such traditional problems as employment, prices, and output.

STUDY QUESTIONS

1. What does the phrase *consumer economics* mean to you? List topics you would include under that heading. Can you differentiate the big questions from the little questions?

2. In a poor economy, what are the principal problems facing the population? How do they contrast with the problems of an affluent economy?

3.   Over the past generation, many small neighborhood stores have closed and have been replaced by chain stores or regional shopping centers. Explain this process in terms of market development. What do such changes imply for consumers?

4.   Suppose your father says, "My old Model T was a better car than that clunker we've got now." In what sense is he right? Could the fact that the "clunker" is a better car make it a worse car?

5.   We have said that consumerism is an outgrowth of affluence, yet poverty remains a problem in the United States. What does this situation imply? Does it mean that the poor do not have to worry about consumer problems?

6.   Outline the ways in which the environmental problem and consumer problems are related. Show how both are features of a highly developed economy.

7.   There has been a widespread revival of interest in arts and crafts in recent years. How can this revival be related to market development and specialization? Can you think of any other reactions to these developments in the market?

8.   A man in California recently burned his car in front of the agency that had sold it to him because he could not get it to work right. What does this action tell you about today's consumers and their problems?

9.   Many in the "under thirty" generation wear faded jeans with patches. What does this tell you about changing attitudes towards consumption?

10.   What does the word *theory* mean? What is the test of a theory? How can you tell a good theory from a bad one?

SUGGESTED PROJECTS

1.   Consult the *Reader's Guide to Periodic Literature* or some similar index and check for articles relating to consumerism over the past ten years. What pattern emerges concerning the frequency of such articles?

2.   Look through a standard introductory economics textbook. What do you find about consumer problems? Comment.

3.   Look through some advertisements in your favorite magazines. Do you see anything in the ads that reflects the consumer movement? Did you find any ads that tried to capitalize on consumer concerns?

4.   Conduct your own survey of consumer attitudes (see Appendix). Ask the same questions of people in different parts of town, and if possible,

in smaller towns in the area. What differences would you expect from consumers in different areas? Explain.

5.   Do the problems identified under Project 4 follow from the overall problem of consumer isolation in a sophisticated, specialized economy? Classify the responses according to the development presented in the text.

6.   Consider again the problems identified. Which of them would have been significant a generation ago? a century ago?

BIBLIOGRAPHY AND SUGGESTED READINGS

1. *Economic Report of the President*. Washington, D.C.: U.S. Government Printing Office, 1972.

   An annual report on the American economy containing discussions of key problems. Also more statistics than you will ever need to know. A good source of basic information that also offers insights into what policymakers think the problems are.

2. Ferber, Robert. "Consumer Economics, A Survey," *Journal of Economic Literature*, December 1973, pp. 1303–42.

   A recent review of what economists are saying about consumer economics. Even though some material is technical, it is the best survey available. Contains an especially valuable bibliography.

3. Fusfeld, Daniel R. *Economics*. Lexington, Mass.: D. C. Heath and Co., 1972.

   For an analysis of national income and the role of the consumer, see Parts II–IV.

4. Galbraith, John Kenneth. *The Affluent Society*. Boston: Houghton Mifflin Co., 1958.

   We shall be using this book a great deal and also other works of Professor Galbraith. He was among the first to inquire into the impact of affluence on an economy, and his analysis—in Chapters 9–11—on economic organization helps to explain consumer impotence.

5. Magnuson, Warren, and Carper, Jean. *The Dark Side of the Marketplace*, 2d ed. Englewood Cliffs, N. J.: Prentice-Hall, 1972.

   A guided tour through the horrors of consumer fraud with a prescription for legislative action. Senator Magnuson has been a leading supporter of consumer protection in Congress.

6. Mitchell, Wesley Clair. "The Backward Art of Spending Money." In *The Backward Art of Spending Money and Other Essays*. New York: McGraw-Hill Book Co., 1937.

   A collection of Professor Mitchell's writings covering the first third of this century. The title essay is a splendid examination of the problems involved in spending. It is a perceptive analysis; Professor Mitchell deserves special credit for having identified the problem when it was first emerging.

7. Nader, Ralph, ed. *The Consumer and Corporate Accountability*. New York: Harcourt Brace Jovanovich, 1972.

   Vintage Nader. A collection of readings that illustrate a range of consumer problems from product quality to consumer power. The various selections take an advocate's position, while exploring many timely problems.

8. North, Douglass C. *The Economic Growth of the United States, 1790–1860*. New York: W. W. Norton and Co., 1966.

   An excellent analysis of the spread of markets and increasingly complex production in United States economic history. Features application of economic theory to historical developments.

9. *Restoring the Quality of Our Environment*. Report of the Environmental Pollution Panel of the President's Science Committee. Washington, D.C.: U.S. Government Printing Office, 1965.

   An early report on the environment and the importance of ever increasing levels of consumption in the problem.

10. Shaffer, Harry G. *The Soviet Economy*, 2d ed. New York: Appleton-Century-Crofts, 1969.

    Consumer problems in a centrally planned economy are different from those in a market system. Problems exist, however, and are covered in a series of articles reflecting both Western and Soviet views. See especially Section 8. Consumer goods have presented the Soviets with particular problems, the most serious being that Soviet consumers want more of them.

11. Silberman, Charles E. " 'Identity Crisis' in the Consumer Markets." *Fortune*, March 1971, pp. 92–95.

    A look at the impact of changing consumer attitudes on marketing and product lines. Considers what these developments portend for the future.

12. Smith, Adam. *The Wealth of Nations*. Modern Library edition. New York: Random House, 1937.

    Generally accepted as the first economics book in the English language. Chapters 1–4 concern specialization. Students who can absorb the richness of Smith's eighteenth-century style will find him well worth reading.

13. Solow, Robert M. "The New Industrial State, or Son of Affluence." *Public Interest*, no. 9, Fall 1967, pp. 100–108.

    One of America's leading present-day economists comments on Professor Galbraith's approach. His comments are relevant to the sorts of problems we shall be facing in the coming chapters.

14. Veblen, Thorstein. *The Theory of the Leisure Class*. New York: Mentor Books, 1953.

    Classic social commentary on consumption and consumers by an economist whose own tastes were somewhat unusual. That Veblen is still read indicates the depth of his insight. He fathered, among other things, a whole school of economic thought.

2

There Is Nothing
So Futile as a
Marginal Utile

THE ECONOMIC PROBLEM—AGAIN

In the Beginning

We have argued that economic analysis offers the most fruitful approach to investigating actual consumer problems. We now need to support that argument by demonstrating how theory, seemingly so abstract and detached, can be applied in this case. To do that, we must begin at the same point economic analysis begins. Identifying that point is easy enough because all of economics rises, like an inverted cone, from one proposition. The billions of words written on economics all follow from this simple fact: There isn't enough of everything for everybody.

In more conventional terms, the problem is scarcity. Scarcity arises out of two conditions. The first is that human wants, taken all together, are insatiable, or limitless; it would be impossible to add up all the things that everybody wants. On the other hand, the goods and services available to satisfy these wants are limited. They are limited because you cannot make something out of nothing. Resources or factors of production are required to produce things; because there isn't enough land on which to plant crops or build buildings, labor to put things together, or capital to build factories, things are scarce. Limit*less*/wants into limit*ed* resources won't go.

That is the economic problem humans have always faced. The task of any economic system is therefore to satisfy as many of these wants as possible. This establishes consumption—the satisfaction of human wants—as the goal of all economic activity. In a sense, *consumer economics* is a redundant expression, like *historical history* or *chemical chemistry*, because all economics is about consumption. Indeed, the word *economics* is derived

17

from the Greek *oikonomikos,* meaning home management or household finance. With this identity established, economists' neglect of consumer economics is difficult to understand. Yet the neglect exists, so that consumer economics has come to be thought of as something quite different from economics per se. Examining this alleged distinction, think for a moment what things would be like if the basic problem of economics, scarcity, were removed. If there were actually enough things for everyone, there would be no economics and no consumer problems either. Individuals could care for all their wants without experiencing any of the problems of being a consumer. That is obviously not the way things are. Consumers are forced to economize, to stretch their incomes as far as possible. The idea of scarcity, then, emerges as the logical beginning of this analysis.

Either/Or

Because it is impossible to produce enough to satisfy everybody's wants, it follows that economics involves *choices* about which goods are going to be produced. Decisions introduce the idea of cost. The fact of scarcity means that the economy cannot have more of everything, assuming that available resources are being fully used. To produce more of one good, say pretzels, it is necessary to produce less of something else, say beer. Since to get additional pretzels, the economy has to give up the opportunity to have the beer, it is correct to measure the cost of the pretzels in terms of the beer given up.

Logically enough, this measure is called *opportunity cost.* If the same resources can be used to produce either a case of pretzels or a case of beer, the real cost—the opportunity cost—of the pretzels is the case of beer that did not get produced and hence is not available for consumption. The point can be further illustrated by the so-called TANSTAAFL principle, or There Ain't No Such Thing As A Free Lunch. Resources used in one pursuit cannot be used in another. The commitment of resources to the lunch means they are unavailable for alternative use. Thus, in order that the lunch be supplied, some other product or service did not get produced.

The problem for the consumer mirrors the problem for the economy as a whole. Think of all the things you would like to have and you will see that the individual consumer has limitless wants. Why don't you have all those things? Because your income is limited. The typical individual consumer must also make decisions that involve costs. This means giving up some things in order that others may be enjoyed. Unfortunately, this point is often confused by the statement "I can't afford. . . ." Some things are indeed too expensive for most buyers; few of us could afford a villa in the South of France. But very often the statement should be translated as "I don't want to give up what I'd have to in order to get it." If someone who has just purchased a color television set tells you he cannot afford a washing machine, he is really saying that he was unwilling to give up the set in order to get the washer.

This illustration clarifies two important points about the theory of consumer demand. First, it is a theory of choice. Consumers must choose what they want from among all the goods and services available. Costs are involved since consumers cannot have everything they want and therefore must forgo some goods. But how do they decide which goods to consume? That is the second point. The consumer always chooses the good valued most highly, which is to say, the good that will bring the greatest amount of satisfaction.

THE CONSUMER, THEORETICALLY SPEAKING

More Bang for the Buck

We have now identified the basic elements involved in our theory. All that remains is to explore the details of the process by which the consumer reaches equilibrium, that happy state of being as well off as possible.* Since the whole question revolves around the satisfaction of wants, we assume that the goal of the consumer is to maximize satisfaction or utility. This is a commonsense assumption, for it only says that a person wants to be as well off as possible with the income he has.

It should be clear that if consumers follow the principle of always purchasing the good or service that brings the greatest amount of satisfaction, they will automatically reach this maximization position. If each individual purchase represents the best buy, all such purchases taken together must add up to maximum satisfaction. We are saying simply that if you have done the best you can, you cannot do any better; if you bought the good you wanted most each chance you had, there is no other way you could have spent your money and been better off.

You should notice that this is a very personal process. No one tells consumers which good they want most; they make that decision themselves according to their own tastes and preferences. Who knows what you want? You do, and if you make *rational* decisions, meaning purchases designed to fulfill those wants, you're on your way to maximizing your satisfaction. To this we must add that you are *certain* of your preferences; if you were not, you would not know what it was you wanted to satisfy. From that it follows that you would not know what goods to buy.

So now you are certain of what you want and you are going to make rational decisions accordingly, but you are still not ready to buy. You won't be ready until you know how well each good available to you will fulfill those wants. You know what you want the goods to do, but you need to know which goods will actually do it. Therefore, you must have perfect *knowledge* of the goods available. Only with this information can you evaluate all possible alternatives in terms of your preference.

The specific manner in which this evaluation takes place can be demon-

* Students may wish to review the chapter on consumer equilibrium in an introductory economics text. See references [1] or [3].

strated in different ways. However, since they all begin at the same place and end in the same place, we need not be too concerned with these differences. The simplest approach is classical marginal utility analysis, which assumes that since consumers have perfect knowledge and a given set of preferences, they know how many units of satisfaction—called utiles—are derived from each good consumed.*

Utility, however, is a sometimes thing, changing as consumption changes. Taken altogether, your wants are limitless, but your desire for a particular good at a particular time is not. This process is given the elegant name *diminishing marginal utility*. All it means is that as you get more and more of something, each extra unit will bring you less satisfaction. Certainly a steak would have different utility for someone who was starving than for a person who had just finished a seven-course meal. Anyone who has ever wondered why he or she took that last drink knows the meaning of diminishing marginal utility.

Diminishing utility helps explain how people end up with a particular mixture of goods and services. The first unit of a good they consume is the one that gives them the most satisfaction, or the most utiles. As they get more of that good, however, additional units of it bring them less satisfaction. A point will soon be reached when more of the first good will bring less satisfaction than some alternative, which means it is time to switch. This illustrates the rule of always making the purchase that gives the most utiles. By repeating the process over and over until income is gone, consumers maximize their satisfaction. A specific example will show the process at work.

Suppose you have a dollar to spend, and you can buy either beer or pretzels, both of which cost a quarter. It isn't necessary that we assume that there are only two goods, but it does make our illustration a lot simpler without changing the results. Further, assume that the marginal utility to be gained from different quantities of the two goods is represented by the data in Table 2.1. Where did we get those numbers? They are hypothetical, but they are meant to represent the amount of satisfaction you will get from the two goods, based on your relative preferences for them. Now, with an income of $1, you can buy four beers or four bags of pretzels or any combination of the two costing $1. Which combination will you actually buy?

As the arrows indicate, the maximum position is three beers and one unit of pretzels. You prefer the first beer to the first bag of pretzels (10 utiles to 5), and while the second beer gives you less satisfaction than the first, it still gives you more than the first bag of pretzels. So you buy a second beer. You now have 50 cents left to spend and find that the first bag of pretzels and the third beer offer the same utility (5 utiles each). So you buy one of each, and you are broke.

* Indifference curve analysis is currently a more popular approach. It does not require that a consumer know precisely how much utility is obtained from a good, but only that one good is preferred to another. The conclusions reached from indifference curve analysis, however, support conclusions derived from the classical approach.

TABLE 2.1   Maximizing Satisfaction:
            Illustration
            (Income = $1)

| | Utility per unit | |
Quantity	Beer @ 25¢	Pretzels @ 25¢
1	10	5
2	8	2
3	5	1
4	2	0

You have gained 28 utiles from your dollar; from your preferences, as shown in the table, there is no other way you could have spent your money and been better off. Try some different combinations and you will see that this is true. If you had drunk four beers, you would have gotten only 25 utiles of enjoyment, the same amount you would have received from two beers and two pretzels. By choosing the unit that gave you the most satisfaction each time, you reached equilibrium, a position of maximum satisfaction—consuming three beers and one bag of pretzels.

Note that for the last units purchased the utility was the same. This will always be true, for if it were not, the consumer could always improve his position by buying more of the good with the greater utility. When prices differ, marginal utility must be divided by price before a comparison can be made; equilibrium is attained when marginal utility divided by price (MU/P) is the same for all goods, or $MU_a/P_a = MU_b/P_b = \cdots = Mu_n/P_n$. Thus, when there is no other way consumers could spend their money and be better off, they have maximized their satisfaction.

His Majesty, the Consumer

The analysis of consumer equilibrium is now summarized, with the consumer in the happy position of being as well off as possible. Our theoretical treatment of the consumer is not yet complete, however; one more matter requires investigation. We have been considering the impact of consumer choice on the individual's level of satisfaction. Consumer choices have an impact beyond the consumer, however, reaching to the producer and therefore to the entire economy. In the theoretical development of the market economy, consumers do not exist in a vacuum; they are an integral part of the system.

When you buy a hamburger, your interest in it may go no further than your stomach, but you still have done something more than just buy it. You have voted for the hamburger. In voting for a political candidate, you are saying "I want this person to have the job." Similarly, when you buy the hamburger, you are telling the producer, "I like it; produce more." To vote no, you simply don't buy. Ford's best efforts could not save the Edsel, nor could *Women's Wear Daily* turn the midi-skirt into a national craze. Both were greeted with "no" votes, which means no buyers.

Consumers, by the pattern of their purchases or the way in which they cast their dollar votes, dictate to producers which goods will be produced. Thus, consumers emerge as the decision makers, using the market system as a communications mechanism. This is called consumer *sovereignty*. It is important from the viewpoint of the whole economy, since it ensures that the goods that are produced will reflect the actual demand of individuals.

It is also important to individual consumers, for it means they are not merely passive takers but active participants in production. The lines of causation are clear; consumers direct producers and therefore it is the consumers who have effective power. Instead of being lost in a complex marketplace, consumers emerge as its masters, holding life-and-death power that ensures that their wishes will be respected. We have seen that just as consumption is at the heart of economics, the consumer is at the heart of the economic system.

COMING BACK FROM WONDERLAND

"Curiouser and Curiouser"

Some students may feel light-headed at this picture of the consumer as king. It takes time, after all, to adjust to the rarefied air of unreality. Indeed, the whole analysis needs only a talking rabbit to underscore its Alice-in-Wonderland quality. The Queen of Hearts is as likely a sovereign as the consumer, and the Cheshire cat is no less believable than the marginal utile. Certainly, many economists have come to that conclusion. One such critic, labeling himself a curmudgeon, risked professional disembowelment by dismissing the theory of consumer choice as nothing more than "a set of moderately dull exercises," which have survived only because "several generations of graduate students have been taught to jump through these hoops" [6, p. 410]. Mind you, that is an economist speaking. Since the theoretical treatment is hardly a mirror of reality, there is the strong temptation to dismiss it as unworkable and without value in investigating actual consumer problems.

A more careful examination, however, indicates that such conclusions may be premature. Think about it for a minute. The theory starts from a very realistic position. It assumes that consumers have limited income and that they want to get all they can from it. That is a fairly exact description of most of the flesh-and-blood consumers I know. Yet while the theoretical consumer blissfully maximizes satisfaction, the typical consumer has to muck around in a quagmire of problems where bliss is noticeably lacking. Since they both start from the same place with the same goal, why does one make it and one fall short?

The curmudgeon quoted above gives a hint when he asks of what use economic theory is

> in buying a hi-fi set, or perfume, or a house? Most of my friends . . . are not technical experts on hi-fi sets or automobiles. To a great extent, they are not even always sure of what they want; they are not particularly expert on judging quality; their decisions are made under uncertainty, and they regard the amount of time they spend making their decisions as often being a considerable cost to themselves. [6, p. 410]

Does this curmudgeon have particularly dumb friends? No, they are not much different from the rest of us. They are unsure of themselves, facing an uncertain world in which they lack adequate information to make decisions. The theoretical consumer would not face any of these problems; without doubting, shopping, or making mistakes, the theoretical consumer just maximizes.

That is the point. Economic theory is not much use in buying hi-fi sets, perfume, or houses since all of the problems that real consumers meet are assumed away in theory. That these assumptions are not met in real life is the bottleneck that keeps the consumer from attaining the blissful state his theoretical counterpart enjoys.

If that is true, we might echo the curmudgeon's question and ask of what use a theory is that does not pertain to real-world situations. We should be missing the point. The theory sets forth the *conditions that must be met if the consumer is to maximize satisfaction.* In setting them forth, theory provides us with a guide to the problems that consumers face. After all, those assumptions are in there for a reason, and that reason should now be clear. Without them, the consumer is going nowhere—which is about as far as most consumers get.

It follows that investigating these assumptions should lead to understanding actual consumer problems. More important, investigation should also point the way to their solution. The closer real conditions come to assumed conditions, the closer the consumer comes to the goal of maximum satisfaction. Contrary to appearances, economic theory turns out to be a practical how-to guide for the consumer. By telling us what is necessary for maximizing satisfaction, it provides a focus for our investigation. We now know where to look in order to come to grips with consumer problems.

Assuming Away the Assumptions

All that remains now is to restate the critical assumption and indicate briefly how each contributes to consumer problems as we know them. Our basic rule has been that the consumer maximizes satisfaction by always buying the good that gives the greatest amount of satisfaction. If consumers are to follow that simple principle, a number of other conditions must be met. Specifically, they have to be *rational* about their spending and *certain* of their decisions, and they should have knowledge, or *information*, about the products they buy. To ensure that consumers have leverage in the market, it is necessary to add the assumption of *consumer sovereignty*—consumers acting to direct production.

The question now becomes "What happens if. . . ?" Suppose, for example, that the consumer is irrational, either lacking any clear idea of what he wants or buying on impulse. Obviously, he'll be taken, doomed to hours of agonizing over why he let that salesman talk him into putting aluminum siding on his Edsel. In plainer terms, he is a sucker, and to paraphrase W. C. Fields, the market "never gives a sucker an even break." We shall become aware that rationality is a slippery concept; but now we are accepting that the consumer needs to think through what he wants and then to buy accordingly.

What happens if we drop the assumption on certainty? Consumers may know what they want now, but what about the future? About all that is certain (never mind death and taxes) is that income, tastes, and prices will change over time. Consumers must therefore take future possibilities into account when making current decisions. That marks what the consumer thinks is going to happen as an important consideration; misjudging the future can be very expensive.

The assumption of perfect knowledge is almost comical. Ask anyone who has spent the afternoon shopping only to end up even more confused. As the curmudgeon's friends would testify, it takes time, effort, and money to gain information, all of which involve costs. Yet ignorance may be even more expensive. Many sad souls have underscored that statement with their own sweat and tears. They're the ones who bought used cars because "the body looked good" or who "didn't have time" to find out about the interest charges on a loan.

Therefore, the value of information must be balanced against its costs. How can these costs be cut? Advertising, government standards, word of mouth, and experience can all cut, but not eliminate, information costs. Certainly, inadequate information is a fundamental problem that all consumers face; therefore reducing information costs is one of the important elements in this analysis.

Finally, there is consumer sovereignty. Most consumers find it difficult enough to be faithful subjects, let alone sovereign. The market is too large and complex for most individuals to affect it directly. This does not necessarily mean they are at its mercy, isolated and powerless; it does mean that consumers must act to adjust the odds. This they can accomplish both by working through the market and by working to change it.

These fundamental considerations bear directly on the requirements for being an effective consumer. They define our task for us. We now need to look at each of them more carefully, exploring what is involved, and isolating the key elements that affect consumer performance. Our analysis begins with the elusive concept of consumer rationality.

STUDY QUESTIONS

1. Suppose you are figuring out what a year of college costs, and you add your expenses for tuition, books, room, board, and miscellaneous expenditures. Explain why that figure would *understate* the real cost of your education. Is college more expensive for a senior or a freshman? Why is it even more expensive for an all-American basketball player?

2. You use theory every day, even when you are crossing the street. What assumptions do you make if you are crossing a street in traffic? How do you tell if your assumptions were justified?

3. Look again at the example of utility maximization in Table 2.1. From the preferences shown in the table,
    a. What combination would you consume if you had $1.50?
    b. What combination would you buy if the price of pretzels fell to *two bags for 25 cents* (with income of $1)?

4. Suppose a friend who had just bought a new car told you he was dropping out of school for financial reasons. What would you think?

5. There may be no such thing as a free lunch, but what about air? Isn't air free? What about time?

6. We all know people who have trouble making up their minds. How do you think this trait would affect their behavior as consumers?

7. The list that follows contains a variety of topics familiar to most consumers. Categorize them according to the four assumptions we discussed in the text.
    a. Insurance.
    b. *Consumer Reports*.
    c. Buying on time (or credit).
    d. Consumer protection organizations.
    e. The Food and Drug Administration.
    f. Classified advertisements.
    g. Consumer boycotts.
    h. Product guarantees.
    i. Impulse buying.

BIBLIOGRAPHY AND SUGGESTED READINGS

1. Alchian, Armen A., and Allen, William R. *University Economics*. Belmont, Calif.: Wadsworth Publishing Co., 1964.

   An introductory text book that develops the theory at a more sophisticated level than most books. Particularly useful in drawing out implications of the theory and in its consideration of information costs.

2. Friedman, Milton. *Essays in Positive Economics*. Chicago: University of Chicago Press, 1953.

   An outstanding collection of essays on theory and its role in economic analysis. Professor Friedman argues that a theory should be judged on how well it predicts, not on how realistic its assumptions appear. One of the most thoughtful discussions of the topic available.

3. Fusfeld, Daniel R. *Economics*. Lexington, Mass.: D. C. Heath and Co., 1972.

   See especially Chapter 2 on choice and Chapter 23 for a good presentation of consumer equilibrium.

4. Galbraith, John Kenneth. *The Affluent Society*. Boston: Houghton Mifflin Co., 1958.

   Professor Galbraith has modified his position somewhat since this book was written, but Chapters 9–11 are still a good introduction to his view of producer sovereignty as opposed to consumer sovereignty.

5. Katona, George. *The Mass Consumption Society*. New York: McGraw-Hill Book Co., 1964.

   Professor Katona was a pioneer in consumer research. During his many years as head of the Survey Research Center, University of Michigan, he emphasized the psychological and behavioral aspects of consumption. This book considers various influences at work on the modern consumer. We shall use this and other books by Professor Katona extensively in the next two chapters.

6. Shubik, Martin. "A Curmudgeon's Guide to Microeconomics." *Journal of Economic Literature* 8 (June 1970) pp. 405–34.

   This curmudgeon takes an irreverent look at microeconomics; his view should be particularly appreciated by those students who have been baptized into some of its mysteries.

7. Stigler, George J. *The Theory of Price*, 3d ed. New York: Macmillan Co., 1966.

   An intermediate price theory text that is a good reference for students who want to follow through on some of the implications of the theory of consumer equilibrium. Chapter 1 is particularly good for our purposes, containing an excellent, and entertaining, introduction to information costs and a more general consideration of theories.

3

In Search of the Rational Consumer

WHAT DOES IT MEAN TO BE RATIONAL?

Throughout history, scholars have typically had the greatest difficulty in dealing with everyday phenomena. The nature of matter, for example, has been debated since before Aristotle. Yet even now, as scientists are unraveling the secrets of the atom, they still have not concluded precisely how things are composed. Similarly, it took centuries to understand something as commonplace as fire. Medieval thinkers could do no better than the imaginary phlogiston to explain combustion.

Such is the case with rationality, and unfortunately we haven't gotten much beyond the phlogiston stage with it. Think of all the times you have used the words *rational* and *irrational*; then try to remember their definitions. Webster's defines *rational*, "having reason or understanding; intelligent; sensible," which is why dictionaries are not of much value in cases like this. "Sensibility," with its curiously Victorian ring, may do fairly well as a short definition of rationality, but it offers us almost no help at all.

Psychologists have wrestled with defining *rationality* and have produced a variety of definitions. There exists, however, little agreement among the different schools of thought within the discipline about whether or not some particular pattern of behavior is rational. The courts, too, have a long history of involvement in this question. Over the years, a legal definition of *insanity* has emerged, constituting a judgment whether or not a person is rational. This is essentially a process of society's deciding which types of behavior it will tolerate and which it won't. Yet few would argue that all irrational people are in asylums or even that all the people in such institutions are actually irrational.

Since this confusion exists, it seems a bit presumptuous for economists simply to assume that consumers are rational and let it go at that. In so doing, they are obviously ducking a very complex issue. This artful dodge may be defended by arguing that economists have traditionally been more interested in exploring the conditions necessary for maximizing satisfaction than in investigating consumer behavior per se.

However, we cannot sidestep the issue so neatly. We must come to grips with rationality, beginning with the economist's perception of it. Paradoxically, we can probably best approach the question negatively, establishing first what rationality *is not*. According to my friends, rational is what I'm not when I argue with them. People tend to think of any pattern of behavior that is different from their own as irrational. *Irrationality* comes to be equated with *different, strange,* or *unusual*.

From the economist's point of view, such a contention is totally unjustified. Our theoretical consumer of the beer and pretzels maximized utility, or satisfaction, by consuming the combination that gave the most utiles. Where did those figures come from? They came from the individual— from whatever the seat of taste formation is within him. An officer in the Women's Christian Temperance Union would undoubtedly have a different set of tastes and would consume differently. Would she be irrational? Not at all.

Utility is highly individual, and there is no reason to suppose that everyone is going to value things in the same way. There is every reason to suppose that they will not. At the same time, individual valuation, the ranking of priorities according to tastes, is at the heart of the economist's perception of rationality. The rational consumer is one whose purchases are made according to such a ranking.

By now you should perceive a dilemma. We are in a box! The rational consumer makes purchases according to personal preferences, but if only the individual knows those preferences, how can anyone be judged to be irrational? There is a circularity to the reasoning that encourages saying no more about the subject. That is partly, perhaps, why economists have had so little to say about rationality. They have known that if they should try, they would very quickly be confronted with the inherent inconclusiveness. So they have passed over the issue very neatly, unfortunately leaving us nothing very useful to go on.

How can we challenge this fallacy that holds that consumers are rational because we assume that they are rational? The question is difficult, and perhaps the answer will not be to everyone's satisfaction. Yet the very manner of our approach suggests several fruitful lines of inquiry. It is obvious that we cannot assume rationality. True, no one can prove us wrong if we do, but we cannot prove ourselves right either. We need to provide a concrete basis for judgments. The sad truth is that the concept of rationality has been violated. Too often, rationality is defined by imposing one person's standards on another, under the assumption that any departure from such standards is irrational. For the consumer behavior we are considering, such judgment is hardly valid. While we may not be sure what rationality is, we have a fair idea about what it is not. There is so much loose thinking and so many errors of analysis on this topic that if we do nothing more than expose them, we shall have done a lot. Our hope is for still additional insight.

MISCONCEPTIONS ABOUT RATIONALITY

The Human Computer?

Many of the misconceptions that surround rationality stem from the traditional analysis of consumer maximization as we have so far outlined it. Our theoretical consumer carefully attached values to all the goods he was consuming and then purchased according to the number of utiles each offered. It takes nothing more than casual empiricism to demonstrate that consumers do not behave that way. It is easy to take the next logical step and conclude that consumers are not rational at all. That step isn't necessarily logical, but it *seems* logical because of the way in which the theory presents the consumer. Indeed, the consumer in theory is more of a caricature than a representative type. Alas, we are victims of our own analysis.

In other words, economic analysis of the consumer implies particular types of behavior for the consumer. Since we do not typically observe such behavior, there is a temptation to conclude that consumers are not rational, that they are at best creatures of habit, or more likely, behave in a random, impulsive fashion. Such judgments are superficial. It is our task to discover what behavior is consistent with the theoretical analysis.

We must avoid the temptation of jumping to conclusions—there has been far too much of that in the study of consumer behavior. Take an example. Suppose a person buys a bag of frozen French fried potatoes. The immediate urge is to say "Stop! You can get the same number of French fries for a fraction of the cost if you buy fresh potatoes and prepare them yourself." It is true that the cost would be less, but what of it?

We have alternative ways of explaining the consumer's behavior in this case. One is that he is irrational, paying more than he has to for his French fries. The other is that he is in a hurry and doesn't want to take the time to bother with fresh potatoes—it takes two to three times as long to make the French fries yourself. Which explanation is correct? Since we cannot stop and ask the consumer, we really do not know. Which explanation holds is really irrelevant; we merely want to illustrate a point: Consumer behavior is too complex to submit to simple explanations.

Notice that there is a more subtle difference between our two explanations of why the consumer bought the French fries. One assumes random behavior with no explanations or support, while the other explains the consumer's choice within a broad analysis supported by consistent theoretical propositions. We cannot tell which explanation is correct without further investigation, but the second is clearly more sophisticated. It is the difference between saying something happened and explaining why it happened [1, pp. 3–46]. Our theory does not prove we are right, no theory can, but it does support our argument by providing a consistent explanation.

It is hard to tell which is more maligned, the consumer or the economic analysis of the consumer. Both deserve more credit than they typically receive. The analysis of consumer rationality is not so much wrong as it is oversimplified. Its implications are far-reaching and embrace a variety of possible consumption patterns. What, then, is a consistent explanation of consumer behavior in terms of the analysis developed above?

Some Examples

Today's conventional wisdom asserts that consumer behavior, if not generally irrational, features a strong current of irrationality.* Consumers are characterized as bumbling, not very bright creatures who respond only to lower stimuli, seldom, if ever, using what little mental power they may have. The following statements illustrate the sort of evidence that is offered to support such contentions:

Many consumers buy on impulse.
Most shoppers shop at only one supermarket.
Charge-account customers purchase more than cash customers.
Consumers buy name brands, overlooking lower-cost substitutes.

These statements were gathered at random from the literature on consumers. Assuming that they are true, what do they really show?

Precisely what does "impulse buying" mean? Consider the housewife who makes a shopping list and plans to spend no more than $30 at the grocery store. She sees that the store is running a special, one-third off on her favorite shortening. She hadn't planned to buy it, and if she does she will go over her budget. Yet most of us would agree that she would be quite rational to buy the shortening. She would have bought it sooner or later anyway, and by buying now she can take advantage of the lower price.

Consider further the case of the husband who is on his way home and decides to stop and buy some flowers for his wife. It may be pure impulse, but if they bring joy, it is money well spent. The money spent on the flowers may bring more satisfaction than if it had been spent on something else, which clearly sanctions it with the stamp of rationality, according to our analysis. The size of the purchase is an important consideration. Buying a car or house on impulse is clearly dangerous, but if the purchase constitutes only a tiny fraction of the overall budget, it may not be worth the effort to plan the expenditure carefully. Beyond that, the fact that a decision is made quickly does not mean that it is necessarily a bad decision.

---

* *Conventional wisdom* is a phrase John Kenneth Galbraith popularized; it refers to commonly accepted ideas that are uncritically taken as articles of faith.

While impulse buying is widely discussed, it is not a very fruitful line of inquiry. It is not at all clear precisely what constitutes an impulse purchase; and even if that could be established, it cannot always be maintained that such purchases are necessarily bad. It appears that *impulse* is taken to mean "unplanned," in which case it masks many different circumstances that are better analyzed individually. If *impulse* means "random," then an element of irrationality is involved, but very little evidence indicates that such behavior is typical of most consumers.

What about grocery shoppers who shop at only one store? It is probably quite rational. There is considerable evidence that most shoppers know which grocery stores suit them and which do not. The shopper who becomes familiar with the market and then decides that a particular store is best can hardly be considered irrational for shopping there regularly. Such a decision takes more than price into account; it usually comprises quality, service, and location also.

Then there is the statement that credit-card customers buy more than cash customers. That implies that a credit card seemingly turns a normal person into an insatiable buyer. The flaw of logic in this argument should be clear. What type of customer is likely to have a credit card? The wealthy, well-established person—the sort of person who would buy a lot anyway. The credit card merely simplifies the process and provides flexibility; its use does not explain why the person buys more.

Finally, there is the matter of buying name brands, even when lower-priced substitutes of comparable quality are available. The key here is information. If consumers have become familiar with a certain brand, by either advertising or experience, they learn to count on it. Other brands may be as good, but costs are involved in finding out. It will become apparent that in some cases, the market seems to be organized to keep information from consumers. In the case of aspirin, where great price variation exists, misleading advertising confuses consumers and makes it more difficult for them to get information necessary for a decision.

These examples point out that many of the easy conclusions about consumer behavior are unwarranted. They are only confusing and divert attention fom the realities involved. If we can penetrate this confusion, we can clear away some of the obstacles that impede our understanding of consumer rationality.

Conventionality Versus Rationality

There is a common error in the examples cited above. Notice that in each case, there is an implied judgment about how people *ought* to act. One person's (or group's) standards are being applied to others. Since we have already established that consumer satisfaction is based on *individual* preferences, how can one person tell another how to consume? In economic parlance, the dictum is that one cannot make interpersonal utility comparisons. In commonplace language, "there is no accounting for tastes." Yet while this folk idiom implies a great deal of tolerance for differing consumption styles, it belies the fact that such tolerance is often very limited.

Each year stories appear in the newspaper about some neighborhood that is disrupted because a homeowner does not conform to the standards of the area. Usually it concerns someone who neglects to paint his house or mow his lawn, or something like that. Now suppose for a minute that this involved some other area of consumption, say food, and the individual in question happened not to like cheese. No one would think it strange that the person did not buy cheese. Shouldn't the same be true of house paint? If the homeowner gets more enjoyment from other types of purchases, why should he reduce his level of satisfaction and buy house paint?

What we see here is the conflict between community, or social, values and individual tastes, where *community* refers to some group such as a neighborhood, city, nation, or even larger unit. The community defines for itself an acceptable range of consumption based on its value structure, traditions, conventions, or religious beliefs. If members of the group all share in these values, if the group is homogeneous in cultural terms, things should go smoothly. Societies are commonly pluralistic, however, and everyone does not share the same values. In such cases, it is common for one group to try to impose its standards on others. This problem deserves serious consideration; when treated superficially, it is the source of significant misunderstanding. Community standards—conventionality—become the basis for judgments of rationality for all types of consumption. A second point follows from the first. If these standards are enforced, the level of satisfaction of some individuals will be reduced when they are forced to conform to someone else's tastes and preferences.

Any law or standard will reduce someone's level of satisfaction. Take the helmet laws that many states have passed, requiring motorcyclists to buy and wear helmets for their own protection. Unlike other safety legislation, laws about improved braking systems on cars, for example, these laws affect only the driver and do not make the streets any safer for the rest of us. The motorcycle driver might feel that the risk of an injury is not sufficient to warrant the cost of the helmet. The law overrides individual preferences, however, collectively judging welfare. The fact that not all states have passed such laws illustrates the variations in such judgments from area to area.

If motorcyclists are required to wear helmets, isn't there a certain logic for having pedestrians wear helmets too? They would certainly be safer. That is carrying the argument to an extreme, or perhaps beyond it, but it does show the problem. If we can restrict certain types of behavior, should we not try to restrict all types? Historically, the answer to that question has been an emphatic yes. Efforts, largely successful, were made to legislate the details of a person's consumption behavior. When they did not succeed, less formal, though not necessarily less effective, social sanctions were applied.

The smaller the unit involved, the greater the likelihood of intense problems. Consider the relations between parents and their college-age children. The typical vacation is a period of tearful confrontations sparked by the manner in which the "child" dresses, behaves, or spends money. Such confrontations are generally caused by the parents' attempts to impose their consumption standards on their children, the parents not realizing that their standards reflect tastes and preferences that their offspring probably do not share. The disagreements are likely to continue until the tastes of the parents and child converge or until the parents awaken to the realities of the situation.

A far more serious example of misjudgment concerns welfare grants in the United States today. It is safe to say that payments are not offered in a spirit of charity and compassion. Welfare recipients are not free to spend their money as they see fit. They can spend it only in designated ways on specified items. This can be justified only if one assumes that those receiving welfare do not know how they should spend their money, and those giving the money do.

There are no grounds for that assumption. Why should low-income individuals want to spend their money in the same manner in which middle-income individuals do? Forcing them to do so only reduces the effectiveness of welfare. Furthermore, it is demeaning to deny the recipient the rights enjoyed by others in the economy. Acting as if the low-income family does not know what it wants and needs places a stigma on receiving welfare.* The net result is prejudicial to the welfare system and thus to the client and the country.

This denial of individual preferences is not limited to welfare payments. It shows up repeatedly in laws that limit or restrict certain types of consumption. Probably the best (or worst) example was Prohibition. That "noble experiment" outlawed alcoholic beverages. The results were disastrous, which demonstrates that even if a majority of the population favors something (in this case, a doubtful conclusion), it cannot always be forced on the minority.

Unfortunately, that lesson was not well learned. We still have a variety of laws that cover consumption, including controls on alcohol, zoning requirements, blue laws to regulate business operations, and (until recently) limitations on birth-control information and devices. There is obvious disagreement on these restrictions; some readers may feel that all are warranted, others may feel that none are. With such differing attitudes, is it possible to establish any overall guidelines for such cases?

The key here is whether the particular case is purely personal, involving only the individual, or whether it involves (and possibly endangers) the community at large. In the latter case, personal responsibility may be enough to ensure that the interests of the community will be observed. A few irresponsible people, however, can create problems for everyone. If in-

---

* Low-income groups may have a special need for consumer education and information. That does not mean that they are incapable of making their own decisions; it means that they need better information on which to base decisions.

dividuals want to drink, that is their business, but if they then attempt to drive a car, that is everybody's concern.

In recent years, the courts have tended to adopt a broad view of civil liberties, removing restrictions on purely personal consumption decisions. In areas like censorship, efforts have been made to allow adults as wide a range of personal choice as possible, while restricting the choices of children. This represents an attempt to reconcile personal choice and community responsibility. The movement has been uneven and there are still people who take an inordinate interest in the affairs of others, but progress has been made.

Such topics are generally not included in treatment of consumer economics, but you can recognize that they are a fundamental part of such considerations. We are talking about nothing less than what you can consume and who decides whether you can consume it. These questions are going to continue to be important, and intelligent consumers must be able to deal with them in a responsible manner. Public and private responsibility come together here, for each individual is both consumer and a citizen. If individuals are to carry out their responsibilities in both roles, they must be aware of the issues on both sides.

We should now have a clear picture of the problems that arise when rationality is confused with conventionality. The central problem of our inquiry remains, however: How can we turn consumer rationality into a workable tool? We have established how not to judge rationality, and in doing so touched on several points for a more positive approach. To solve the riddle of the personal nature of consumption and get a clear idea of rationality, we must reevaluate what we mean by consumption.

A RADICAL RECONSTRUCTION

The Problem Reconsidered

Although individuals consume according to their own tastes and preferences, consumption does not take place in a vacuum. On the contrary, the consumer's decision is an extension of his background, experience, hopes, and fears. Understanding the individual's consumption encompasses all these elements [4, chaps. 2 and 3]. Consumption must be viewed as a social as well as an economic phenomenon. An important aspect of this relationship is that one person's consumption is commonly affected by how or what others consume. An example is the homeowner who did not want to paint his house. He did not care that the unpainted house detracted from the overall beauty of the neighborhood. If the neighbors care, however, then their level of satisfaction is reduced.

This illustrates what economists call externalities in consumption; in the illustration, they are negative, since one person's consumption interferes with others. Externalities may also be positive, as in the case of the person who keeps a parklike yard that others in the area can enjoy. In an increasingly crowded urban society, such interdependence is becoming more important. If settlement is scattered, there are few opportunities for consumption patterns to interact; if you cannot see your neighbor's house, then you are not likely to care whether he paints it or not. With today's high level of development, however, most people do not live that way. Individuals must now contend with one another's consumption.

There is another way in which consumer interdependence expresses itself. The examples above relate to actual consumption, but consumers' preferences may also interrelate. That is, the way one individual feels about a particular item is commonly influenced by how others feel about it. Often this is little more than feeling a need for approval; if you have bought something, it is nice if others agree that it was a good purchase. It is not uncommon, however, for the attitudes of others to be more significant, influencing the degree to which you want something. Suppose you ask a friend whether she likes a particular product or not. We can assume that her individual reaction to the product will determine her answer. If you had first told her that this product was very popular, would that have influenced her answer? It would have for many people, since their perception of products and the satisfaction they get from them is influenced by others. Harvey Leibenstein pioneered this analysis; he was among the first to specify the different ways in which consumers tastes can interact.

How this interdependence in consumption shows itself depends on the individual. For the *snob*, it may mean that as an item becomes popular, it offers less satisfaction. Snobs will reduce their consumption of a popular item, for they value exclusiveness; if everyone has the product, it loses value. The item is the same, but with increased exposure it becomes less than the particular product they bought in the first place. Snobs also buy uniqueness, and if that quality should be lost, less satisfaction ensues [9, p. 201]. The snob effect is particularly important in fashion. Many people attach great importance to being the first with the latest style; they delight in having it before it becomes generally available. Producers know this, and you will often see that a certain good is in limited edition or in a collector's edition. When the snob effect predominates, lower cost, which means greater availability, may actually mean a reduction in sales.

The opposite of the snobs are the people who are trying to keep up with the Joneses. Their interest in an item increases as others acquire it. This is the *bandwagon effect*, so common in the world of fad [9, p. 192]. A family might not have been particularly interested in color television until their neighbors bought color sets. Suddenly, that family must have one. Like the snob, these bandwagon climbers are not interested merely in the set itself; they are buying their way into what they see as respectability by being in the "in group." With the bandwagon effect, products may enjoy sudden popularity and tremendously increased sales.

Finally, there are the people who think that more is better, especially when applied to price. They buy the expensive good merely because it costs more. They too are buying more than the good itself; they are buying status. This is the classic case of conspicuous consumption that Veblen identified; hence it is referred to as the *Veblen effect* [9, p. 203; 12, chap. 4]. Consumption in such cases is meant to impress others, to show that the individual "has arrived." Such types buy liquor for the label, not for the contents of the bottle, and send their children to "all the best schools," not for the quality of the education but for the name of the institution.

The key element in each of these cases is that consumers are buying more than the goods themselves. The actual goods or services may be relatively unimportant. You may not approve of this type of consumption, and its social value is open to question, but we must admit that the individuals are acting rationally. If snobs really get added enjoyment from being snobs, then they are maximizing satisfaction by acting as they do. Behavior that may appear to be irrational or wasteful is actually consistent with their own preferences.

Similar phenomena may be observed in a variety of different situations. Consider a family that has risen from poverty—one that is not rich but judged financially secure. They might take some of their consumption in not scrimping. That is, they might splurge a little—something that might otherwise be called irrational—and derive great satisfaction since they are experiencing a luxury they had not enjoyed before. This case shows that the way in which people consume becomes consumption itself.

A related aspect of consumption, one that is becoming increasingly important, may not even involve the exchange of money. To buy things, people must work and earn money, but suppose the individual decides not to work? Is that irrational? Not if free time is worth more to the individual than extra money and the things it would buy [2, pp. 432–33]. That is becoming more common; more people are consuming leisure time these days as incomes grow and the pressures of life increase.

In the past, society has stacked the cards in favor of work. The work ethic extols the virtues of honest labor, and some religions equate work and the success presumed to follow with salvation. In the past, however, people had to work harder than they do now. Today, people have come to realize that work should lead to something besides more work and that success (and certainly salvation) is hollow if there is no opportunity to enjoy its rewards. While some people consume leisure in a most unleisurely fashion, the fact that people are not very good at it should not detract from leisure as an important consumption good.

Thus we observe tremendous variation in individual consumption patterns. Since this diversity exists, it is very difficult, and often dangerous, to generalize. Take, for example, common admonition that an individual should spend about one-fourth of his salary on housing. That is an average, and like all averages, it masks a lot of variation. As a rule of thumb, it might not be too bad. More likely though, it is like the "one-size-fits-all" clothing, which means it does not fit anyone. If this rule of thumb is to have any meaning, what must we assume? We must assume that the individual's other expenses—food, clothing, entertainment, travel, and so on—should follow a pattern, so that when they are all taken care of, one-fourth of the individual's income will be left for housing. Now that is assuming a lot about many different tastes. Suppose the person really values housing, that he wants to consume space? Suppose also that he doesn't care about travel or nights on the town? He would therefore spend less on the latter items than the average, but should spend more on housing.

We have made a number of assumptions in this example, but they were explicit. Too often, consumers are offered advice that contains even more assumptions, but they are unspecified. When we take the trouble to look closely, we see again that how an individual allocates his expenditures represents his personal taste.

Redefining "Consumption"

Our definition of consumption has now been broadened to include more than just the goods and services themselves. Our definition includes also the *psychic enjoyment* that goes with them. When a person buys something, it is unlikely that he is buying just the thing itself; typically he is also buying status, convenience, or a state of mind. The way in which the person buys may even become part of consumption, as in the case of the person who allows himself an occasional splurge.

A more sophisticated view of consumption thus emerges. It recognizes that consumers derive utility not only from the good itself but also from properties of the good. This point of view constitutes a departure from the traditional economic position that goods are valued for their intrinsic qualities only. Increasing numbers of economists are adopting the view that "goods are not goods." Their work has been at the upper levels of economic theory and is typically too complex to have filtered down to elementary treatments. We can, however, summarize their approach and in so doing lay to rest a great many misconceptions that surround consumer rationality. By now you should have the idea that such misconceptions arise out of confusion over what it is that consumers are actually consuming.

Kelvin Lancaster, who coined the phrase "goods are not goods," has been an innovator in this area. He summarized his approach in three fundamental propositions. Lancaster maintains:

> 1. The good, *per se*, does not give utility to the consumer; it possesses characteristics, and these characteristics give rise to utility.
> 2. In general, a good will possess more than one characteristic, and many characteristics will be shared by more than one good.
> 3. Goods in combination may possess characteristics different from those pertaining to the goods separately. [8, p. 133]

These remarks follow the tenor of our discussion. Indeed, they represent the logical culmination of the argument we have been developing.

Consider Lancaster's discussion of why a person buys a meal:

> A meal, treated as a single good, possesses nutritional characteristics, but it also possesses aesthetic characteristics and different meals will possess these characteristics in different proportions. Furthermore, a dinner party, a combination of two goods, a meal and a social setting, may possess nutritional, aesthetic and perhaps intellectual characteristics different from the combination obtainable from a meal and a social gathering consumed separately. [8, p. 134]

Now, that may sound ponderous, but the point is simple enough. People who "buy" meals are not really buying meals at all; they are buying a whole set of qualities or characteristics that satisfy their particular needs. A person who is starving is probably interested in a meal strictly for its nutritional value. The person who goes to a hamburger carry-out, however, is buying a meal *plus* convenience, while the patron of an elegant restaurant is buying aesthetics in addition to the meal.

While this point has not, strangely enough, been well integrated into economic theory, parts of it are commonly recognized in everyday speech. Most consumers are aware that they commonly "buy" convenience. Furthermore, you have certainly heard someone say that at a particular restaurant you are "paying for the atmosphere," or that a home in a certain neighborhood costs more "because it's a good address." Still, many commentators on consumers and consumption do not seem to recognize that point. They continue to emphasize consumption in terms of the qualities of the good per se. Such qualities may be very important, as in the case of nutritional values of foods, and more education and information are certainly needed in the area. However, to understand consumer choice and especially to make any judgments on rationality, it is essential to remember that "goods are not goods."

The discrepancy can be explained in the same terms that explain all current problems—high income and an increasingly sophisticated economy. In a low-income, nonspecialized economy, goods are valued primarily for their intrinsic qualities. The pioneer family needed shelter and obtained utility directly from the shelter itself. Anything that met that need—log cabin, sod shanty, and so on—was adequate, since it was shelter that counted, and the family was in no position to be concerned about anything else.

As incomes rose and the immediate need for shelter was met, the family could afford to broaden its concerns and include such elements as comfort and appearance in its consideration of housing. Today, that process has gone so far that shelter is hardly emphasized as a quality of housing.* Any advertisement for a new apartment complex will tell you more about tennis courts, swimming pools, saunas, and game rooms than about the apartment itself. Similarly, most home buyers take shelter for granted and concentrate on finding the right style, neighborhood, and location.

---

* We should note that low-income groups constitute an important exception to this rule. Their concerns are more elemental, centering around the lack of adequate shelter itself. This, however, only underscores the point we are making. The problems of the poor are considered specifically in Chapter 10.

Thinking about consumption has not changed as conditions have changed. We still think in terms that may have been appropriate fifty or a hundred years ago, when consumers' incomes were more limited, but these terms do not fit the realities or today's affluence. As a result, we have tended to treat consumption in terms that are far too simple to account for all its complexities. Investigators have been getting the wrong answers because they have been asking the wrong questions and they have been asking the wrong questions because they have failed to understand what consumption really is.

Many of the judgments commonly passed on individuals' consumption are hopelessly naïve. An observer might note, for example, that a housewife is passing up the "best buys" in her weekly grocery shopping and therefore conclude that she is not a careful shopper. That would be true if she were buying only the good itself, but most likely she isn't. She is buying the good *plus some other set of qualities that she values*. In this case, it is clearly the observer, not the housewife, who is confused.

TOWARDS A "RULE OF REASON"

The Consumer's Habitat

Consumers are probably much more rational than most people think. We have certainly established that most of the evidence mustered to demonstrate that consumers are irrational will not stand up under close examination. Consumption is so complex that no simple axioms can deal with it adequately. Now that we understand those complexities, we are in a position to evaluate consumer rationality more carefully. Doing so, however, requires that we consider not only consumers, but also the environment in which they operate. Most of what we have so far said concerns consumers themselves and how they perceive their consumption. A variety of stimuli from the consumer's environment affect their perceptions. These stimuli, and indeed, the consumer's environment itself, may impede rather than facilitate consumer decision making.

An analogy will be helpful in understanding what that means. A scientist carries out experiments—growing bacteria cultures, for example—under carefully controlled laboratory conditions. If those same experiments were performed outside the laboratory, would you expect the results to be the same? Of course not. In a nonsterile environment, airborne bacteria and other agents would interfere with the experiment, altering and probably invalidating the results. The same thing is true of the consumer. Most evaluations of consumer rationality are written *as though* consumption were carried out in a clinical environment highly favorable to the consumer. Under such conditions, any errors or mistakes can be assumed to be evidence of irrationality and attributed to the consumer. The error in logic should be clear. The consumer's actual habitat is not conducive to careful, rational decision making. Indeed, if we had to characterize today's market, it would appear that every possible obstacle had been erected to prevent the consumer from making a rational decision.

Take life insurance for example. Life insurance is important—but how is the consumer to find out about it? Each company's policies are slightly different from those of its competitors, so that comparing policies by talking to different agents can be confusing. Under pressure from consumers, insurance advertising has improved recently, but some of it still uses scare techniques and does not cover the real differences among types of insurance. It is hardly surprising that some consumers buy the wrong kind of insurance. It may be more surprising that many of them manage to buy the right kind. The different types of insurance policies illustrate what economists call product differentiation. That phrase refers to products that are essentially the same but made to appear different by superficial changes, packaging, and advertising. All of that is not only very expensive, it is also very confusing. The next time you are in a grocery store, pick out some household item— soaps, for example—and notice how many different kinds line the shelves. You may find over fifty different kinds of soaps and detergents, offered in such a confusing array that it would befuddle the most diligent shopper.

Let us look at another way in which the market is rigged against the consumer. American automobile producers resisted safety standards for years, maintaining that "safety won't sell." They pointed to evidence indicating more buyer interest in styling, performance, and comfort. The evidence may have been valid, but we have to ask, Why? The answer is simple enough. Detroit has advertised its products almost solely in those terms, so that car buyers naturally view such factors as important. If fifty years of advertising had stressed safety, quality, and economy, consumers would work from different standards.

You can go on thinking up your own examples. The market is simply not organized in a way to facilitate careful decisions by consumers. Some observers have made stronger allegations, indicating that it is impossible for consumers to think through alternatives and make choices based on their own judgment. Consumers may think they are rational, but in truth their judgment is influenced, if not controlled, by producers.

John Kenneth Galbraith has been a champion of this view, characterizing the consumer as a pitiful creature, brainwashed by advertising and manipulated by corporate image makers, wanting things because he is told to want them. He is, to modify Galbraith's own analogy, in the position of a squirrel that struggles "to keep abreast of the wheel that is propelled by his own efforts" [3, p. 125]. To Professor Galbraith, understanding the economic system and the consumer's role in it "means recognizing that wants are dependent upon production." This view

accords the producer the function both of making the goods and of making the desires for them. It recognizes that production, . . . through advertising and related activities creates the wants it seeks to satisfy. [3, p. 127]

In this context, any talk of consumer rationality is clearly nonsense: consumers merely react to the specific direction of advertisers and to the broader pressures of a society that producers dominate.

We need not accept Professor Galbraith's position to appreciate that he is correct about the obstacles that confront the consumer. Producers do exercise influence over consumers, influence that may be, as Galbraith says, all-pervasive. On the other hand, consumers may overcome these difficulties and arrive at truly rational decisions, and this is our hypothesis. Our purpose here is not to debate the merits of Professor Galbraith's position.* Rather, it is to emphasize that if consumers operate rationally, they do so in spite of, not because of, *the way in which the marketplace is organized.*

Clearly, then, the consumer who tries to choose intelligently among carefully considered alternatives faces a difficult task. Most of the forces in the marketplace impede the consumer. We can see now that any evidence of rationality represents a triumph and means that the consumer has beaten the odds. It suggests that consumers deserve a lot more credit than they are commonly given, and prompts the supposition: If some consumers manage rational decisions under adverse conditions, how much more might we expect under favorable conditions.

The Jury Comes In

In supporting our supposition, we must establish that at least some of the people act rationally some of the time. From our accumulated evidence, it is now time to render a verdict. Happily, in making a judgment we can call on the experience of Professor George Katona, who has probably done more research on consumer behavior than any other scholar. His carefully reasoned analysis is not conjecture, but the result of his years of experience in studying consumption behavior at the Survey Research Center, University of Michigan. Not surprisingly, Professor Katona has found that no simple formula can encompass all the complexities of consumer behavior. He notes that consumers typically do not reach decisions "after careful weighing of alternative courses," although at the same time "consumer behavior is not capricious." That is, even if consumers do not behave in reality the way they do in economics textbooks, their behavior is not random; it can be understood and explained and, as Katona continues, "in this sense, is not conceived as irrational" [5, p. 19].

What can we say then—Is the consumer rational or irrational? According to Katona:

> This is not the right question to ask. The consumer is a human being, influenced by his past experience. . . . He is apt to prefer short cuts, follow rules of thumb and behave in a routine manner. But he is also

---

* You should appreciate that there are numerous other implications of Professor Galbraith's conclusions. We have done little more than introduce the topic here, and will return to it when we discuss consumer sovereignty in Chapter 7.

capable of acting intelligently. *When he feels that it really matters, he will deliberate and choose to the best of his ability.* [6, p. 145, emphasis added]

This view of the consumer is very appealing. It pictures him as hurried, hassled, and a little lazy, but not hopeless. This characterization has more to recommend it than just its basic appeal. In the first place, it meets the requirement we have set, providing evidence that consumers can act rationally. Beyond that, it provides another insight into consumer behavior that looms as significant.

Our entire analysis is based on the complexities of the marketplace and the difficulties the consumer has in handling them. Consumers must buy such a wide range of products that if they tried to study each purchase carefully, they would get very little else done. So they do the human thing—they compromise. Little or routine purchases are relegated to habit, a path of least resistance. The housewife becomes familiar with the stores in her area and then shops at the one that fits her needs best. From time to time she may pass up good buys at other stores, but it isn't worth her time and effort to take advantage of them.

New residents in an area typically find that shopping takes them longer than it did before. That is because they have to find out which stores are best for them. Once they have this information, shopping is quicker. They have simplified the process by eliminating decisions. Or perhaps it is more accurate to say that once they have made the decisions, they do not have to keep repeating them.

Thus, habitual behavior, which is often cited as an example of consumer irrationality, may be just the opposite. It may be a rational (note the use of that word) reaction to the complexities of the market. Since it is impossible to ponder every decision, give the simple ones over to habit and reserve attention to the ones that really matter.

What we have done is to recognize that there are costs attached to making decisions. Were it not for these costs, consumers might carefully evaluate all possible alternatives in making decisions. Since such costs do exist, however, consumers must concentrate on those purchases that take a significant amount of their income. These they consider in terms very similar to those of economic theory that describe the rational consumer. This attention to information costs correlates with Professor Katona's statement.

From all the relevant factors then, we can conclude that consumers are often unfairly maligned. If any court had jurisdiction, they could sue for defamation of character. Consumers really do fairly well, considering that they work with inadequate resources in an unfriendly environment. What emerges as important is not so much rationality as how consumers adjust to the marketplace. It may be that the whole idea of rationality is nothing more than this adjustment.

We began our investigation of rationality by noting that it is a very difficult concept to pin down; it engenders much confusion. We can now see how great the confusion is and how far is has obscured the real issues. What most people mean by *rationality* really involves consumers' knowing what they want and what particular items will give it to them.

THE LAST WORD

Know Thyself

If rationality has any meaning for typical consumers, it concerns their knowing precisely what they want. Consumption decisions are made in line with individual preferences and tastes. If individuals do not know what they want, they are not going to be able to make intelligent choices. That is such a commonplace observation that we may be tempted not to take it very seriously. After all, we may rightly assume that most people generally know what they like and what they do not like. What more is there to say? Well, there is more, because at a particular time an individual has a whole structure of wants and likes and these must be fitted together.

At this moment, for example, you may want a cup of coffee, a new car, and a trip to Europe. Those are quite different commodities, but they have one thing in common: each of them costs money. Since the money you have is limited, you must decide which of the three you want most. The cost of a cup of coffee is so small that it will not much affect your ability to buy either the car or the trip. Buying a car, on the other hand, would probably put such a dent in your checkbook that you would have to put off any idea of going to Europe. If you really want the car, you should buy it, but you should not turn around and complain about not having enough money to go to Europe.

You may recognize that we have returned to the opportunity-cost argument. Consumers must have an overall idea not only of what things they want, but also of how much they want them. With this perception, they can order their consumption accordingly. We may generalize on this point, for it appears that consumers do not always think through what their purchasing implies. If they buy something, the car, it means they have that much less money to spend on something else, the trip. Notice that we are not saying that the consumer should spend money in this way or that. We are not attempting to establish any typical, normal, or accepted pattern of consumption. Rather, we are saying that however consumers decide to spend their money, they should evaluate individual purchases against overall preferences. Doing that will ensure that the particular purchase is the one that will give the greatest amount of satisfaction. Here is where so much of the consumer advice that is offered misses the mark. It is too often geared to telling consumers how to consume rather than helping them evaluate alternatives.

This distinction is vitally important. Suppose a middle-income couple wants to go to Europe. Conventional wisdom might suggest that it is beyond their means, but the onlooker has no right to make such a judgment. We already know that consumption cannot be evaluated solely in terms of the good itself. The actual trip may be relatively unimportant. The couple may be more interested in fulfilling a lifelong dream, status, visiting the graves of their grandparents, or any of a number of things. Potential advice in this case should indicate alternatives that confront the couple and what the trip means measured against other consumption choices. Thus we might say that if the couple takes the trip they must put off buying a new car, finishing the basement, and getting braces for their ten-year-old's teeth. They are then in a position to decide how they rank these alternatives.

We can conclude that even if consumer performance in evaluating choices is not what it should be, consumers are not entirely to blame. They have not been getting much help. In a complex economy, decisions are difficult, and the consumer needs help in making them. Unfortunately, most of the advice consumers get not only fails to offer real assistance but confuses the issue by distraction. It is clearly time to stop telling consumers how to consume and begin providing them with information that will help them to make intelligent decisions.

Consumer education shows up as tremendously important. Despite the fact that all American schoolchildren are consumers, few of them get any real instruction in what that means. We do not let people drive without instruction, yet we expect them to take on the far more complex role of consumer without any training. It is true that rationality cannot be taught. Much of what is called rationality, however, is bound up in awareness of alternatives and establishing and attaining goals. These concepts can be taught, and consumers can increase their knowledge of their environment and the way in which they must deal with it.

The Information Gap

The consumer's environment becomes the other element involved in what is commonly called rationality. Even if consumers are well aware of their own wants, they still must know which goods will satisfy them. Thus, it is impossible to consider consumer rationality without also considering the consumer's environment.

It may be difficult in practice to tell whether a consumer needs more information or whether the problem is not knowing precisely what he wants. Take vodka, for example. Vodka is vodka; it is a liquor distilled from potatoes and diluted with distilled water. Thus, if it is the liquor you are interested in, the cheapest brand will suffice. Now let us assume that two people go into a store and both buy the most expensive brand of vodka on the shelf. We cannot tell much about the background for these purchases until we are more informed.

The first person knows the more expensive brand is no better, but buys it for status; that is the Veblen effect. This person is more interested in the bottle than the vodka, and if the status is really worth that much, the decision is rational. The second person, however, was interested in the vodka itself, but erred in thinking that the more expensive brand must be better. Since that is not true, the person made a poor purchase. It would be a mistake to call the second person irrational; the issue is information, not rationality. The error is common. There are far too many examples of poor purchases. To cite them as examples of consumer irrationality, however, serves no useful purpose. What is needed is an improved flow of information, not condemnations of consumers. Information is available, but it is often expensive and difficult to obtain.

Improving the flow of information to consumers should therefore improve consumer performance. Better information will make it easier for consumers to make better decisions. That is where the focus should be. Confusing inadequate information with irrationality only complicates the situation. Rationality stresses consumer knowledge of what consumers want and what goods will best satisfy those wants. These important considerations are best analyzed directly, and not under the heading of rationality. The confusion on this point has surely not served the consumer well. A better understanding of all factors separately can only improve the situation.

STUDY QUESTIONS

1. Suppose that you go home for the weekend and your parents immediately begin to bicker with you about your hair, your friends, and the way that you spend your money. If you can keep your head through all of this, what can you say to them?

2. The law prohibits some types of consumption. Marijuana, for example, is illegal, even though its effects are not fully known. Consider the relation between individual choice and social control in this case. What sorts of controls do you feel would be warranted?

3. Analyze each of the following statements:
a. I used to buy that kind, but I don't now because everyone has it.
b. Cash on the barrelhead, that's my motto; if you can't pay for it, don't buy it!
c. I figured it was so cheap, it couldn't be any good.
d. If I had known then what I know now, I would never have bought that car.
e. I know what's best for you.

4. Ask some friends what *impulse buying* means to them. Make sure they define it. Can they answer the questions about it that were raised in the text? Discuss.

5.　How do you explain, assuming that consumers are at all rational, that fraud and deception are so common?

6.　How does the concept of consumer rationality change with growing affluence? Why did it mean something different when your grandparents were young from what it means now?

7.　Under what circumstances would saving be irrational?

8.　Why is habitual consumer behavior so important? Does it prove anything about consumer rationality?

9.　Suppose that a particular firm employs two mail clerks. Both are poorly paid, but one buys expensive clothes at the town's most fashionable shop; the other dresses poorly, but is sending his daughter to college. Does this tell you whether or not they are rational? Does it tell you anything about their preferences? Which pattern is likely to be approved? Is there any real basis for this judgment?

SUGGESTED PROJECTS

1.　Read the consumer advice columns in a magazine or your local newspaper. What do you think of the quality of the advice? Would the individual be wrong in not following it?

2.　Survey the facilities for consumer education in your community. Are courses available in the schools, and if so, are they worth while? Are there any adult education programs or private groups offering educational opportunities to consumers?

3.　Go to a grocery and price five prepared foods. Then get as good an idea as possible of the price if you bought the basic food and prepared it yourself. What is the average price differential?

Next, figure the time it would take to prepare the foods yourself. What is the cost of the time you are saving? How much time would it have *cost* you if you had prepared the food yourself?

4.　Compare prices in a convenience store with those in a regular grocery store. Do the price differentials vary with different goods? How much are you actually paying for convenience?

5.　Look at several advertisements for houses, apartments, and automobiles. Do the ads tend to emphasize the product itself or other qualities which it has? Is there any relation between the price of the product and the degree to which basic properties are emphasized?

6.　Discuss within the class or with friends bad purchases that any of you have made. Do these represent irrationality? Can you identify the cause of the mistake in each case? Can you identify a pattern among the causes?

7.   Investigate local laws that relate to individual consumption or affect it in some way. (You will probably be surprised at the number and extent of them.) Do they fall into any pattern? On what basis can they be justified? In your estimation, should there be more laws like this or fewer?

8.   Can you devise a test of consumer rationality? What is the relation between being a rational consumer and being a careful consumer? Could you conduct a survey to test the latter?

BIBLIOGRAPHY AND SUGGESTED READINGS

1. Friedman, Milton. *Essays in Positive Economics*. Chicago: University of Chicago Press, 1953. Chap. 2.

   The role of theory again. Friedman's first essay, "The Methodology of Positive Economics," provokes dispute, but remains a classic. It is particularly valuable in exploring what theory can and cannot do.

2. Fusfeld, Daniel R. *Economics*. Lexington, Mass.: D. C. Heath and Co. Chap. 2.

   See Chapter 23 for a good discussion on the economics of work and leisure in terms of individual preferences.

3. Galbraith, John Kenneth. *The Affluent Society*. Boston: Houghton Mifflin Co. Chap. 1.

   Review of the dismal view of the consumer. These ideas will figure heavily into our later discussions of consumer power and public consumption.

4. Hamilton, David. *The Consumer in Our Economy*. Boston: Houghton Mifflin Co., 1962.

   An intelligent discussion of the consumer with economic theory as an outline. Chapters 2 and 3 are relevant here on the cultural aspects of consumption.

5. Katona, George. "Consumer Behavior: Theory and Findings on Expectations and Aspirations." *American Economic Review, Papers and Proceedings*, May 1968, pp. 19–30.

   An exploration of consumer behavior on which we shall draw further in the next chapter.

6. Katona, George. *The Powerful Consumer*. New York: McGraw-Hill Book Co., 1960.

   Katona is required reading for anyone interested in rationality. He has broadened the narrow, traditional economic view into a meaningful concept. Chapter 9 on rationality is particularly valuable.

7. Lancaster, Kelvin. "Change and Innovation in the Technology of Consumption." *American Economic Review, Papers and Proceedings*, May 1966, pp. 14–23.

A less technical presentation of the ideas presented in the text about goods and consumption. Has especially valuable applications to consumerism.

8. Lancaster, Kelvin. "A New Approach to Consumer Theory." *Journal of Political Economy*, April 1966, pp. 132–57.

The basis for our argument in the text that consumers are not consuming the good for itself but for some set of characteristics that the good has.

9. Leibenstein, Harvey. "Bandwagon, Snob and Veblen Effects in the Theory of Consumer Demand." *Quarterly Journal of Economics*, May 1950, pp. 189–207.

A classic article on demand theory. You will see in Professor Leibenstein's work a suggestion of the approach that Professor Lancaster later developed. Previously, economists had largely ignored interdependence in consumption.

10. Robertson, Thomas S. *Consumer Behavior*. Glenview, Ill.: Scott, Foresman and Co., 1970.

Analysis of the determinants of consumer behavior from a marketing point of view. Valuable on attitudes and motivation.

11. Strumpel, Burkhard, et al., eds. *Human Behavior in Economic Affairs*. San Francisco: Jossey-Bass, 1972.

A valuable collection of original essays by leading economists on different aspects of consumer behavior. We shall use this collection increasingly as we go along.

12. Veblen, Thorstein. *The Theory of the Leisure Class*. New York: Mentor Books, 1953. Chap. 1.

Veblen on conspicuous consumption. A primer for anyone interested in the topic.

4

The Crystal Ball
Is Clouded

LIVING IN A WORLD OF "IFS"

Cider in the Ear

Sky Masterson, the high-rolling gambler of *Guys and Dolls*, based his philosophy of life on a saying that his father passed on to him. Roughly translated, it goes liké this: "If someone says he can make a shrimp jump out of his pocket and spit cider in your ear, don't bet. Sure as you do, you'll end up with cider in your ear." That is good advice, even though it is unlikely that anyone will offer you such a wager. The future is unknown and no matter how outrageous or contrived a situation may sound, you cannot be sure that it will not happen. Just because you have never heard of a trained shrimp with a taste for cider, that does not mean that there is not one around somewhere.

We may have an understanding of the past and some grasp of the present, but the future is conjecture. We may not like to admit that, but it is true, and one of the few things we can be certain about. We still try to ignore it, making statements of fact about the future when we know they are subject to limitations. You may say to a friend, "I'll meet you for dinner at eight," when what you really mean is "If nothing unforeseen happens to either of us, we'll have dinner at eight." Simply stated, it is impossible to make an unconditional statement about the future; we do not even know whether we have a future.

Yet we pretend that nothing too drastic is going to happen. We try to plan our lives in an orderly fashion based on the idea that the future will be pretty much like the past. The philosopher David Hume was talking about this when he said that only mathematical truths are known with certainty: all else is habit. Just because the sun has come up every day in human memory, that does not prove that it will come up tomorrow. Yet everyone acts as though they are sure it will. That makes sense as far as

49

day-to-day living is concerned, because it would be impossible, and certainly depressing, to ponder all of life's unknowns and account for all potentialities.

We still have a pervading, some would say perverse, interest in the future, and it seems to be growing. Soothsayers, seers, and fortune tellers of all kinds do a booming business from people who want a glimpse of what is to come. The revival of interest in astrology reflects this same phenomenon and is a rejection of the rational, scientific approach to coping with change. Perhaps it is a matter of daring fate, of the individual's standing up to the unknown. In this respect, people haven't changed much over the years. For all our technological advances and increased understanding, we still face the future alone.

The Future Is Now

It may appear that we have strayed a long way from consumer economics. The considerations just mentioned do seem esoteric, and we could put them in the same category as pondering the possibility of converging parallel lines if it were not for one fact. The future is now. We are not talking here, as it has become fashionable to do, about the pace of change being so rapid that it overcomes us. No, we are saying that present actions have an impact beyond the present; they extend into the future. Therefore, future developments must be considered in current decisions.

The catch is that no one can be sure about what those future developments are going to be. Yet since such developments must be taken into account, it is individuals' perception of the future—what they think is going to happen—that becomes important. The point is, then, that things that have not happened yet and indeed may not happen have a direct bearing on the way we behave.

From the consumer's perspective, that means that possible future developments affect present consumption. We can see this in different ways. There is the young married couple who puts off buying furniture because they aren't sure that they will still like Danish modern five years from now. Or the construction worker who decides not to buy that color television, even though he has the money, because he is afraid he might be laid off. Consider, too, the college student who would like to major in English and be a writer, but who takes business courses instead because she is worried about job opportunities after graduation. And finally, there are the insurance salesmen, selling security and reducing life to a set of probabilities.

In each case, we see that the future influences present actions. Even though no one knows what the future holds, we form expectations about what we think is going to happen and these expectations influence our current behavior. The future may be an abstraction, but it significantly affects the way we behave in the present. As in the examples above, people make consumption decisions according to what they think is going to happen. That clearly marks out such expectations as a very important ingredient in consumer behavior.

In economic theory the consumer faces none of these complications. No uncertainty is allowed to creep in and muddle his computerlike computations. When we have tried to make sense out of consumer rationality, we have not admitted the possibility of uncertainty. That was because we already had enough to worry about, but now we must recognize that consumers are influenced by what they see in the future, as well as by what has happened or is happening to them.

Even though consumers make purchases according to their own tastes and preferences, these are affected by possible future developments. The key word here is *possible*, for uncertainty is a fact of life for consumers and must be faced as such. Then we must ask, If uncertainty cannot be eliminated, can it at least be reduced? The answer is yes. We may not know what is going to happen in the future, but by concentrating on the most probable developments and weighing them in our decisions, we can at least come to grips with the problem.

EVALUATING FUTURE DEVELOPMENTS

Pie in the Sky By and By?

There are three points to keep in mind throughout our evaluation: (1) The future hasn't happened yet. (2) Some of it will not happen for a long time. (3) Some of it may never happen. Now, those are not three of the most profound ideas you have ever run across, but they underscore the premise. Each of the three points is relevant in evaluating the impact of future developments on present consumption decisions.

If the future is unknown—our first point—then even if you have an idea about what is going to happen, you can't be sure about it. As a result, that future event cannot be weighed as heavily in your decision-making process as some event that is known with certainty. Reducing the weight (or importance) of future developments is known as *discounting*. It means simply that you do not take the event at face value but reduce the significance attached to it.

If you can't treat future events like present ones, how much weight should they be given? Our second and third points provide the key to that question. In deciding how much importance to give a possible future development, you must consider the length of time until the expected event and the likelihood of its happening. Depending on the answers to those questions, a future event may be given nearly as much weight as current happenings, or it may be disregarded altogether.

Time is one factor. Human nature puts things off. We may be worried about tomorrow, next week, or next month, but our concerns generally do not extend much further than that. We may, in our more contemplative moments, wonder where we'll be ten years from now, but such reflections always seem to be pushed aside by the pressures and demands of the present. This suggests that the further an event in the future, the smaller its impact on present decisions.

Planning about future income can be summarized by the statement: A dollar now is worth more than a dollar a year from now. It is true that if you put your dollar in savings, it will earn interest so that in a year you will have say $1.05. But have you ever thought why you are paid interest? It is essentially a bribe to induce you to give up the use of that dollar for a year. If you have a dollar now, you can spend it and get the enjoyment from whatever you buy; you cannot do anything with next year's dollar until next year. Thus, you would not give it up unless you were paid interest to do so.

To put it differently, if someone offered you the promise of a dollar a year from now in exchange for a dollar now, you would not make the trade because you would lose the use of your money for a year. If you saved your money and earned five cents interest, the dollar you have now would be worth more than one dollar in a year's time. So the promise of a dollar in one year is not worth as much as the dollar you now have. You have to reduce the value, or discount, next year's dollar to obtain its present value, meaning its value to you now.*

For the same idea in less abstract terms, suppose that a rich uncle dies when you are twenty and stipulates in his will that you are to receive $1 million on your twenty-first birthday. You would probably increase your spending immediately, going on a buying binge even though it meant using credit and going into debt. After all, that money from your uncle will be yours in a few months and you will have more than enough to cover your accounts.

Suppose, however, that your uncle mistrusted foolish youth, and while he left you the million, he said you could not have it until you were 65. Forty-five years is a long time to wait, even for a million dollars. Using the formula we gave above, the present value of $1 million in 45 years is only $31,327.88, with an interest rate of 8%.* It might influence you in terms of buying insurance or retirement benefits but would probably have no impact on your current consumption levels. The money is simply too far away to have very much value. As you grow older and there is less time left for you to wait, its value would increase, but that is small comfort when you are twenty.

From these examples, we can see that even when future events are virtually assured, they must be adjusted because they are in the future. The further in the future their potential occurrence, the greater the adjustment.

---

* Accounting students will recall that in a mechanical sense, present value is given by the formula $PV = C/(1 + r)^n$, where C is the income flow, r is the interest rate, and n is the number of years. If the interest rate is 5 percent, the present value of $1 in a year is $1/1.05, or about $0.95. The present value of a dollar in two years is $1/(1.05)^2 =$ $1/1.1025, or a bit less than $0.91.

* Higher interest rates are commonly used in such calculations, since future interest rates are themselves unknown. Whatever rate is used, it is clear that the value of the money will be significantly reduced.

If you are thinking of buying a car, you might buy a more expensive model if you think you are going to get a raise next year. On the other hand, if that raise is two or three years off, you probably would not take it into account in buying the car. Suppose, though, that you thought you were going to get a raise and therefore bought the more expensive car. Then, the boss does not come through with the extra money. You would be in a fix. That further illustrates the point we have been making: you can't be certain about the future. We used the phrase *virtually assured* above, but future events are rarely virtually assured. Therefore, they must be adjusted further, according to the probability that they will happen.

If an event is unlikely, it will not have much impact on current actions, even if its potential impact is very great. If you buy a sweepstakes ticket, for example, that gives you a one-in-a-million chance of winning a million dollars, this outlook should not have much impact on your consumption because the odds against you are so great. If you happen to win, you could invite all your friends and have a tremendous bash, but it would not be wise to make the arrangements in advance.

Taking these two factors together, we can see that the greater the probability of the event and the sooner its happening, the greater its influence on your current actions. The range of possible future developments must be evaluated in these terms. A one-in-a-million chance for a million dollars at age 65 would not rate even a second thought from most college seniors. But those same seniors will be out buying cars, clothes, and maybe even furniture because in a few months they will have jobs. The jobs will not pay a million dollars, but the job market entrants can be relatively sure of getting their money, and soon. Thus, the high probability of getting even a small amount of money in the near future will affect consumers more than the remote chance for a large sum some time in the distant future.

This is the way that consumers take future events into account when making current decisions. Time and probability are the key elements. These elements apply to income, and they operate in other areas too. These forces work on the consumer in different ways and various expectations interact to affect consumer behavior.

The Range of Expectations

Consumer expectations about developments in other areas may be as important as income expectations in determining current consumption behavior. These other areas may be any of the different factors that affect consumer behavior. In particular, expectations about tastes and prices are significant. These factors along with income appear to affect current consumer behavior the most.

The time and probability rule can be applied here also. For the consumer who is buying something that will last a long time, there is a chance that tastes will change over the lifetime of the product. Therefore, when he is making the purchase, he must think of the possibility of changing tastes. This applies particularly to housing and consumer durables (automobiles, home furnishings, and appliances) [8].

If the item will be used up rather quickly on the other hand, such considerations are not going to be very important. The nature of the item is important too. If it is purely functional, like a garden hose, then it is unlikely that tastes are going to change. A garden hose may last for years (assuming it is brought indoors in the winter), but it is hard to imagine how changing tastes could have much of an impact; a hose is meant to get water from one place to another, and the ordinary model is the best way.

The expense of the item and its relative importance in the consumer's budget must also be considered. Tastes in clothing, for example, change annually—some fashion fads do not even make it through one season. Yet if the item is relatively inexpensive, the consumer may go ahead and buy anyway. Thus, if a particular type of wild tie is currently the rage, a man might buy one, knowing that even if the fad doesn't last, he is not out very much money. That same man, however, might buy a more conservative suit that is likely to be in style for a number of years. The greater expense of the suit makes him cautious and forces him to consider changing tastes.

Our general time-probability rule suggests that the more uncertain a consumer is about changing tastes, the less likely he will be to buy. The time element is important in the example of the newly married couple who put off buying furniture because they are not sure what they are going to like in five years. No one can be certain that tastes will not change over time; probably most people expect that they will. The key question is, Is there any reason to suspect that tastes will be changing soon? If the answer is no, the tendency would be to go ahead and buy. Possible changes of taste in the distant future are too remote to have an impact on the present.

Happily, we can analyze consumer expectations about changing prices in a more straightforward manner. In a period of inflation, and most of the years since World War II can be categorized under that heading, consumers form expectations about continued inflation. Any feeling they have that prices are going to continue to rise is built into their consumption behavior. This may be shown in many ways. It appears in union contracts, for example, where there is added pressure to include a cost-of-living adjustment. Short of such an agreement, the negotiator may ask for a 10 percent increase, 5 percent to cover inflation and 5 percent as an actual increase. In individual decisions, expectations of higher prices tend to encourage current consumption. Why wait if things are going to cost more later? Such an attitude tends to discourage savings, especially if consumers feel that even with interest the purchasing power of their savings will decline [10, chap. 14].

If, on the other hand, consumers feel that prices are going to fall in the future, they would tend to postpone consumption. While this has not been the case with the overall price level in recent years, it has been true for particular products. Color television sets are again a good example. Many consumers put off buying because they expected prices to fall. This effect was so pronounced that industry spokesmen felt compelled to counter it by maintaining that there would be on significant decline in price. They were not particularly successful; buyers waited and prices fell. That pattern is typical of most new products.

CONFRONTATIONS WITH THE FUTURE

The Future in Retrospect

This is a good time to summarize what we have said thus far and to be more specific about how it affects the consumer. Consumption decisions must take into account not only what has happened, but also what the consumer thinks is going to happen. It is in this way that consumers' current consumption is affected by their perception of future events.

It may be useful to think of the future as both a *challenge* and a *resource* to the consumer. It is a challenge because it is unknown, and the consumer must therefore be prepared for various eventualities. This preparation commonly takes the form of savings or insurance, both of which offer the consumer a hedge against adverse developments in the future. Viewed differently, *they represent the application of current resources against the future*, since money used for savings or insurance cannot be spent on current consumption goods; the level of current consumption is depressed.

The future is also a resource, however, in that it represents potential earnings. All but the oldest consumers can look forward to earning money in the future and *the possibility exists of transferring that money from the future to the present*. That is a fancy way of saying that consumers use credit or go into debt. If you think about it, debt means spending money you have not yet received, and then paying it back as you earn it. We hinted at this above when we talked about college seniors spending the earnings expected from jobs they had not yet begun.

We can now see that there are two elements involved here. Consumers' perception of the future determines how they will spend their current and future income. *They may either transfer current income into the future (savings, insurance) or transfer future income to the present (debt).* This offers flexibility—consumers are not limited to present resources but can draw on future resources also.

Transferring income forward or backward raises abstractions and complexities. Some abstraction is necessary to summarize the argument, but it is easy enough to translate these ideas into everyday terms. The complexities are more difficult to handle. In essence we are investigating how the consumer balances the demands of the present against the demands of the future. To understand the process and cut through some of the complexities, let us look first at the general pattern. In doing so, we assume away many of the complexities, something economists are fond of doing. "Assume all else is equal" is one of their favorite phrases. All else is not really equal, but if we assume for a moment that it is, we can isolate key factors. It is a matter of clearing away confusing detail so we can see what is happening. Once we have sorted out the various elements involved and identified a general pattern, we can drop the all-else-equal assumption and admit individual variations. In this way, we can use the general case as a reference against which to measure the effect of individual variations. This should bring us closer to an explanation of observed consumer behavior.

Tomorrow's Dollars Today

In establishing a general pattern for the transfer of income, we begin by looking at the consumer's entire lifetime, considering both income and needs. Not surprisingly, this approach, which has become a common feature of economic analysis, is called the life-cycle or permanent income hypothesis [6]. When we take this view, we realize a difficulty immediately. Individuals' income comes in unevenly over their lifetimes. Typically, income is lower in the early working years and then follows an upward trend until individuals reach their maximum earning years in their forties and fifties. Then income tends to level off or fall slightly before dropping sharply with retirement. Unfortunately, this pattern does not match the individual's need for money.

Expenses are high for a newly married couple. Even the most frugal find that it is expensive to set up housekeeping. There are appliances to purchase, clothes for work, and a car. Soon the couple wants a home, and if they have children, costs increase even more. Older citizens do not face the same problems, but they too find that costs are high relative to income. Medical bills in particular are likely to increase; even if health is not a factor, simply enjoying retirement is expensive.*

Thus, the bulge in income comes during the middle of an individual's working years, while the bulge in expenditures comes at the beginning and the end. The obvious solution is to transfer income from the peak earning years around middle age to the periods when needs are greater. Income and expenditures are then matched and evened out. This recalls our reference to diminishing marginal utility. Diminishing marginal utility applies to money too. Thus, we can buttress our commonsense argument with the more elegant contention that individuals' total level of satisfaction over their lifetimes will be greater if they transfer money from periods when its marginal utility is low to times when it has a higher marginal utility.

Transferring income is relatively simple. It means going into debt or taking money out of savings when expenditures are greater than income and saving or paying off debts when income is greater than expenditures. Note that we are not talking about a net increase in purchasing power, but merely transferring purchasing power from one period to another. Once

---

* The pattern here is also affected by the availability of comprehensive medical insurance. If such a program is available for the elderly, medical costs may actually decline.

money is spent, it is spent, so consumption can be increased during one period only at the expense of consumption in another period. The consumer's level of satisfaction is increased, however, because money is available when it is needed most.

So we have the young couple borrowing money and going into debt. Then, as their income rises, they pay off their debts, accumulate savings, and buy life insurance. The key is that during this period their income has grown not only in absolute terms, but also relative to their expenditures; otherwise, they would not have money to live on. Later, when income declines relative to expenditures, the couple draws on savings and collects on insurance.

This formulation has much to recommend it. Young couples do go into debt for cars, appliances, and housing. If most of us waited until we could pay cash for a house, we should all be living in apartments. Once these fixed costs are taken care of, there is more money left over. With incomes rising, families can pay off debts and begin more significant savings. These savings will be important in later years when income declines again. There are simplifications involved here, of course. People buy many cars, appliances, and even houses over their lifetimes. Similarly, costs may be high during middle age, too, particularly if there are children to educate. However, we are only trying to establish a general pattern; we are not claiming that it is representative of every case.

It is now time to drop the assumption that all else is equal. In doing so, we are asking what influences would either keep consumers from following the pattern laid out above or prompt them to conform to it. In other words, we are analyzing the forces at work on consumers when they distribute their lifetime income. The analysis involves individuals' expectations about their futures. To understand how the individual operates within the general framework, we must look closely at expectations.

FORMULATING CONSUMER EXPECTATIONS

Impact of a Changing Environment

Consumers base their expectations of the future on their experience in the past. Consumers relate to their environment and become familiar with it. They come to know that certain things remain constant over time and they utilize them in forming expectations about the future in the same way that ancient navigators used the stars to navigate through uncharted waters. There is nothing mystical about these consumer guideposts. They are nothing more than lessons learned from experience and passed along from person to person, from generation to generation. Recent college graduates, for example, can look forward to increasing incomes, having witnessed the experience of friends or relatives. A person with 50,000 miles on her car knows that she should expect higher repair bills. People moving from the country to the city should expect higher living costs.

The people in these examples may have no personal experience to go on, yet because of the experience of others, they have a reasonably sound basis for formulating expectations and planning for the future. They cannot be certain of course—some college graduates don't make it and some cars run forever (I'm told) without needing repairs—but enough people have faced similar experiences to pass along a fund of useful knowledge. There is no guarantee that this information will apply in every case, but it does at least give the individual a basis for making judgments.

The individual develops a sense of the probabilities, what is likely to happen and what isn't. Suppose your car has 50,000 miles on it; should you replace it? You know that typically cars need more repairs with that much mileage. You also know your car's own repair record. You might ask a mechanic what he thinks. While you will not be able to get a definitive answer, you will be able to get a reasonable idea of what you should do. Consumers base their expectations on a certain perception of order and structure, which allows them to project into the future and to reduce the uncertainty. That works fine as long as the situation is stable, but when this structure is disturbed and the signposts to the future are changed, consumers naturally become confused.

Recall our earlier comment that if consumers expect prices to continue rising, they will tend to buy now. If consumers have come, however, to view a particular price level as *normal* (their signpost from experience), they may cut back consumption in anticipation that prices will return to the norm. That seems to be what happened recently with interest rates. After years at lower levels, interest rates rose in the late 1960s. That trend continued, somewhat unevenly, into the 1970s. Consumers, who were used to thinking of interest rates in the neighborhood of 4 or 5 percent, had a hard time accepting rates of 7, 8, and even 9 percent as "normal." Thus, many consumers are waiting for the rates to go back down, even though the best evidence is that they will remain high for some time to come. Such changes in established patterns disorient consumers because their experiences no longer hold.

The same sort of change is evident with vocational choices. For years we have heard of a teacher shortage in this country, so that any student enrolling in a college of education could be sure to find a job on graduation. Suddenly we hear of a teacher glut, and many graduates with teaching degrees are being forced into other lines of work. To a prospective teacher, this sort of change is difficult to accommodate. If you had planned to be a teacher and were conditioned to thinking of a bright employment picture, the change in outlook required would be considerable.

In an even more fundamental sense, the same thing is true of the value of a college education. The idea that a college education means a better job and higher earnings is an article of faith for most Americans. Many high-school students grow up with the idea of continuing their education; it is not something they think about, it is just accepted. Now, however, we find that in many areas there is a surplus of college graduates. The best jobs seem to be available to those with vocational training, many of whom do not have traditional four-year degrees.

It is not yet clear whether or not this educational development represents a long-run change. If it does, it means that the whole society will have to reorient its thinking about the importance of higher education. The basis on which expectations have been formed in the past will have to be changed. During the period of flux, when the signals about the future are confused, there may be no good basis for forming expectations. Such a catch-as-catch-can situation tends to be not only confusing but also nerve-wracking.

If the general rule we established earlier is correct, periods of great uncertainty should cause consumers to postpone purchases. When people are not sure what is going to happen, there is a tendency to wait and see. Instead of going right ahead with higher education, more and more high-school graduates work for a year or two after getting out of school. They may plan to go on to college, and a few years ago they might have gone on directly, but now they are temporizing, and seeking a better picture of what lies ahead before making a decision.

The confused economic situation of the early 1970s provided another example. Despite inflationary pressures, which tend to promote current consumption, consumers postponed buying. Savings, which tend to be very stable, rose. There was a backlog of purchasing power, but because signals about the future were mixed and it was not clear what was going to happen, consumers were not buying. This situation continued until conditions stabilized and consumers were able to develop a consistent basis for forming expectations about the future.*

We can see, then, that while consumers are not necessarily creatures of habit, they do come to depend on certain features of their environment in judging the future. In a setting that either is static or features controlled change, expectations can be formed with some confidence. More significant change not only disorients the consumer, making it difficult to read signals about the future; it also affects the consumer's own attitudes and outlook. Turning from the consumers' environment leads us to the consumers themselves.

The Role of Consumer Attitudes

Consumers are individuals. If we cannot expect everyone to have the same tastes and preferences, we certainly cannot expect everyone to have the same expectations about the future. Different people react to uncertainty

---

* There was a paradoxical circularity in this situation. Consumer expenditures were one of the main elements that would determine what was going to happen. Thus, while consumers were waiting for some clearer signals about future developments before they committed themselves, those signals could not be forthcoming until consumers actually decided what they were going to do.

in different ways, just as they react to goods differently. It is like that old saying about the difference between an optimist and a pessimist looking at half a glass of water—one says that it is half full, while the other maintains that it is half empty. Two individuals can confront the same situation with the same amount of information and draw radically different conclusions. When those conclusions have to do with future possibilities—about which no one can be certain—the range of variation becomes even greater.

The difference becomes clear when we observe how people confront the future. Some people have an aversion to risk; they will try to hedge against future developments by saving, buying insurance, or generally following a conservative strategy. Others, like gamblers, adventurers, or speculators, seem to seek out risk. Most of us are somewhere in the middle or move from one group to the other depending on the circumstances. No single strategy fits everyone. When we speak of those topics that relate to future consumption, like debt and insurance, we must account for individual variations. Thus, there is no right amount of insurance. What is right for one person may be too much for a second individual and too little for a third. The right amount of insurance can be determined only from an individual's preferences.

Expectations, like so many other factors that affect consumption, reflect deep-seated personal attitudes. These are evolved from cultural, ethical, and religious beliefs. If an individual's religion places a high value on thrift, this is going to be reflected not only in the way that person consumes but also in savings patterns and attitudes toward debt. Consumer's reactions to the future are shaped, if not determined, by cultural factors, following a fundamental aspect of human behavior.

Thrift, which somehow ends up being the antithesis of debt, is highly valued in the American tradition. Everyone is familiar with homey little admonitions like "Waste not, want not" and "A penny saved is a penny earned." Those, it seems, are always followed by a recitation of Polonius's advice, "Neither a borrower nor a lender be." If a society's collective wisdom is summarized by such statements, it is a pretty good clue about prevailing attitudes.

These attitudes color our thinking and provide another dimension to formulating expectations. Put differently, this means that while individuals may form expectations according to their own personal judgments, these judgments are influenced by social pressures. This fact suggests that there should be a degree of continuity and stability in such judgments. That is particularly true when members of the society share common goals and aspirations. Any change in attitudes, then, has far-reaching implications that are likely to be disquieting.

That is not just a passing observation; it is a highly relevant comment on recent developments in the United States. Everyone is aware that we are witnessing important changes of attitudes in this country. To appreciate what has been happening, it is necessary to realize that these changes are closely tied to changes in expectations. To understand these developments fully, then, requires an explanation of the change in expectations. For that we must roll back the calendar some forty years and look at the bleak decade of the 1930s.

A Digression on Depression

Probably no event in America's recent experience has had as great an impact on the nation's psyche than the Great Depression of the 1930s. It may seem unusual to use the word *psyche* in reference to a nation, but it is quite appropriate in this case. The depression was nothing less than a national trauma. It shaped the thinking of the people who lived through it to such a degree that neither they, nor the country, would ever be the same again.

Those in their thirties or younger may not remember the depression or any direct impact it had on them; nevertheless, it has considerably affected their lives because of the tremendous impact it had on the lives of others. The statistics are startling enough. Income in 1932 was only half of what it had been in 1928.* Today we worry if unemployment goes above 4 percent, but during the depression, it was as high as 33 percent; that is, one worker out of three without a job. Average unemployment for the decade was 17 percent.

The true meaning of the depression cannot be measured with statistics. Its impact was much greater than even these data would suggest. The society seemed lost in a sea of despair as old landmarks were swept away and cherished assumptions were questioned. Economists and policymakers alike groped for new solutions, and while some of their efforts were salutary, in retrospect we can tell that most never really came to grips with the problems.

The years of unparalleled prosperity that lie between us and the Great Depression have brought many changes. Social welfare programs have been expanded and a policy of full employment has come to be taken for granted. Most people feel that the experience of the 1930s will not be repeated; there is an apparent psychology of prosperity [11, pp. 174–76]. Yet the depression did leave a scar; it is less ugly now that years have passed, but it is still visible.

This residual depression psychology is subtle and not easily isolated. It may be at work even though individuals feel that a severe depression is unlikely. The very fact that they are concerned about the possibility betrays their thinking. Asking younger Americans if they fear a recurrence of the Great Depression is meaningless. It makes as much sense to ask them if they are afraid the British will burn Washington again; they cannot relate to either event. Thus while older Americans are concerned about maintaining prosperity, those who are young take that for granted; this is where the difference in perception comes in.

These differences are apparent in both attitudes and motivation. In-

---

* In money terms. Real income only fell by one-third because of the decline in prices.

stallment credit is one example. Those who endured the depression are not likely to use credit freely, fearing the worst about the future. Younger people, who have no such fears, are more willing to use credit. In a slightly different vein, labor leaders find that the depression, which served to forge American labor into a solid unit, means little to younger workers. They are unmoved by the stories of how bad things used to be or of the labor victories of the 1930s. The increasingly restive and critical stance of many young workers reflects their changed concerns.

The depression psychology shows itself in other ways. Typically, college students find that their parents are more interested in their vocational aims than they themselves are. Students who want to major in a nonvocational area or who want to take a year off from school often find that their parents have little sympathy for such ideas. "Will that help you get a job?" or "You have to start thinking about your future," are common responses in such situations. This could be dismissed as the generation gap, but it is more than that. Parents, who know what it is like to do without, feel more strongly about security than their children. The latter, who have been largely secure, are interested in more than security. Thus, they tend to criticize their parents for being preoccupied with security. Parents in turn look upon their children as ungrateful.

This may suggest to you some of our earlier analysis of how affluence changes the character of consumer demand. To the depression generation, goods were valued primarily for what they would do, not for the combination of other characteristics that bring satisfaction. Until recently, home appliances were available only in white, reflecting the fact that demand was primarily functional; consumers were more interested in how things worked than how they looked. Now appliances come in a wide range of colors with optional "decorator accessories." If you are interested primarily in what the appliance does, this additional play to appeal is frivolous. The net effect is certainly to make consumer durables less durable, since if you redecorate your kitchen, you may suddenly find that your flaming red refrigerator does not go with your new avocado color scheme. This move into the realm of esthetics would have been unthinkable even a generation ago. It clearly reflects both greater affluence and the numerous young buyers in the market.

Appliances are a trivial example of the more fundamental changes that are taking place. As the depression generation passes, change will accelerate. Many younger consumers are living the life that their parents could only dream of; but they have discovered that very often it is anything but dreamlike. Thus, we can expect more questions about the system, material gains, and consumption itself, as we witness the passing of the depression psychology.

Time and Change

These changes in thinking can be related to expectations. The two matters have a connection, since expectations are largely concerned with the changes that will be taking place. For example, expectation of higher income should increase current consumption; similarly, expectation of higher interest rates will affect savings and borrowing patterns. What about the expectation of change itself, however? We might argue that if consumers expect change to be built into their lives, other expectations become less important. Consider the contrasts between a couple buying a home today and a similar couple buying a home a generation or two ago. The latter lived in a less mobile society; when they looked at a home, it was probably in lifetime terms. Thus, they had to find one that fitted them exactly, giving careful consideration to the future related to family size, tastes, income, and taxes. Today's couple, is most likely thinking about a much shorter time horizon. They may be planning to be in the house no more than two or three years. Therefore, they need only be sure that the house meets their current needs and the immediately foreseeable developments.

If consumers see every move as temporary, then long-run elements are not going to figure very heavily in their decisions. Lack of permanence is a function of change within the society. We have become conditioned to change, expecting it and accepting it. We see this not only in increased mobility, but also in new products and in new variations on old ones (as in the colored appliances).

In such a transient setting, expectations remain important, nevertheless. The couple probably would not even be buying the house if they didn't expect a favorable income trend in the future. However, long-run expectations are not going to be very important, for in a sense there is no long run. Instead, consumers see only a sequence of short runs. That may sound like double talk, but it means simply that if consumers do not see their decisions as final, they will be influenced mostly by immediate considerations.

This, then, is the meaning of our earlier statement that the key expectation may be that of change itself. Change has become such a part of our lives that we take it for granted. It is hard to imagine that the situation was ever otherwise. Yet a static environment has characterized most of human history. Even in this country, which has always been relatively dynamic and mobile, the real impact of change was not felt until recently, when technological breakthroughs in organization, transportation, and communications made greater mobility possible.

It is easy to overemphasize this point. Evidence can be brought to refute it. Many people still live in the same town, even in the same house in which they were born. Many consumers still think of large purchases in long-run terms, so they expect to have their refrigerator or automobile more than just a few years. It is also possible to argue that beneath all the apparent change, attitudes and lifestyles remain surprisingly constant.

That evidence can be granted and is worth remembering, particularly by those who say that ours is a "plastic" or "throwaway" society. At the same time, it is impossible to understand what is happening to today's consumer without recognizing that for a significant proportion of the population, there has been a fundamental shift in perspective. For these people, long-run considerations are less important; it follows that long-run expectations are less important too.

It is difficult to know precisely how to evaluate the shift in emphasis. Our present condition is relatively new, brought about by a combination of rising income and technological developments, so we really have not had the time to evaluate it. We do not even know whether it is just a passing phase or represents a lasting condition. Until these determinations are made, we must reserve judgment. We can see, however, that today's consumers differ from their counterparts of earlier generations, and our contention is supported that there are characteristics peculiar to present-day consumer problems that reflect a highly developed economy.

On Measuring Expectations

We have examined different aspects of expectations and linked them with consumer behavior, but have yet to specify the mechanism by which expectations are formed and translated into action through current purchases. It is logical to begin by looking at past experience. When things are going well, individuals have a tendency to think they will continue that way. Conversely, a series of reversals will make consumers more cautious about the future. Such experiences establish a trend, a pattern by which to measure the future. These are subject to change, but the overall tendency is consistent. Success establishes a favorable psychological climate and encourages optimism about the future, and failure does just the opposite.

Individuals basing their interpretation of the future on their past experience reflect differences that are observable and measurable. Individual variations will occur, for as George Katona notes, "Only in certain lower-order responses do we find a one-to-one correspondence between the stimulus and the response" [10, p. 34]. Human response is complex, influenced by different influences (*intervening variables*, in psychological parlance). Nevertheless, a pattern should be discernible that allows us to explain consumer behavior from expectations.

We have indicated that this pattern derives from past experience, which Katona identified as "molding our habits, motives and attitudes." He continued by noting:

> Expectations are a subclass of attitudes that point to the future, since our time perspective extends both backward and forward in a highly selective manner. There is no place for a sharp distinction between attitudes toward the past and the future. . . . [10, p. 34]

What emerges is a complex picture. We see attitudes bound closely to an individual's past experience, to future aspirations, and to the environment in which he lives. Various studies have been undertaken to test this point, and despite mechanical problems and the complexities of measurement, they have shown that expectations affect consumers significantly. As you might suspect, this is clearest with durable-goods purchases, since in most cases, these purchases can be postponed if necessary. By asking questions like, Are you making as much as you were a year ago, or more, or less? and, Do you think prices will go up in the next year or so? consumer attitudes can be categorized [4, p. 365]. When these attitudes are measured against actual purchasing behavior, they clearly show a link between expectations and consumption.

That is not a complete answer to how such expectations are formed. Evidence in this case supports the idea that attitudes are in a continual state of flux, changing as the consumer's environment changes. Again, in Katona's words:

> Wants are not static. Levels of aspiration are not given once for all time. They are *raised with success and lowered with failure.* Success and failure are subjective concepts indicating the individual's perception of his accomplishments as well as disappointments. They are group determined by being viewed in relation to the success and failures of others in one's group. [9, p. 21, emphasis added]

To test his hypothesis, Katona classified people according to what had happened to their income in the four-year period just past and what they expected was going to happen during the next period. Thus, two values were involved for each individual, one actual and one expectational. All individuals whose income had gone up were classified with a plus (+). If they expected income to continue to rise, they rated a second plus for expectations (++). If, however, they felt income would now level off, they would be classified as equal (+=). Those who felt income would now fall were designated with a minus (+−) [9, pp. 24–25].

Thus, there are nine different possibilities. People start off with actual income increasing (as above, +), stable (=), or decreasing (−), and then form expectations about future changes. They may therefore be classed as (++), (+=), (==), (−=), and so on. The (++) group are the most optimistic; they are individuals whose income has gone up and who consider that it will continue to rise. Those whose incomes have not changed and who expect no change are (==), representing a static situation. Individuals who have met with failure and who foresee continued disappointments are the most pessimistic, or (−−). Using these categories, Katona collected information on individuals in different groups, seeking first to find out about purchasing intentions and then checking those against actual purchases. Significant results emerged.* The (++) group emerged clearly as the most avid consumers. Despite past purchases, they expressed buying intentions more frequently than other groups. They proved to buy 50 percent more durables than groups with no (+), and were three times as prone to use credit [9, p. 27].

We can therefore conclude that consumer expectations are important

---

* The results were adjusted to take into account other variables like age, sex, and family size.

in current consumption and that these expectations are a function of experiences in the recent past. While this example concerned income expectations, similar studies have shown similar results for expected changes in prices and other variables [4 and 8]. Our basic approach that emphasizes expectations as a factor in consumer behavior seems justified.

TOWARDS A STRATEGY FOR TOMORROW

The Elements of Time Preference

Expectations are thus a criterion by which consumers divide present and future income. Economists call this division time preference, which for us simply means the value attached to consuming now as opposed to consuming later. We already know that with all else equal, consumers would rather spend now and enjoy their consumption directly. But what about when all else is not equal?

Time preference can be illustrated simply. Suppose it is April and you are thinking of buying a $1200 sailboat, but you only have $600. If you save $45.50 a month for the next year, you will have enough to buy the boat for the following summer. If you want the boat for the coming summer, however, you would have to borrow the $600; paying that back over the next year would cost you $54.50 a month.*

Either way, you will have the boat paid for next spring. Either way, you will have to cut back your spending over the next year so that you have money to save or make your payments. Which should you do? It is clearly cheaper to save and buy the boat next spring; borrowing will cost you $108 more. If you wait, though, you will not have the boat to enjoy for the coming summer. The question can only be answered in those terms. If this summer's sailing is worth $108 to you, then you should go ahead and buy now; if the things you could buy with the extra $9 a month over the next year are worth more to you, however, then you should wait.

If time preference were the only consideration, a decision would not be hard. Suppose two people confronted that situation and one bought the boat now while the other waited; we should say that they were merely demonstrating a different time preference. If we reintroduce uncertainty, however, the situation changes. Maybe one person is unsure about next year's tuition money. In that case, he probably would not want to go into debt. Savings, on the other hand, would make a lot of sense; he could draw on it for tuition if need be, and if he did not need it, he could go ahead and buy the sailboat. These are the kinds of considerations that enter into analyzing time preference.

---

* This assumes you can earn 6 percent interest on both the $600 you start with and the savings you accumulate over the year, and that if you borrow, you will have to pay a 9 percent interest charge.

Notice that we did not say that saving is good and debt is bad. There are no grounds for making such an arbitrary statement. Rather, we perceive a series of conditions, and depending on those conditions, either saving or borrowing may emerge as the better choice. Both have their advantages, but neither one is going to be right for all situations. The distinct features and implications of both savings and borrowing indicate how consumers may use them to advantage. A definition of savings will focus our thoughts. Economists define *savings* simply as "money not spent"; consumers accumulate wealth by postponing consumption. Consumers can do several things with this "money not spent." They can hold it as cash, put it in checking or savings accounts, buy bonds, or put it in the stock market, housing, art, or land. That is quite a variety of choices, some of which are commonly thought of as investment, or even consumption, rather than savings.

A commonsense definition of savings will satisfy our purposes. To arrive at it, we shall apply a *liquidity* criterion. An asset is liquid if it can be easily and safely converted into spendable form. Cash is clearly the most liquid asset, since it is immediately spendable. However, since it earns no return, it is not a very good form of saving; the same is true of checking accounts. Savings accounts are highly liquid, as certain government bonds are. These are the classic forms of savings, offering both earnings and security.

Common stock is less liquid, for while it is generally easy to sell, there is more risk involved and it may be necessary to sell at a loss. Other assets are even less liquid. Housing, for example, may be an excellent hedge against inflation, providing a service at the same time, but it cannot be sold on short notice, and selling carries both costs and a risk of loss. The same is true of art and land, for it is very easy for the amateur to make a bad buy in these areas.

You may have noticed, as we have gone through this list, that earnings potential increases as liquidity decreases. This suggests that an individual's savings should be varied or balanced (*diversified* is the word brokers use). It makes sense to have a mix of assets, some of which are liquid and some of which have big earning potential. The consumer with even modest savings will want to strike some balance between the two.

Striking a balance may not be easy—*there are information costs attached to savings.* Consumers need information about the general types of savings and specific information about the particular type they select. That is, consumers must first choose among stocks, bonds or banks, and then decide which bank or which bond would be best. The information costs may be relatively small, amounting to nothing more than shopping around to see which savings institution (bank, savings and loan, credit union, and so on) offers the best interest. For assets of high yield and low liquidity, however, information costs can be significant. To make a good buy in land, for example, one must know the market, which requires an awareness of population trends, growth rates, and other factors affecting demand. Collecting and analyzing such information requires time and effort beyond the means of most individuals.

The same thing is true of the stock market, although help is generally available through brokers. In that case, the broker assumes the information costs and charges the client a fee. People may set a few dollars aside each week to "play the market" because they enjoy it, but for them it is a hobby, essentially consumption. Those who are seriously interested in the stock market, however, would do well to seek professional advice. No broker can tell you what the market is going to do, but because of his specialization, he is equipped to deal with information costs.

Cornelius Vanderbilt offered sage advice about buying a yacht: "If you have to ask how much it costs, you shouldn't be buying it." The same advice holds true for the type of assets we are discussing here. If you can afford to lose money, well and good, but if not, be cautious. It may make good sense to buy land for a summer place or just to have room to get away from it all, but don't expect it to make you independently wealthy.

The careful reader will recall that this whole discussion was the first of two points; happily, the second point is closely related. It is merely that the structure of the economy hinders, rather than helps, consumers in making these decisions. That is not a new point, but it is worth reemphasizing here.

Consumers are expected, indeed required, to master the ins and outs of saving and borrowing in the same way they are expected to learn how to ride a bicycle. No one can teach you how to ride a bicycle; either it comes naturally or it doesn't. If it doesn't, you keep trying until you get the feel of it. The worst you can pick up is a few bumps and scratches along the way. Unfortunately, if you try to master money management that way, you can pick up a lot more than bumps and scratches. Yet most people are forced into a hit-or-miss approach for lack of an alternative. This is doubly unfortunate because while the problems are real enough, they are not overpowering. In short, good alternatives are not an impossible dream; they could be realized. What is needed is an increased educational effort, which incorporates a wide range of approaches. In addition to formal classroom training, these could include such things as short courses for adults, public service broadcasting, enforced informational broadcasting by financial institutions or any other means that will distribute information cheaply and easily.

It may seem strange that in considering uncertainty we should be so concerned with information costs. At the same time, however, you can see that how best to hedge against the future is intimately bound up with information. While consumers must accept that the future is unknown, they can prepare themselves to deal with it. To do so, they need a consistent strategy, which in turn requires a knowledge of the particular mechanisms involved in hedging against uncertainty. Thus, information about these mechanisms emerges as a proxy for information about the future itself.

That Proverbial Rainy Day

In American folklore, savings or frugality runs a close third to the flag and apple pie. That would be all well and good if the folklore reflected reality. In fact it doesn't. Debt is actually the American way, whether you are talking about the modern suburbanite, the colonial plantation owner, the early capitalist, or the nineteenth-century homesteader.

Virtue, of course, is often promoted and then forgotten, but the issue runs deeper than that. Savings is promoted as a virtue, but the reasons why it is a virtue are seldom made clear. That's actually not quite correct, for there is usually some notion of a rainy day associated with the need to save. At a time when weather forecasters give the chances of rain in terms of probabilities, you would think we'd be able to do better than that.

There are different reasons for saving, all of which fall into two broad categories: saving for some particular goal and saving as a hedge against the future. The sailboat goes into the first category, the rainy day into the second. There is really not much more that we can say about the first type of saving. People do save for houses, vacations, college education, or many other things (a few people may just save to save, but they are in the minority to be sure). The saving is specific; the consumer has a particular target or goal in mind, and saves for it [13].

The rainy day presents more problems, mainly because no one is sure precisely when it is going to rain or how hard or how long. The question then becomes, How much should I save? One savings and loan advertises that "saving 10 percent of gross income means financial security," which means that few Americans are financially secure. On the average, savings in 1971 was only 7 percent of personal income (income before taxes), and the figure for earlier years was significantly lower [5, pp. 212–13]. The answer to how much—one is tempted to say "the obvious answer"—is that there is no set figure that is the *right* amount of savings for all individuals. That should hardly be surprising, since we have been continually emphasizing the importance of individual variations. The right amount for the individual depends on many factors like age, amount and type of insurance, private pension plans, and debt level, as well as on less tangible things like lifestyle and aspirations.

The function of savings has changed significantly over the past generation. In earlier years, the elderly were the responsibility of their children, but that arrangement cannot work well in an urban society. Thus, the need for savings rose, but to do away with the need for large savings, new private and public insurance plans emerged. The best known are social security and Medicare, which do not assure older citizens a financially secure life, but do affect the need for cash savings. Another form of insurance is given by the pension plans in business. Because of improved fringe benefits, many workers earn retirement benefits to supplement social security and personal savings. In a sense, this is a form of forced savings, augmented by employer contributions.

Not all contingency saving is for old age. Again, however, the amount of savings varies. If the individual has adequate medical coverage, including provisions for long-term illness and disability, the need for personal savings will be reduced. Similarly, a single person will have need for less savings than a married couple with children and a mortgaged home.

There are two points here, really. The first is that savings takes different forms in modern society. In a sense, some insurance premiums, social security contributions, and payments to pension funds are savings. As a result, most people really save more than they think. Simultaneously, with these other forms, the need for personal cash savings is reduced. The second point is that it is probably counterproductive to name a percentage of income and say that individuals should save that much. Personal variation is simply too great for that to make much sense. This variation pertains to both reaction to risk and the financial position of the person. The only sound way to make a savings plan is to sit down and take a good look at both your lifestyle and your finances. Out of this should come some picture of your savings needs.

Here is a place where professional advice would be helpful. Happily, it is available to at least part of the population. Your bank is a good source for such help, even while it has, in a literal sense, a vested interest in your savings. But capable professional advice is not as readily available as it ought to be. Poor people are again at a particular disadvantage; they may not be aware of where to go for help, and even if they knew, that help might not be forthcoming. There is a tremendous need for improvement here, at both the public and private levels.

We must admit, then, that while it makes sense for most people to save some money, it is difficult to say much more than that. Individuals need to work out their own savings plans for themselves. Notice that we have not said that savings are unimportant; they offer, on the contrary, needed security against possible adverse developments in the future. It is merely that different individuals have different needs and hence different savings requirements. Consumers should not save out of either fear or vague social pressures. They should be aware of what they are saving for and why. That knowledge is the basis for an intelligent personal savings program.

Insurance: A Policy Statement

So far when we have mentioned insurance, our primary concern was with savings. Now we are reintroducing insurance in a new guise—as it is related to the future. It is the classic hedge against the future and relates directly to how consumers divide income between the future and the present. If you want to insure yourself against future developments, current income must be used, which means that present consumption levels must be reduced.

In its effect, insurance has a lot in common with rainy-day savings; both are a hedge against possible future adversity. However, insurance has a unique feature that distinguishes it from other types of hedging. The amount you collect from insurance is not necessarily limited to a certain sum, while the amount available from savings is limited to the amount you have saved plus interest.

There is another side to the coin. If you do not need the insurance, you get nothing back (with some exceptions), but with savings the money is always yours to use as you wish. The return from insurance is consistent with the principle of insurance. If you knew that you were not going to have any serious illnesses, it would not pay you to buy health insurance. Similarly, if you knew that you were going to be alive at age 70, it probably would not pay to buy life insurance. You cannot know these things, and most people do not want to take the risks involved in the absence of accurate knowledge. That is where insurance comes in; insurance companies can cover risks that would be impossible for the individual to bear.

They can assume risks because they operate under a fundamental law that has nothing to do with governments or courts and is always in force though never enforced. It is the law of large numbers. If you have a red marble and put it in a bowl, you certainly would not bet that anyone reaching into the bowl would come up with anything but a red marble. Even if you add a white marble, the odds are only fifty-fifty. Suppose, though, that you add 999 white marbles to the one red one and mix them all thoroughly. You would probably be willing to make a fairly big wager that the person would not draw the red marble. It is not a sure thing, but the odds of 999 : 1 in your favor make it as good a bet as you are likely to get.

Insurance companies make that kind of bet all the time, although the analogy would probably not be appreciated in Hartford. When you buy health insurance, you are saying "I bet I get sick," and the company is saying "I bet you won't." Just in case you do, however, the company is making the same bet with thousands of other people. You may get sick, along with several others, but the odds are against everyone's getting sick. Thus, while you may collect, the company still comes out the winner because it is receiving payments from thousands of policyholders and paying out to only a few.

Probability is the essence of insurance. By studying records of sickness, accidents, and mortality, the companies can determine the probability of occurrence of any of those events. They know, for example, that the odds against a forty-five year-old male's dropping dead are 30 : 1 (hypothetical figures). They then know how many men they must insure and how much they must charge in order to come out ahead. The company, then, is covering its bets, and in so doing providing a service to the individual that he could not provide for himself. The odds may be 30 : 1 that he will not die, but if he happens to be the one, that's it. Thus, his premiums are an insurance against that chance.

Now that all sounds simple enough, and it is. In the administration and sales of insurance, however, many very difficult questions emerge. Insurance is not always available to all people, and it sometimes seems that the choice of who is insurable is made on very unsound grounds. Then there are questions about the earnings of insurance companies. The companies invest premium payments, earning a further return on their investments. The role of the public interest is not always clear in this instance. We are mentioning these problems because it would be improper to imply that all issues on insurance are covered here. These questions are vitally important to the consumer and are subsequently considered as aspects of consumer power and government protection. Our interest here is with how the consumer can hedge against the future.

Insurance can perform many functions. It may be more than insurance; it may also be savings. Straight life and endowment policies carry a savings feature. You pay more for such insurance, but if you live, you receive the cash value of the policy when it matures. The companies therefore are selling you insurance and collecting your savings. These are in turn invested and the money is paid back to you at the end of a specified period or to beneficiaries on your death.

How well does the insurance company do in managing your savings? Most do fairly well. There is something to be said for this approach, especially when information costs are considered, since it is the company that assumes these costs. Furthermore, individuals who lack the discipline to save may find that such a program of forced savings enables them to save more than they could on their own. Individuals who can manage their own savings, however, will find their efforts well rewarded. With effort, individuals can better the performance of insurance companies on their own. Here is how it works. The cheapest kind of life insurance is called term insurance because it is purchased for a particular period, or term. It is pure protection, with no savings features. However, term insurance is cheap, so you can buy it and then put the difference between what it costs and the cost of a straight life policy into some form of savings.

If you did that, how would you come out? The magazine *Changing Times* asked that question [2]. The magazine's staff compared a $10,000 straight life policy with a $10,000, thirty-year decreasing term policy, both purchased at age 35. The study assumed that the difference between the premiums on the cheaper decreasing term insurance and the straight life would be invested in a mutual fund; brokerage fees were included.* For age 65, the cash value of the mutual-fund holdings was figured at *more than three times* the cash value of the straight life policy. This approach therefore enables you to cover your risks with term insurance and accumulate savings far in excess of what the combined savings-insurance program would have provided.

There are several facets involved in this sequence. Mutual-fund performance varies over time and among different funds. Furthermore, there may be tax advantages to the individual who saves through insurance. The key considerations, however, are information and convenience. Managing your own savings, even through a broker, takes time, effort, and discipline. Once such a program is well established, information costs can be minimized, but they still remain a consideration.

The potential advantages of the independent approach may still be sufficient to convince many individuals that the extra effort is warranted. Again, it is impossible to say that one approach is the right way. That de-

---

* With decreasing term insurance, the value of the policy declines over time; a policy worth $10,000 at the age of 35 might offer only $5,000 coverage at age 50. It was assumed in this example that the earnings from the mutual fund were reinvested.

termination can only be made relative to the individual's own situation. If consumers know the alternatives, they can make their individual decisions in full understanding of what is involved in each case.

Life insurance furnishes the bulk of insurance savings. Most people obtain health and accident insurance through their jobs. The cost of such protection varies, but in most cases it represents a significant savings. Health insurance is a particular problem. Differing national health insurance schemes are under consideration, though it is not certain whether any comprehensive program will be adopted very soon. The need for adequate health care is great; health insurance, even for persons with group policies, is one of the main health care considerations in the United States today.

As far as other types of insurance are concerned, there is a simple rule: It pays to shop. Policies do differ from company to company, but that is not the only point to consider. Service is important, and it is also necessary to find an agent whom you can trust. You may have to read or otherwise inform yourself on insurance so that you will have a better idea of what is going on. Such an investment of time and effort will most likely pay handsome dividends in providing you with improved service and coverage at reasonable rates.

The consumer must contend with the fact that the industry is not organized in such a way as to facilitate comparisons. Policies are written in complex language, which makes just understanding them difficult. Furthermore, similar policies from different companies may differ enough to make direct comparison difficult. The industry's advertising, while it has improved, still provides the consumer with little useful information.

Happily, though, some improvements can be noted. An important step was taken towards better information flow when the Pennsylvania Insurance Department published its *Shoppers Guide to Insurance* [12]. This publication ranks companies in terms of the costs of their policies and the benefits they provide, offering one of the most comprehensive evaluations yet made available to consumers. While it created quite a stir when it was issued, at least one company included the report in its advertising, encouraging people to write for it.

A Dollar Down and a Dollar a Week

Anything that can be said about the need for improved information and life insurance can be redoubled and applied to credit and debt. It is often maintained, that people do not care about interest charges, but only about how much they have to pay and for how long. The extent to which this is true measures public misunderstanding. It would be premature to issue a blanket condemnation of the public because they are uninformed. Although credit and debt are very complicated, individuals get very little help in figuring them out.

Like life insurance companies, lending institutions often advertise, but they provide little information. You may learn that Bank X is *giving away* china (if you deposit *just* $1,000), but more substantive information is hard to come by. Finance companies hold out the hope of "solving your money worries," but seldom mention interest charges or even hint at improving household management. The possibility that the number of nagging little bills being consolidated will constitute one back-breaking load is not broached.

The lack of information is not much different for insurance and for credit and borrowing. The ads give barely a hint of the real issues involved. There are two differences, however, which make the lack of knowledge about credit more serious. The first is the very nature of debt. After all, you cannot be taken to court for not saving nor repossessed for buying the wrong insurance. Mistakes in those areas can be devastating enough, but mishandling debt means financial disaster.

The nature of debt, spending future income, leads to the second difference, reduced future consumption levels. Future income is already encumbered or marked for repayment of debts. While consumers have some flexibility about future consumption levels, the adjustments that can be made are limited. Some costs are fixed, like food and shelter, and cannot be escaped. In the extreme case, consumers may find that they are unable to meet current demands on their income because of the prior demands made by debt service or installment payments.

We have been undergoing a credit explosion in recent years. Credit has become readily available to more people than ever before. This is most obvious in the ubiquitous consumer credit cards, which have become the symbol of the modern consumer. Beyond that, bank loans of all types are more available. Banks even advertise their loans, which must come as a shock to traditionalists who remember banks as the staunch defenders of financial conservatism and personal frugality. Financing is also available from other institutions, often from businesses themselves. They may cater to people who are high credit risks and therefore had difficulty getting credit elsewhere. Not surprisingly, such credit charges are typically very high, though they are buried in such complex language that individuals do not really know what they are. They may not find out even after the truck pulls up to their door to take back their furniture.

There are a variety of horror stories commonly told about such cases, stories mustered to show that consumers are foolish and indifferent. They do not demonstrate that at all; rather they underscore the need for better information flow and more consumer education. Public awareness simply has not kept pace with expanding credit availability. Many people have access to credit today, but too many of them do not know how to use it. The public has had difficulty in coping with the change.

If that is the problem, what are the issues involved in using credit or debt? The basic one is that you do not get something for nothing. If you use credit, you pay for it through interest charges.* Moreover, these interest charges are compounded. That means you pay interest on the interest, and

* This does not apply to 30-day accounts or charges paid within the month.

if you carry that very far, the expense mounts. The variations and complexities are almost endless. While we cannot cover all the possibilities, we can illustrate the most common problems and set out a few basic rules.

The most obvious need is for consumers to find out what interest charges they are actually paying. Some progress was made in this area with the federal truth-in-lending law, which requires that lenders state interest rates in annual terms. Thus, a seemingly minute 1½ percent monthly charge emerges in its true form as an 18 percent annual interest rate. Even that does not complete the picture, however, for that is a simple rate that doesn't take compounding into account. If you pay off a $100 debt at $10 a month, for example (usually the minimum payment), and the interest charge is 1½ percent a month, your effective annual interest rate is over 21%. That means whatever it was you bought cost over one-fifth more than the price tag indicated. All this is very confusing, even if you sit down with a pencil and paper (or better yet, a calculator) and try to figure it out.

One basic principle should be clear. The smaller your monthly payments and the longer they are drawn out, the greater the amount of interest you pay. That should make sense, because the interest rate is applied against the principal, and the more slowly the principal is reduced, the larger the interest charges are going to be. Notice that we have not said this is necessarily bad. It would be quite sensible for the person who values current consumption highly, or in other terms, who applies a very high discount rate to future income. It may be argued that people do not actually discount future income, and that is true in the sense that they do not carry out formal calculations. Most people, however, are well aware of what they want now and what they want later. Further, they know how much it is worth to them. In that sense, they do discount the future. Those who place a relatively low value (a high discount rate) on future income would find small payments and high interest rates quite to their liking.

There are limits to the strategy of using credit. Some people find that they can only make payments to cover interest charges and they never reduce the principal. Theoretically, they could go on paying for ever. If the amounts involved are large, this will place a serious drain on the individual's financial resources. Very few people would be able to carry on for very long under such conditions.

That is the sort of financial disaster we mentioned earlier. It happens all too frequently when people get in over their heads, or more realistically, over their pocketbooks. This may result from some unforeseen development like the loss of a job or illness in the family. More often, however, it happens out of ignorance. This brings us full circle, back to the twin concerns information and education. By now their importance should be self-evident. Not only must consumers know how they value consumption now as opposed to consumption in the future, but they must know the implications of the various alternatives open to them. Without this knowledge, they are in no position to decide such matters. Improved educational programs and better information flow can only improve performance.

Wesley Clair Mitchell, in 1912, felt there was reason for optimism. He observed:

> With greater confidence we may rely upon progress in physiology and psychology to make wider and more secure the scientific foundations of housekeeping. But such progress will have little practical effect unless the results of research are made available to far larger circles. This work of popularizing scientific knowledge, however, promises to become increasingly effective. [14, p. 18]

We can only wonder what Mitchell's reaction would be if he realized that over half a century later most of these promises were still unfulfilled. The need for "popularizing scientific knowledge" still exists. The means are at hand to do it; it is possible to give consumers the information, training, and assistance they need to operate effectively in the marketplace. Carrying out such a program is something else again. The needs illustrate how interrelated consumer problems are. Part of hedging against uncertainty is obtaining adequate information.

STUDY QUESTIONS

1.   You can put a dollar in the bank and let it earn interest so that in a year it will be worth more. How, then, can a dollar now be worth more than a dollar a year from now?

2.   If the interest rate is 5 percent, would a bond worth $5,000 in five years be a good buy at $3,750 now? Suppose the interest rate were 7 percent? Would it be a good buy at 5 percent if it did not mature for eight years?

3.   Suppose you are asked to observe the consumption behavior of two couples, each earning $9,000 a year. One is made up of recent college graduates, while the other is made up of grandparents in their late sixties. How would their consumption patterns differ? Would you expect any similarities between the two?

4.   Briefly explain how expectations might affect current consumption behavior in each of the following cases:
   a.   A teacher who expects both income and prices to go up in the future.
   b.   A construction worker whose wages have been going up steadily, although he has been laid off several times in recent years.
   c.   A person who is now 25 and will inherit $500,000 when her 55-year-old aunt dies.
   d.   A farmer who expects his income to go down in the future.

5. Suppose a middle-income worker in his mid-twenties buys $250,000 worth of life insurance. What does this tell you about his reaction to uncertainty?

6. A university administration announces an increase in retirement benefits that requires an increase in payroll deductions. Younger faculty members oppose the move, while older ones support it. Should the administration have expected this reaction? Explain.

7. Why does inflation favor current consumption? Does it also favor going into debt? Explain.

8. Suppose you have your savings in an account earning 5½ percent and your neighbor tells you that you could be earning 6 or 7 percent. Assuming all savings are insured, should you switch your savings? What do you need to know before you answer?

9. Art of good quality appreciates tremendously over time. Why, then, don't more people put their money in art, for which a high return is practically assured?

10. People typically save and go into debt at the same time (that is, they have both a mortgage and a savings account). Others gamble and buy life insurance. Are these combinations of behavior consistent? What do they tell you about the individuals' attitudes towards risk and uncertainty?

11. Under what conditions might it be wise for a person to
  a. Have no savings.
  b. Have no life insurance.
  c. Have neither savings nor life insurance and go deeply into debt.

SUGGESTED PROJECTS

1. We are all familiar with homey little sayings like "A penny saved is a penny earned"; "A bird in the hand is worth two in the bush"; and "Eat, drink and be merry, because tomorrow we die." Write up a more comprehensive list of such sayings. What do they tell you about reactions to the future? Can they be used to gauge society's attitudes?

2. We have suggested that since the expansion of credit is a fairly recent development, younger people should be more prone to use credit than older ones. You can test this hypothesis by developing a set of questions that reflect people's attitudes towards debt. You might ask questions like:
  a. Is going into debt wrong?
  b. Should debt be used only for purchasing homes?
  c. Should debt be used for buying cars but not appliances?

    d.   Should debt be used only in emergencies?

    e.   Should you ever carry a credit balance over 30 days?

Allow people to agree, give no opinion, or disagree (or add strongly agree or disagree, see Appendix). Sample different populations such as students, parents, urban, rural, random groups, and so on. Do any significant differences emerge? Do these follow the pattern you expected? What factors besides their classification might influence people's reactions?

    3.   Have several members of the class contact different insurance companies about the same type of policy. How do price and coverage differ? Ask the different agents for their recommendations and compare what they say.

    4.   Make a comparative study of interest rates:

    a.   Check at different savings institutions for rates on different types of savings. Compare rates among institutions and different types of savings programs. What pattern emerges? How is this affected by government regulations?

    b.   Survey loan rates. How do rates vary with length of time, type of loan, and amount? Include financing offered by sellers in your study. What can you conclude?

    5.   Companies that use games or sweepstakes as sales promotions must now publish the odds of winning. Collect several of these advertisements and estimate the expected value of the prize by multiplying its price times the probability of winning. Is this sufficient to induce you to buy the product? Is it sufficient to cover the cost of a stamp and the time necessary to enter? Would you expect different people to react differently to such offers?

    6.   There is a famous problem in expectations and probabilities called the St. Petersburg game. Players flip a coin and as long as it comes up heads, they win the value of the coin and the chance to flip again; it it comes up tails, they are out. Thus, they stand the chance of winning an infinite amount of money (assuming they continue to toss heads). Why wouldn't you pay very much for the chance to be in such a game, even though you could win a great deal? Can you figure precisely what the chance to play would be worth? Try it and see what average winnings are.

    7.   Do people really discount the future and take this into account when they consider future income, debt, and savings? Discuss how you might devise a means of testing this question.

    8.   Analyze the advertising of various financial institutions (banks, savings and loans, finance companies, and financing offered by individual firms). Do these ads offer significant information to the consumer? Would any of them confuse the consumer? (See Chapter 6 for more detailed consideration of this question.)

BIBLIOGRAPHY AND SUGGESTED READINGS

1. Adams, F. G. "Consumer Attitudes, Buying Plans and Purchases of Durable Goods." *Review of Economics and Statistics* 46 (November 1964).

   A famous study on the topic that technically oriented students with an interest in the area will find well worth reviewing.

2. *Changing Times.* Kiplinger publication. October 1962.

   Worth checking for information on insurance and related questions. As indicated in the text, this magazine has produced some good comparative studies, providing information that is typically difficult to obtain elsewhere.

3. Devletoglou, Nicos E. *Consumer Behavior.* New York: Harper & Row, 1971.

   Economics students may enjoy looking through this unorthodox book. It illustrates the possibilities with the analysis we have developed over the past two chapters and reaches some unusual conclusions.

4. Dunkelberg, William C. "The Impact of Consumer Attitudes on Behavior: A Cross-Section Study." In *Human Behavior in Economic Affairs,* ed. Burkhard Strumpel, et al. San Francisco: Jossey-Bass, 1972, pp. 347–71.

   Another study relating attitudes to consumer buying patterns and intentions to buy. Valuable for practical illustrations of problems involved, including actual questions asked.

5. *Economic Report of the President.* Washington: D.C.: U.S. Government Printing Office, 1972. Chap. 1.

   Data, current and historical, on income, savings, and consumption patterns.

6. Friedman, Milton. *The Theory of the Consumption Function.* Chicago: University of Chicago Press, 1957.

   Imaginative and thorough study of the relations between income and consumption; basis for development of the permanent income hypothesis. Also contains interesting material on uncertainty and how it affects economic analysis.

7. Halter, Albert N., and Dean, Gerald W. *Decisions Under Uncertainty.* Cincinnati: South-Western Publishing Co., 1971.

   Illustrates problems of decision making under uncertainty. Latter parts are less analytical and give practical applications. Good for students seriously interested in these subjects.

8. Juster, R. Thomas, and Wachtel, Paul. "Uncertainty, Expectations and Durable Goods Demand Models." In *Human Behavior in Economic Affairs,* ed. Burkhard Strumpel, et al. San Francisco: Jossey-Bass, 1972, pp. 321–45.

   A study of the impact of consumer expectations on the critical area of consumer durables. Another good illustration of statistical techniques applied to real problems.

9. Katona, George. "Consumer Behavior: Theory and Findings on Expectations and Aspirations." *American Economic Review, Papers and Proceedings,* May 1968, pp. 19–30.

Important and understandable study on the formulation and impact of expectations. For all its $(++)$ and $(--)$, this paper offers a straightforward approach.

10. Katona, George. *The Mass Consumption Society.* New York: McGraw-Hill Book Co., 1964.

11. Katona, George. *The Powerful Consumer.* New York: McGraw-Hill Book Co., 1960.

Anyone who reads nothing else on uncertainty and expectations should read these two books. Students will find them understandable and interesting. They are particularly valuable because they apply to actual developments and assume a broad, interdisciplinary approach to the problems.

12. *Shopper's Guide to Insurance.* Harrisburg, Pa.: Pennsylvania Insurance Department.

The best available comparison of insurance policies. Makes dollar-for-dollar comparisons so that consumers can evaluate policies. An excellent comparison of costs and benefits. Pennsylvania plans to offer similar studies in other areas, a good illustration of a service that state regulatory agencies can, but commonly do not, offer.

13. Troelstrup, Arch W. *The Consumer in American Society*, 4th ed. New York: McGraw-Hill Book Co., 1970.

One of the best personal finance textbooks, offering a broader perspective than most. Contains some good material on the mechanics of savings and insurance. See especially Chapters 13 and 14.

14. Mitchell, Wesley Clair. "The Backward Art of Spending Money." In *The Backward Art of Spending Money and Other Essays.* New York: McGraw-Hill Book Co., 1937.

5

A Little Knowledge Is a Dangerous Thing

THE PROBLEM OF BEING INFORMED

The Informed Consumer—A Fable

It was sad that night about a year ago when I went to the refrigerator to get a beer. I reached in and took out the can, but my heart sank when I opened it. The happy "snap" was followed by an unfamiliar "glurg." Tearfully I screamed to my wife, "The refrigerator is freezing my beer!" "So," she replied, "it's been freezing the lettuce for six months." Even in my disoriented state I understood that there was no use in pursuing the topic with someone who did not understand the difference between freezing beer and lettuce. Sadly I concluded that the time had come to buy a new refrigerator.

That sounded simple enough, but one problem became clear as soon as we began our search for a new box (that is what a refrigerator is called in the trade, a "box"). I knew nothing about boxes, or refrigerators either. How many cubic feet did we need? Where did we want the freezer? What were the advantages of a side-by-side model? Did we really need the model with an automatic icemaker that served drinks through the door? I had always thought of refrigerators as things that keep food cold, but I soon discovered a whole set of confusing specifications and features.

As I wandered through the multicolored world of no-frost refrigerators, I could have consoled myself with the thought that I was not alone. Most people do not know much about refrigerators. Most people do not know very much about most of the things they buy. Even if that thought had comforted me at the time, it is hardly a very encouraging note on which to begin our consideration of the consumer's overall problem of information.

In my confused state I may have been typical of most consumers, but I had nothing in common with the consumer prototype from economic theory. Economic theory admits no such problems. It assumes that consumers have perfect information about all the products they want. If I had known one of these theoretical consumers, I should not have had to search at all; I should merely have had to asked my perfectly informed companion.

Such an encounter is an impossible dream, but it emphasizes both the importance of information and the distance between theory and reality in this case. It is obvious why the assumption of perfect knowledge is necessary; without it the consumer could never reach equilibrium. The same thing is true of the real-world consumer. Information is required to reach maximum satisfaction, but in this case we are not in a position simply to assume the problem away. We have to deal with it.

We have already come to realize the importance of information. Many issues viewed in terms of rationality or irrationality really break down into questions of information. What appears to be an irrational purchase may reflect a lack of information. When there is uncertainty, there is a need for information about the future. Moreover, information emerges as the critical ingredient in evaluating matters associated with savings, insurance, and debt. Many problems in these areas are linked to the expense and difficulty in getting information. Our main emphasis has been on consumers themselves and their subjective evaluations of their own wants and needs. While these matters have external aspects, they are essentially internal and personal. The products that satisfy consumer wants, however, are external, and to judge them, the consumer needs to know what the product will do. The performance of a particular product is definite; it does not depend on any subjective evaluation. Either a refrigerator will hold 17 cubic feet of food or it will not; that is all there is to it.

The consumer may still ask, Should I buy the refrigerator? The answer to that question depends on personal priorities and tastes and expectations about the life of the current refrigerator he owns. Those are largely personal decisions, but they cannot be made intelligently without information about cost and performance of the new refrigerator. Information again emerges as the key to the consumer's decision. Since information is so important, consumers' ignorance about many of the things they buy looms even larger. Yet we cannot place all the blame on the consumer. Things are so complex that it is impossible to know everything about everything. This would be a problem even if the market were static, but it isn't; products are always changing. The stereo buff might find that with the advent of quadrasonic sound he has to relearn everything about the field. Pity too the poor car buyer who has spent a lifetime understanding all about cam shafts, pistons, rods and points, who suddenly confronts the rotary engine.

The High Cost of Ignorance

It is hardly an exaggeration to conclude that information is the most important element in the whole consumer approach. If there were no information problem, consumer problems would not go away but they would be significantly reduced, and the solutions to those that remained would be greatly simplified. If you doubt that, consider for a minute what the alternatives are. It should not even take you a full 60 seconds to come up with the answer; the alternative to information is ignorance.

Ignorance means that consumers lack adequate information on which to base their decisions. It follows that *ignorant consumers are also defenseless consumers*. Unless they have information, consumers cannot be sure that the product they are buying is the right one for them. They cannot even be sure that the product or service is what it claims to be. If you pick your car up after having it in the garage, for instance, how can you be sure the mechanic took care of its difficulty if you know nothing about automobiles?

Senator Warren Magnuson offers a more graphic illustration. He quotes a postal inspector who was investigating complaints of consumer fraud in Oklahoma. The inspector reported that high-pressure salesmen

> induced more than 1,000 financially distressed persons in Oklahoma to sign purchase contracts and promissory notes for the purchase of major household appliances . . . at the grossly inflated price of $660.96 on a three-year payment contract. . . . [12, p. 19]

Would these same people have signed the contracts if they had known, as the report continues, that identical appliances could be purchased in the area for "less than $300 each, and some for less than $250"? They certainly would not, but without that information, they lacked a basis for comparison. They were no match for the viciousness of the unscrupulous salesmen.

In short, *knowledge is power*. The consumer who has it can make intelligent decisions, or in other words, consumers who have information can look after their own interests. We have been saying that all along really, for we have emphasized that individual consumers will make choices in line with their preferences. We can now see that while that is true, it assumes that consumers have the information on which to base their decisions.

Improved consumer information is actually a form of consumer protection. That is why there is no mention of consumer protection laws in economic theory; they are not needed because consumers can protect themselves. In reality, consumer protection laws remain important because while information flow can be improved, perfect information is impossible. The market is simply too complex for everyone to understand about all the products in it.

Nevertheless, the case for improved information remains strong. It is impossible to legislate against every possible type of consumer fraud. Further-more, a law once enacted must be enforced, and that takes time and money. Thus, it makes sense also to give consumers the power to protect themselves. The more the consumers are equipped to look after themselves, the less the government or some other agency will have to look after them. From a policy point of view, that is a very important point. It means that government can help not only by passing specific laws that protect the consumer, but also through legislation that improves the flow of information. We can sum-marize that idea by saying that while the government needs to help con-sumers directly, it also needs to help consumers help themselves. That re-quires giving them the tools to make intelligent decisions. Notice that this approach reflects a particular view of consumers. It assumes that given the wherewithal to do it, consumers can look after themselves. They are not stupid and irrational, as they are so often portrayed, but merely ill equipped to do the job they are supposed to be doing.

There is one additional advantage improved information has over legislation; it can protect consumers from themselves. No law can do that.* Everyone makes mistakes, but with better information, such mistakes should be minimized. Consumer protection legislation would have helped in the case of the appliance salesmen mentioned above, but if the salesmen had been able to convince consumers they were getting a great deal, such legisla-tion would not have done much good. Better information is needed to stop such frauds, marking the consumer as the first line of defense against such abuse rather than as an easy touch.

Therefore, in considering everything about better information, we are discussing the cornerstone of the system. If individual choice is to have any meaning, individuals must have the information to make those choices. Given that information, consumers can emerge as a powerful force within the marketplace. Without it, they are no better than sheep, and the best they can hope for is that some benevolent shepherd will look after them.

The High Cost of Information

There is no doubt that ignorance is expensive, but so is information. For consumers to find out about the things they buy, they must be prepared to absorb these costs. That is the point that is too often overlooked. It is easy enough to come out against ignorance, but that begs the question: everybody is against ignorance. The costs of reducing ignorance have to be weighed.

There is nothing mysterious about these costs. They include the time, effort, and money expended in obtaining enough information to make an intelligent choice. In plain terms, a consumer has to shop around in one

---

* Some laws can help though. One example is legislation that gives consumers three days to change their minds after signing a contract. This so-called cooling-off period helps offset high-pressure sales techniques. Consumers who were pressured into signing might on re-flection think better of it. See Chapter 8.

way or another before making a purchase. One of the everlasting glories of economics is that it can take something as simple and commonplace as shopping and give it an imposing name like "information costs." It is, however, an appropriate term. You don't really shop for products, you shop for information about the product, and that involves costs.

Consider again my quandary with the refrigerator. It would hardly have been wise for me simply to go out and buy one, any one. I had to become familiar with the market for refrigerators, their features, and their prices before I could know what to do. Such activities took time—time I could not use for doing other things. It also took gasoline and operating time on the car. And remember the babysitting money—nothing makes shopping more painful than dragging two preschoolers from store to store. All of these costs have to be taken into consideration and added to the cost of the refrigerator itself.

Information costs may vary considerably from person to person. If an appliance dealer's refrigerator were to start freezing his beer, he would have less trouble than I would in picking a new one; he would already be familiar with the elements involved in the decision. That is an important point; we pick up bits of information as we go along. Some comes from experience, while some we just pick up as random information. It may seem useless at the time, but at some later date, it could come in handy. This accumulation of knowledge is *residual information*. The more residual information a person starts out with, the shorter the search that will be required. I knew almost nothing about refrigerators when I started out. That is true as far as particulars were concerned, but I did carry along some residual information. I knew, for example, that the compressor is the heart of the refrigeration mechanism, which means that the guarantee on the compressor is most important. I also knew that frost-free varieties use more electricity. So there were some things I didn't have to learn; or perhaps it is better to say that I knew enough to know where to start finding out more.

The most important residual information is knowing that the product exists. That may seem so obvious that it hardly deserves mention, but under certain circumstances it can be a significant factor. While most everyone knows about refrigerators, at least part of the population is unaware of many available goods and services. You may be confounded by a wet basement, for example, while if you only knew of a new waterproof paint, you could care for the difficulty quickly and inexpensively.

A more significant example is the family that does not know the basic nutritional requirements. The shortcomings of the family's diet may be contributing to ill health, and the family does not know what is wrong. Most people are informed about nutrition and take the information for granted. However, given the tremendous variation in information levels, one cannot assume universal information conditions. Too often, an information gap forms the basis for serious biases. It may be said, for example, that a certain group of consumers does not shop wisely. In part, this reflects the effort of one group to impose its tastes on another. To the extent that such contentions have a basis in fact, however, they are likely to reflect a lack of information rather than irresponsibility or irrationality.

This situation serves to complicate the information-cost question. It means we need to be concerned not only about information on certain products or services, but also basic information on market operations and product types. It also means we must be concerned with getting this information cheaply and easily to the people who need it, for the information itself is usually available. The problem lies in the transferral mechanism, which means that although the information is there, it is not well distributed.

Inadequate flow of information affects all consumers to some degree. It means that consumers must incur the costs of obtaining their own information. In my case, it meant shopping in the literal sense. I might have stayed home, calling appliance dealers on the phone; or I could have read *Consumer Reports* to see how they rated refrigerators. Certain ways of obtaining information are more efficient than others, but regardless of my approach, I would still have faced costs.

As the marketplace has become more complex over the years, these costs have risen and the consumer's position has deteriorated. This recalls the low level of specialization usual within the family. The wide range of products that families purchase and the complex organization of the market make it most difficult for either families or the individual consumer to cope with information costs. There is, moreover, little opportunity for greater specialization. The only alternative is to develop mechanisms to disseminate information cheaply and easily to all consumers. We need to analyze the nature of information costs as well as available sources of information and how they can be improved. To do that, we must be more specific about precisely how information costs affect the consumer.

The Optimal Quantity of Information

While the consumer needs information to make purchasing decisions, that information is seldom free. This implies that *the consumer must weigh the cost of the information against the benefits obtained from it*. This, in turn, suggests the rather surprising conclusion that it might not always pay the consumer to seek additional information. That conclusion is surprising because it means that the optimal amount of information—the amount that is right for that consumer—might not be the maximum amount of information available. Such a contention seems to run counter to both our discussions of the theoretical consumer and popular notions of the responsible, well-informed consumer. Cost is clearly at the heart of the matter. Consumers in theory are perfectly informed, but they do not have to face information costs. If knowledge is free, it makes sense to get as much of it as you can. Since knowledge isn't free for the typical consumer, however, that rule no longer holds.

That point seems to be missed all too often in popular discussions. The virtues of information are extolled and the well-informed consumer is held up as the ideal model for all of us. Such exercises are certainly counterproductive; when we mere mortals set out to emulate the ideal type, we find the process not only expensive, but nearly impossible. Having come up short, we appear to be failures. It is quite likely that the myth of the stupid consumer is founded in such unrealistic prototypes. These not only discourage individual consumers, but also mask the real issues involved and thus inhibit the movement towards a workable solution to the problem.

Realistically, then, how can we expect the consumer to cope with information costs? To answer that, let us go back to my experience with the refrigerator. As I continued my shopping, I began to feel that I had heard it all before. I found that as I visited additional dealers, they didn't tell me anything about refrigerators that I didn't already know. Furthermore, the variations in prices I was quoted by the next dealer were smaller and smaller. I could be fairly sure that the price quoted by the next dealer would be somewhere between the highest and lowest prices I had already received. In short, it appeared that there was not much to be gained by shopping further.

That rather simple statement really answers the question. I could have gone on, visited more shops, made more phone calls and read more reports, but would it have paid? I might have found a tremendously good buy that would have made it all worth while, but that was highly unlikely. Even if I had found a slightly lower price or uncovered some desirable feature that I had not been aware of, it probably would not have been enough to warrant all that extra effort.

Thus, we can offer this rule about the optimal quantity of information: *The consumer should search until the expected savings from additional search is equal to the cost of that search* [15, pp. 216–19]. Suppose you are just beginning to search; you can reasonably expect that the information you gain will be more than enough to compensate you for your time, effort, and money. Certainly, then, you should continue searching. There comes a time, however, as in the example of the refrigerator, that the cost of extra search is higher than the expected savings. When that point is reached, it does not pay to seek additional information.

If we change our argument only slightly, we can cast it in terms of diminishing marginal utility. As additional units of a good are consumed, the utility gained from that consumption will decline. The same thing holds true for searching out information. After a point, additional search yields less additional information. Since savings and information are related, expected savings will decline as the quantity of new information uncovered declines. This includes both direct savings through lower prices and savings associated with finding the most desirable features and the best item for the consumer's needs.

There is nothing mysterious about this process. It merely reflects the probabilities associated with the statistical properties of a sample. When political pollsters take their polls, they do not talk to every voter; they select a sample that reflects the character of the population as a whole. If their techniques are correct, they can feel reasonably safe in attributing the ideas expressed in their sample to the entire population. When you go shopping, you may not think of it in terms of taking a sample, but that is what you are doing.

You visit a few stores—say, five out of fifty—and obtain information about price and performance. This sample should give you a pretty good profile of the market, including price dispersion and available features. If you feel that your sample is a good approximation of the rest of the market, there is no sense in searching further. You make your decision based on the information you have, assuming that the rest of the market is similar to the portion you have canvassed. You may be wrong, but if the cost of finding out is greater than the potential savings, it would not be worthwhile to make the effort.

The optimal amount of search will vary with the individual. It depends in part on residual information; the person who begins with no information has a bigger task. It also depends upon the individual's reaction to risk. Some people naturally are risk averters. Since there is some risk involved in buying with less than total information, we should expect such people to search more.

The character of the market also determines the search. The individual who finds that prices at the first five stores visited are all very similar might stop searching, concluding that the odds are against finding any significant variation. On the other hand, one who finds significant variation with no clear pattern would feel that additional search is warranted; since extreme variations exist, even greater variations and even lower prices are possible. The simple geography of the market has something to do with this. If stores are grouped so that it is easy and cheap to visit several, search costs will be lower than if the stores are spread out.* You might have to drive all over town to visit three junkyards, while you could visit three clothing stores in a single shopping center [15, pp. 218–19].

Finally, the product in question must be considered. Our rule says that the consumer will shop more when expected savings are greater. The higher the cost of the item, the greater the potential or expected savings. We can predict, therefore, that consumers will shop more for expensive items than for cheap ones. For the latter, it may not even pay to shop at all. Suppose you are looking for a ballpoint pen, the kind you can pick up for 20 cents. Sometimes you see them on special for a dime, but it would not pay you to shop around for a special. You would not save enough to make the search worthwhile. On the other hand, if additional search would save you 50 percent on a car or an appliance, you would continue to search; the expected savings would clearly make it worth the effort [15, pp. 218–19; and 16, pp. 1–4].

---

* This is primarily why stores tend to cluster. Their proximity helps all of them, since customers will be attracted by the fact that they can shop easily at many stores. All the stores benefit from the fact that customers' information costs are reduced. Students interested in location theory will find considerable literature on this topic. See [13].

Search may have consumption value for some individuals. That is a fancy way of saying that some people like to shop. In such cases, the individual may search beyond the point at which expected savings equals cost; this is rational so long as the individual gets sufficient enjoyment out of shopping to cover the additional cost. The buff, or enthusiast, represents the extreme example of this type. The camera buff will read magazines and reports and so on about cameras, obtaining information quite in excess of that needed to buy a camera. The same is true of other hobbyists; for them, there is consumption value in the information itself.

The consumption value of search will vary not only among individuals but also among types of searches. Some people simply do not enjoy shopping. Others may enjoy only particular types of shopping; the automobile expert might be a virtual encyclopedia of information about cars but hate to shop for furniture. Finally, the situation is important. It is one thing to shop in a leisurely manner when there is no pressure. If however, your water heater just broke and you have to replace it immediately, there is no time for relaxed shopping. In such cases, search will be purely functional, valued only for the information it uncovers.

Towards an Information Policy

Establishing the optimal amount of information for the individual has brought us closer to our goal of improving information flow to consumers as a group. We now know what is needed to bring about such an improvement. The two key elements that determine the amount of search are *expected savings* and *the cost of search*. Since consumers will not continue searching past the point where the two are equal, that equilibrium should be the focus of our attention.

Since we have established the requirements, improving information flow is simple enough. *It is necessary either to increase expected savings or to reduce the costs of search.* At equilibrium, the two are equal ($ES = C$), but if expected savings increase so that $ES > C$, it will be worthwhile to seek out more information. Reducing information costs has the same effect. For a given level of expected savings, it would pay to obtain more (of the now less expensive) information. In either case, additional search is required to restore the equality, and this increases the flow of information.

To a degree, these two alternatives are merely different aspects of the same process. Information costs are actually involved on both sides of the equation, since they bear on expectations. Information is an important element in forming expectations. We have considered how the individual takes into account information from past experiences and the experience of others in framing expectations about the future. The same thing is true of expected savings; individuals must have some idea of what to expect and that idea must be based on information.

In other words, better information leads to more realistic expectations. Individuals who feel that all dealers charge the same price, for example, might not search at all. In most cases, they would be passing up significant savings. Accurate information about those potential savings would have changed their expectations and induced them to seek out price information. For people who lack basic information about nutritional qualities of food, better information would help them expect more from their diet and hence affect their shopping habits.

In a sense we are talking about residual information, how much information a consumer begins with. It is residual information that is important in framing expectations, in giving the consumer an idea of what to expect. Consumers who start with a reasonable level of information will sense the market accurately and have a sound basis for their expectations. Or expressed differently, the consumer's level of uncertainty is reduced and his confidence in the marketplace increased. Surely, greater confidence should make better consumers, which in turn should improve how the marketplace functions.

Improving the position of the individual consumer and the operation of the marketplace thus requires providing the consumer with high-quality, low-cost information [9]. The rationale we have developed to support that claim buttresses it with more than intuition or common sense, and justifies suggesting ways in which information costs can be reduced. Some of the proposals we are about to suggest may seem startling; they constitute a significant change from the present methods. If information were not so important, the bother might not be warranted. Fundamental change, after all, is necessary only if there is some fundamental issue involved. Since information costs meet that requirement, they not only deserve our attention but also require action.

STRATEGIES FOR CUTTING INFORMATION COSTS

Government and Information Flow

Consumers face a gigantic task in their quest for information, but fortunately they do not have to bear the entire burden themselves. Government, recognizing the importance of these matters to the consumer, has assumed some of the weight. This recognition has been uneven, however, and the government has proved at best an uncertain ally; thus consumers may look to the government for help but should not expect a total solution.

Some of the difficulty lies in the fact that government should really be plural. Public agencies involved in providing information to consumers operate at the state, local, and federal levels. In the case of the first two, there is a great deal of variation, so that citizens in one area may enjoy considerably more help than those in others. Variation exists even within the federal government; one agency may be active and aggressive, while another languishes. This inconsistent pattern is troublesome for the consumer.

Government policies affecting the flow of information constitute consumer protection. Rather than protect the consumer directly, these policies equip consumers to protect themselves. The need for such laws is apparent, for the market is so complex that it would be nearly impossible for consumers to collect sufficient information on their own. *Nearly impossible* means here that the costs would be prohibitive. For analytical purposes, the various public policies that affect information flow can be classified under three main headings: *legal limitations, standards,* and *direct information.*

The first category, legal limitations, covers a broad range of government activities. Any consumer protection law can be considered to be in this category. Whereas improved information leads to consumer protection, consumer protection leads to improving information. To the extent that consumer protection laws are effective, they should free the consumer from having to worry about fraud and deception.* The government in this case is acting like an umpire, setting and enforcing the rules of the game. Consumers can then operate within the rules, freed from the need to investigate such questions on their own and able to concentrate on obtaining supplemental information.

Historically, this is the oldest form of government protection and involves such basic matters as contract rights. If the consumer signs a valid contract, he can be sure that it will be enforced. In this sense, the extensive legal framework that has grown up around the marketplace can be considered as a part of the information-flow mechanism. Unfortunately, these limitations are effective only if they are enforced and if consumers are aware of their rights.

Some consumer protection laws directly apply to consumer information. If a business advertises a special sale, with all merchandise marked down, it will naturally attract customers. It has not been uncommon for businesses to use this as a gimmick, with so-called sale prices actually reflecting no savings at all. That is now illegal; merchandise cannot be offered for sale unless it has been marked down a given percentage, having been offered for sale previously at the higher price. Such regulations can be evaded, but they do offer consumers some protection by cutting information costs; if something is advertised as on sale, consumers will know it is really on sale.

Similarly, if firms advertise merchandise at special prices, they must have adequate stocks on hand. It used to be common for stores to advertise an item at an extremely low price, but when the customer arrived to see it, the item was inevitably sold out. This is called "bait and switch." The ad is the bait; the switch comes when the customer is told there is a similar product available that although somewhat more expensive, is really a better buy. The advertisement merely attracts the customer to the store so that salesmen can push a more expensive item. Now, the consumer knows that if a store advertises a special price, it must have the product at that price.

---

* We shall discuss the particulars of consumer protection legislation in Chapter 8; they are considered here since they affect information flow.

Despite remarkable progress in recent years, serious problems still remain. New deceptions are practiced and old ploys remain. Many important areas of consumer protection that relate to improved information have not been adequately covered. Even when the laws are passed, however, enforcement is spotty. Consumers' information costs are reduced only when they can count on enforcement of the laws. Here is where enforcement variation causes problems, for if consumers cannot rely on the effectiveness of government protection, they will be forced to seek out information themselves and in so doing lose the benefits of lower information costs.

While government officials are sometimes lax and once in a while actually dishonest, the biggest problem of enforcement does not lie in lack of zeal but of resources. While dedicated officials may work hard for the public, there are too few of them for the jobs that need to be done. The Federal Trade Commission has been criticized for moving too slowly against deceptive advertisements; they probably have been slow, but the FTC's total budget for such activities is less than most big companies spend advertising a single product. This is clearly an area where public support and pressure are needed so that such agencies can get the resources to do the job.

Many people do not know what protection is available to them or what their rights are. This is especially apparent among low-income consumers, but it is by no means limited to that group. If knowledge is power, then such people are clearly powerless. They become vulnerable to pressure and easy prey for both the deceptions of fradulent operators and the indifference of more established businessmen. Better laws and even better enforcement cannot be really effective if the total population is not aware of such protection. Unfortunately, most agencies do not have a sufficient budget to publicize their activities, and efforts to use the media have been inadequate. Private groups have had some successes in spreading such information, but their operations have generally been on a small scale.

A large-scale campaign is needed to spread information to the people who need it most. That is an easy conclusion to reach, almost a platitude, but only a concerted effort can open channels of information. Channels include the schools, media, community groups, and legal establishment. Unless people know what their rights are and the degree to which they are actually protected, their rights cannot be assured and protection cannot be effective.

The second way that the government supports the consumer, imposing standards, directly affects information costs. The standards take many forms, but compose two main categories. They are (1) inspection and licensing, and (2) setting standards for information that producers and sellers must provide to the public. As an example of the first, health departments license establishments that serve food, attesting that they meet minimal health standards. Similar inspections are made of many different businesses. In each case, the idea is to assure the public that the product or service meets minimal standards of safety or quality. Meat inspection is a good example of imposing standards. If the government inspects meat, buyers can assume that it is safe and free from contamination. The government's role does not stop with inspection; meats are graded also. This offers another service to consumers, providing information about relative quality of meats as measured by specific standards. Since most consumers are not experienced meat graders, they would be unable to make independent judgments.

There has recently been pressure for extending government standards into new areas. Much of it has focused on automobiles, stressing safety and pollution control. Safety provides a good example, for most people were unaware of the potential hazards in their automobiles. That illustrates the point that what you don't know *can* hurt you. Standards are now being imposed on other products like toys and clothing, with fireproofing a prominent concern for the latter.

The various government regulatory agencies may be considered under the same heading. These agencies are charged with overseeing specific parts of the economy such as medicine and drugs (the Food and Drug Administration), radio and television (the Federal Communications Commission), transportation (the Interstate Commerce Commission), and so on. The rationale for these agencies is based in part on information costs. Regulation is imposed in areas for which market operations alone are judged insufficient to protect the public interest.

Part of the reason that markets do not work well in some instances involves the complex and technical nature of the products themselves. To evaluate the safety and effectiveness of drugs, for example, requires technical information beyond the means of all but a very few consumers. Since consumers cannot get necessary information on their own, they cannot effectively check the operations of firms in the drug industry. For this reason, government takes on the responsibility of ensuring that drugs meet specified standards of safety and effectiveness and that they are sold at reasonable prices.

Because of the wide range of government activities in inspection and regulation, they continually touch consumers' day-to-day lives. To appreciate that fact, think of the degree to which information costs would rise if there were no regulation. While alternative channels of information would probably develop, the consumer would still be seriously hampered, if not overwhelmed, by information costs. The fact that most consumers do not think about such problems shows the degree to which they have come to rely on information that the government provides. Our central thesis, that consumer problems are an outgrowth of a highly developed economy, is again confirmed. Two centuries ago modern drugs were unknown, the transportation system was primitive, and electronic communications did not exist. Information costs in these and other areas were therefore minimal; consumers could rightly be expected to get whatever information they needed on their own. The industrial revolution and the technological changes that accompanied it have changed the situation, creating the need for agencies that take the burden of information costs from the consumer in these key areas.

These changes make quality of enforcement tremendously important. If enforcement is lax, consumers may be lulled into a false sense of security. This situation can be worse than having no standards at all, for consumers who think they are protected will not be on the lookout for problems. Meat inspection is again a good example; there are periodic scandals about unsanitary conditions in the industry that can only undermine consumer confidence. This will increase information costs as consumers finally conclude that they cannot trust supposed standards to be a true representation of quality.

Even when standards are effective, they may have side effects that do not serve the consumer's interests. Occupational licensure may work in the same way. In many professions, ranging from practicing medicine to cutting hair, practitioners must be licensed. This may ensure quality, but it can also be used as a way to limit entry into the profession and thus give those already in the profession more control over price and output. Licensing, which is meant to help the consumer, emerges as a means of maintaining a professional monopoly [7, pp. 137–60].

There are other problems with government regulation. Not only do regulatory agencies perform unevenly, but they often seem to represent the interests of the industries they are supposed to regulate rather than the interests of the public. The ease with which industries come to dominate these agencies makes them uncertain vehicles for protecting the public interest. Even when such agencies are not prejudicial to the public interest, they may afford consumers little real protection. We raise these possibilities now to point out that standards and regulation do not represent a cure-all for consumer problems. It follows that imposing standards as an automatic reaction to a problem should be questioned. If standards are wisely chosen and carefully enforced, they can benefit consumers. That implies, however, that they are imposed only after careful consideration and that once they are in force, their operation is continually monitored.

The second area of government involvement in standards has developed more recently, and in light of the problems we have just mentioned, it may hold considerable promise. This approach is slightly different in that the government does not set standards on product or performance, but sets instead *standards for information that producers or sellers must provide to the public*. Truth-in-lending laws are one example. These laws, by forcing disclosure of effective interest rates, provide consumers with better information on which to base their own decisions.

A similar argument can be made for truth-in-packaging laws, which require that the package accurately represent what is inside. Packages are often misleading about both the quality of the contents and the quantity; large packages are often used to make it appear that the contents are comparable, but when you open the box, it is only three-quarters full. Unit pricing is a variant on this approach. With family sizes, giant economy sizes, and personal sizes, it is almost impossible to figure out which is the best buy. Unit pricing requires that cost per unit (3¢ an ounce, $1.35 a pound, 50¢ a quart, and so on) be clearly marked on the package. This would facilitate comparisons by the consumer both among brands and among various sizes of the same brand. It would end the confusion caused by the multitude of different-sized containers.

This illustration provides an object lesson in the difference between the two approaches to standards. The government could require standardized packaging, but that might be subject to abuse. If unit pricing were required, there would be less incentive for companies to promote so many different-sized packages, since consumers would already have the information the packages were meant to conceal. Thus, there would be a tendency for sellers to move to more standardized packages on their own. The result is the same, but in the second instance market forces are the effective agent; consumers, however, must receive the necessary information so that such forces can operate.

One aspect of the disclosure approach should be emphasized. That is the need for information to be given clearly and understandably. If unit prices are not clearly marked or if contents are stated in technical terms that the average consumer cannot understand, the whole effect is lost. Some education of consumers is necessary too so that they will be able to take advantage of information that is provided. However, the most important point is that the information should be in a clear, usable form [11].

The third area of government involvement with information costs lies with the provision of pure information. Governments at all levels, but particularly the federal, collect and distribute vast amounts of information. The United States Government Printing Office has publications available on nearly every sort of consumer interest from meats to babies, and back again. There is even a publication indexing other publications for the consumer [8]. Some of the same services are also available at the local level. County extension services are most valuable in this regard. They were established about a century ago primarily to aid farmers and others in rural areas, and they are now available to those in cities as well. The services range from financial planning to nutrition and yard care. Some big cities also have departments that distribute information to consumers.

The government collects information for its own use that could be valuable to the consumer. The General Services Administration (and other agencies) sets specifications for the products that the government buys. If this information were released on a systematic basis, consumers would clearly benefit from the prior evaluation that the government carried out. While some of this information is released, much of it is jealously guarded (even though it involves only mundane products) and has even been the cause of lawsuits.

The government information services are an example of the faulty distribution of information. The information is available, but the delivery system is inadequate. Merely collecting the information and making it available (even at minimal cost) is not enough. The situation calls for an aggressive policy to get the information to the people. Some progress has been made. County extension services, for example, are being offered in store-front offices in some low-income areas. This brings information and expertise to the people and as the workers become an accepted part of the community, they can work with the people more effectively. Despite promise, such efforts are only beginning and mainly underscore how much remains to be done.

Perception of responsibility has to be pinpointed. Currently the government acts in a largely passive role, collecting information but not really marketing it. There is a clear need for a more active government policy that would recognize the government's responsibility for distributing information. The government must soon face this fact. Consumer problems follow an imbalance of power in the marketplace, and corrective measures will be required to keep the imbalance from becoming even more pronounced. Consumer pressure will be required to bring such changes about, and as the need becomes more obvious, that pressure will increase.

Private Information Sources

While public agencies may help consumers cut information costs, the final responsibility for collecting information still rests with consumers themselves. Either individually or collectively, they must obtain the information they need to operate day after day in the marketplace. Given the current state of affairs, they often do this in a hit-or-miss fashion, but they still have to do it. We need to look, then, at how individuals or groups can cut information costs.

It is impossible to escape the conclusion that there is no substitute for experience. Any residual information the consumer can command has been gained mainly from experience. Although experience can be costly and calling it into play can be inefficient, it is currently the most important source of consumer information. There is nothing mysterious or complex about it. As consumers buy more things and do more repetitive buying, they accumulate knowledge that they can call on in the future. They learn about the features of the most important products they buy, the brands they like, and the dealers they can trust. That last point should be underscored. Since it is impossible to learn everything about every possible product, finding the right dealer can be a tremendous help. You may not know much about meat, but if you can trust your butcher, you will eat well. You need also to be able to trust mechanics, appliance dealers, plumbers, and others who serve the public. Confidence is the key word, and that takes time to build, but it is worth the effort. Most good consumers are good consumers because they deal with sellers they can trust.

Unfortunately, the pattern of American life over the past few decades has worked against the development of such arrangements. Increased urbanization and mobility are two of the most important factors involved. True, the consumer has more options in an urban area, but it is often more difficult to find the right store and since businesses tend to be larger, it may be more difficult to develop a good working arrangement. Contrasting the urban situation with a small town and its personal relations illustrates the point.

Even if the consumer does develop a pattern of trust with certain businesses, the odds are that he will move to a new area and have to start all over again. For many if not most Americans, the day is gone when they can expect to trade with the same merchants whom they knew as children and whom they have grown to trust. Even the small town, which we have tended to romanticize in this analysis, is changing. Many stores are closing and if they are replaced, it is by national chain stores, which have no particular attachment to the local population.

Increased mobility works against consumers in other ways too. It is quite likely, for example, that they will be removed from family and friends. This cuts them off from potentially valuable sources of information. There was in the past a sort of internship associated with becoming a consumer. When children went out into the world on their own, they did not go very far; members of the family were available if help was needed, including help about purchasing decisions. Very useful information could be passed along in this way. Now, it is common for families to be spread across the country (or even the world), so that this learning process cannot be continued.

Sharing of information is called pooling, and while it may be more difficult now, it is still possible. You might ask a neighbor or friend, for example, where he takes his car for service. If he knows a good mechanic, you can save yourself a lot of time, effort, and probably money. This is not a foolproof method; advice is only as good as the person who gives it. Differences in taste also enter the picture. If you like modern furniture and your neighbor's house is furnished in colonial, you might not want to ask advice on furniture stores.

Efforts at pooling have recently gone beyond the informal exchange of information. Consumers have joined together to share information in an organized manner. These efforts, like so many other recent developments in consumer affairs, have taken differing forms. In some cases they are nothing more than clubs or interest groups, gatherings of friends from either the neighborhood or work. At the other extreme there are formal organizations, for example cooperatives, with legal status and businesslike organization.

Some of the co-ops have gone beyond merely exchanging information to purchasing goods for members; this applies particularly to food co-ops. Most, however, concentrate on information, often specializing in a particular product or type of product. Businesses have even sprung up that provide a similar service. These operations are really a shopping service; for a fee the consumer can receive the information they have collected. The quality, and even the honesty, of the different firms varies widely, but they do illustrate a market response to a consumer problem.

While this sort of business operation to provide information to consumers is relatively new, the idea of businesses organizing to provide specific information to consumers is not. Some businesses have recognized that a better-informed consumer is in their own interest, and thus they provide information services to the consumer. Although there may be certain biases built into such offerings, they are still of potential value to the consumer.

The broker, or agent, is a familiar example of a business providing information. Stockbrokers provide information on stock and bond markets, information that would be too expensive for the individual to collect. Insurance agents, at least the good ones, provide a similar service. Most people are also familiar with real estate agents, though they may not have thought of them as a means of reducing information costs. Yet that is what they do. It is possible, and probably desirable to a degree, for individuals interested in buying a house to visit houses on their own. If they are working with a good agent, however, they can tell the person what features and price they are looking for, and the real estate agent can save them a lot of effort by eliminating the houses that do not fit their needs. The same is true for the person selling a house; the agent can bring in the type of person most likely to buy.

A word of warning is in order here. These are salespeople, and each has his own interests at heart too; they have a product to sell, and while they may provide information in the process, they are primarily interested in making the sale. There are other considerations. Many real estate agents have a poor record on racial issues involving housing segregation, and the fee structure of the whole real estate industry is open to question. Realtors generally charge between 5 and 7 percent on all sales, a figure that is inflated in light of the services provided in certain cases. Nevertheless, if the consumer is alert and uses the services wisely, they can work to his advantage.

Businesses, particularly at the local level, have an interest in promoting consumer satisfaction. The individual consumer has more leverage at this level, so that a dissatisfied consumer could be potentially harmful to business. For this reason, businesses in most areas have organized Better Business Bureaus, which keep a file on local businesses and distribute such information to the consumer. There are two main ways in which the BBB can help the consumer. It can provide information before the sale or transaction and help the consumer afterwards if he is not satisfied [1].

Suppose you need some service on your house, say a new roof, and neither you nor your friends have any experience with companies in the business. You can get estimates and then call the BBB to see if it has any record of complaints on those firms. This should help you get some idea of the reliability of the firm. If you have made some purchase that has turned out badly, the BBB can also help. Officials will go to the business in question, get its side of the story, and then try to work out some mutually satisfactory settlement.

BBB's are financed by businesses and they naturally have a business perspective. Their goal is "promoting consumer satisfaction," but that may mean nothing more than soothing words and efforts to defuse the consumer's wrath. They may make you feel better without really solving your problem. Opinion is divided on the overall effectiveness of BBB's, partly because it appears that their effectiveness, varies from area to area. Some are apologists for business, and others work hard to bring business and consumer together. The rise of consumerism has revitalized lagging operations in some areas, forcing them to be more responsive [4].

Business also provides information to the consumer by guarantees and warranties. The information is uneven, and the history of such agreements is checkered at best; properly used and understood, however, they can be of benefit to the consumer. In the past few years, the record for guarantees and warranties has improved. It was common for an item to be "unconditionally guaranteed," but when the consumer tried to collect he found that a series of exclusions and exceptions rendered the guarantee worthless. The worst abuses have been curbed, so that now warranties must state explicitly what is and what is not covered, as well as set out terms of the coverage.

What this means to the consumer is very simple: *Read the fine print!* Here are some questions that you should ask about any warranty; the more yes answers you get, the better it is.

Is it the responsibility of the seller, not the consumer, to activate the warranty (send in registration card, and so on)?

Does the warranty cover the whole product, not just specified parts?

Does it cover parts *and* labor?

Is it valid for a reasonable length of time?

If repair work is necessary, can it be done locally instead of sending the product to some regional repair center (and thus losing its services for weeks or months)?

If it has to be sent away, are packaging requirements reasonable and does the company pay postage fees?

Are there any other exclusions that seriously limit the usefulness of the warranty?

If you cannot answer yes to most of these questions, then the warranty will not be of much value. If it does measure up to these standards, it can cut information costs because you will know that if you have trouble, you can get it taken care of quickly and easily [3].

It almost goes without saying that the dealer is important too. If you know you can trust the seller, that should give you more confidence in the guarantee. That applies especially to verbal agreements. These have no validity beyond the integrity of the individual. That means that unless you are absolutely confident about the seller (and perhaps even if you are), you should demand everything in writing. An offhand "Oh, we'll take care of that" is easily forgotten or denied.

No discussion of private efforts to distribute information would be complete without including Consumers' Research and Consumers Union. The former is the oldest product-testing service in the United States. While its growth has not kept pace with Consumers Union in recent years, the basic idea of the two groups is similar. Consumers' Research has also been important in exposing consumer fraud.

Consumers Union currently represents the most significant private effort in the United States to evaluate products and pass this information on to consumers. Its monthly publication, *Consumer Reports,* provides the results of tests on literally thousands of items, in many cases representing the only available source of such information. There is also an annual *Buyers Guide,* which summarizes information on many different products.

For many years, CU stood alone, representing a voice in the wilderness of apathy towards consumer problems. There is no question that during that time it served the consumer well. Anyone who has ever looked at a copy of *Consumer Reports* is familiar with the quantity and quality of the information provided. CU devotees swear by these reports and would not think of buying so much as a pack of razor blades without first checking the CR rating. Nevertheless, CU has come under increasing criticism, most of it originating from newer consumer groups. Part of this is nothing more than the younger generation being impatient with those who have gone before, but beyond that are some genuine concerns. The first of these is not new and perhaps cannot be escaped by any private testing group. This has to do with audience. Product testing is expensive, and since to maintain its integrity CU has never accepted advertising, it must depend on membership fees to support its activities. That means the information goes to those in middle-income groups and above, and while these people need the information, they need it less than those in low-income groups. We have the same old problem, then, of the information not getting to those who need it most.

Consumers Union has also been criticized for the products tested. They have not concentrated on particular products, but rather have sampled from the whole range of consumer goods. This means that some of their tests cover products that while not necessarily frivolous are at least not of pressing importance to consumers. This might not be very significant, but it does betray a certain perspective, and perspective has emerged as a critically important point.

At the heart of the question is the attitude of the organization itself. Consumers Union has largely confined itself to providing information, while some observers feel it should take a more active role. They would like to see it become more of an active agent on behalf of consumers, pressing consumers' interests through investigation, legislation, and the courts. The organization has become more active in these areas of late, but its main thrust is still information. Were it to change its focus, it would be taking on a much more difficult job and in the process could become a much different organization [19].

These disputes are being fought out within the organization. Whichever view prevails, CU will probably become more activist; the change will represent degree rather than kind. It would be unfortunate if the organization were to assume the advocate's position completely, both because its information function might be lost and because it would run a high risk of failure, endangering the careful progress that has been made over the years. The whole dispute has detracted attention from the key question—How can information be gotten to the people who really need it? That question must not get lost along the way.

It is almost a requirement of examinations like this that they conclude by referring to the need for more education. So as not to disappoint anyone, we shall follow that tradition. Education has the potential for improving the level of consumer performance. We take the word *education* in its broadest context. It includes formal educational efforts, which need to be enlarged, but it is by no means limited to them. Primary and secondary schools offer a unique advantage, in that nearly every American is at least exposed to them. Thus, they offer the opportunity to reach all segments of the population. Primary grades are purposefully mentioned. Habits are learned early, which means that even young children need instruction as consumers. At the same time, adult and community education programs are tremendously important. These can be provided through the schools but can also be organized independently by community groups. Finally, there are the media, with their potential for reaching the entire population. Of the group, television is particularly significant; while its record is hardly outstanding, it offers the greatest potential for consumer education. Television is still very young, so it is not unreasonable to expect that its potential will be developed in the future.

DEVELOPING INFORMATION POTENTIAL

A National Information Policy?

You may have already been struck by the thought that while there are numerous sources of information available to consumers, there is a distinct lack of coordination and organization among them. The consumer must still seek information on what amounts to a hit-or-miss basis. While the government has moved to reduce information costs, and has *failed to develop an overall policy*. The need for such a policy should now be clear. The goals we have outlined suggest that the policy should aim at providing high-quality, low-cost information to all consumers. The question then becomes, What are the mechanics involved in carrying out that policy? It is useful to look to see what success other countries have had in providing for the consumer.

While the United States has been lagging, the Swedish government has moved, often in cooperation with private groups, to develop a comprehensive policy towards consumer information. There are two key elements in the Swedish approach, one of which is the State Institute for Consumer Information. Despite its imposing sounding name, it is little more than a public version of Consumers Union. Paradoxically, since it is public, it cooperates more with businesses than CU does. The board of SICI is made up of both public and private members, including members of Parliament and also labor and business representatives [17, p. 50]. The other basic part of the Swedish program is a private group, although it is partly financed by the government and it cooperates closely with governmental agencies. It is the Swedish Institute for Informative Labeling, which sets standards for information on labels. Its goals are to standardize labels and increase consumer awareness of them. The institute specifies a format, sets product specifications, and issues licenses for labels that conform to its standards [17, pp. 51–52]. Sweden has also had a consumer council for over fifteen years. It functions somewhat as a cabinet-level department of consumer affairs would work in the United States. It is charged with coordinating information efforts, voicing consumer viewpoints, and promoting research [17, p. 53]. It has had an uneven history, due in part, apparently, to a lack of clear direction and weakness in leadership.

Another Swedish effort that deserves mention is a remarkable publication called *Weak Points of Cars* [20]. It is published annually by the Swedish Motor Vehicle Inspection Company, which itself is supported by public and private (including industry and consumer) groups. Each year, every car in Sweden over three years old must undergo a safety inspection. Like similar programs in the United States, its primary goal is to keep unsafe cars off the road. However, all the information collected in these inspections is tabulated and published in *Weak Points of Cars*, providing consumers with a clear, understandable profile of every make of car on the Swedish roads. Since the inspection is so comprehensive, it is statistically sound; comparisons with average values make it easy to identify particular problem areas of any given make. The service is also valuable to manufacturers, for it allows them to identify structural or technical problems and correct them on subsequent models. While Sweden has gone further than most other countries towards informing consumers, its efforts are not unique. Most other industrial countries have similar organizations. As in Sweden, the outstanding feature of these groups is their public-private nature.

In Europe particularly, there is extensive public support for private groups and private cooperation with public efforts [18]. The European Economic Community (Common Market) has moved towards a common consumer policy. As in so many other areas, however, developing a communitywide program has not been easy. The Consumers Liaison Committee, founded in 1962, was never financed adequately, and it finally languished. Recently, efforts have been made to revive it and promote cooperation with national consumer groups. Nevertheless, a European consumer policy has yet to emerge [10, pp. 20–22]. The Common Market's experience emphasizes the difficulty of coordinating policies across national boundaries.

From our perspective, we might add that it is also difficult to make comparisons among countries. Sweden, for example, is a much more homogeneous country than the United States, with fewer ethnic groups and a more even distribution of income. Thus, what works in Sweden might not necessarily work here. At the same time, you may have observed that none of the elements in the Swedish program are really new. In most cases, similar programs are being carried out in this country. Thus, while a parallel effort would require some definite changes, they would be largely organizational and procedural and would not represent the wholesale importation of alien ideas or entirely new concepts.

Indeed, we should not want simply to import the apparatus from Sweden or some other country. While most of the procedures are relatively advanced, they still have their shortcomings. The basic one is getting the information to those who need it most, which is our problem in the United States. Even in Sweden, efforts at information distribution have not been entirely successful. The Swedish people have experienced many of the same problems we identified with similar efforts in this country [17, pp. 54–55]. One of the most important lessons Americans can learn from the European experience has to do with the benefits of public-private cooperation. There is a tendency in this country to think that public and private groups will never meet, that there is an innate antagonism between them that marks them as distinct entities incapable of acting in concert. Such ideas are carryovers from an outdated concept of rugged individualism, which never did describe the American economy very well and certainly does not now.

Popular notion does not reflect reality. Government and the private sector cooperate in many ways. Public groups encourage private business development through research activities and through cooperation with private groups in developing new markets. This process is most obvious in agricultural development. Through extension services and land-grant universities, the Department of Agriculture has acted as partner in American agriculture. Indeed, the interrelation has gone so far that it is difficult to distinguish between the private and public undertakings. Active collaboration between public and private groups on providing information would therefore represent no significant departure from established procedures. This collaboration could take different forms. It might mean public funding for private groups, or it could mean a joint public-private venture. In any case, there is a clear need to recognize the common interests of the private and public sectors. That recognition is the key to any collaborative effort.

Actually collecting information may be the least of the difficulties involved in a comprehensive information policy. The government already has vast amounts of information; product testing is well established in both the public and the private sectors. What is needed is to unite and coordinate these efforts. This could be done through a product-testing institute, which could occupy a position similar to the United States Bureau of Standards. It should be responsible, however, not just for product testing, but also for coordinating information gathered by other groups.

Labeling is an important part of information. We currently have laws that require that certain information be provided on labels. However, merely passing a law is not enough; an active policy must promote informative labels and help consumers understand them. To this end, a cooperative effort is needed among business, consumers, and government. The successes and failures of the Swedish effort should be instructive.

All of this is really a prelude to getting the information to the people. No country has really come to grips with that issue; some distribute information more actively than others, but none have really begun to merchandise information. What Americans could bring to this approach is a talent for merchandising and marketing. We have developed these skills far beyond most other countries. All that remains is to apply them to information. For a country that takes justifiable pride in its sales techniques, no problem should exist. If we can sell soap, cars, and political candidates, we can sell information. We can, that is, if there is a will to do it. Ultimately we must decide whether we really have the desire to carry through such a program. Motivated by the desire, we can overcome the mechanical problems. Without it, the situation becomes impossible.

The overall record here is hardly encouraging, but there is still reason for optimism. Americans have shown a willingness to come to grips with their problems. In automobile safety and pollution control, for example, American standards are the highest in the world. The progress has been uneven, but it has been made despite objections from industry and even from some consumers. What is needed now is to extend such efforts over a much broader front. That will not be possible without public pressure, and the necessary public pressure will not be forthcoming until there is a broadly based recognition of both the importance of information and the possibilities for improvement. When consumers realize how improved information flow will serve them, they will press for bringing it about. The first problem in developing a comprehensive information policy appears to be information itself.

Costs are relevant to an undertaking of such magnitude. Any effective program would undoubtedly be expensive. Costs must be considered comparatively, however. The real comparison is between what a comprehensive information policy would cost and what the present system (or nonsystem) costs. Consumers now must bear not only most of the costs of obtaining information, but also the costs of bad decisions made with inadequate information. An effective information policy should reduce the private costs to consumers. There is every reason to believe that this savings would more than offset the costs of operating an information program. A large-scale program of information distribution should be much more efficient than individual search. There would thus be a net social savings.

Some Daydreams About Tomorrow

Most of what has been said thus far is highly conventional and traditional. There have been some innovative proposals, but they are within the framework that is familiar to all of us. Since product testing, standards, and the like are already familiar ground, our analysis has taken off from there to deal with ways in which these various tools can be sharpened to improve information flow. Looking forward, however, calls for considering some new possibilities. The technology of consumption really has not changed very much over the years. It is still in the horse-and-buggy era compared with technology for other parts of the economy. Consumer problems, on the other hand, are of the space-age variety. It would be impossible to think of sending rockets into space using the technology of the 1870s. Why then should our thinking about consumption be limited to techniques that are even older? Today's technology should be used to meet the problems of consumers, just as it is used to meet problems in other areas.

This is an area where fiction, particularly science fiction, has gone beyond fact. The computer, for example, has fascinated science fiction writers for years. Recently, household applications of the computer have made their way into popularized science magazines. Most of these pieces have been highly futuristic, written by people who understand neither technology nor computers. Yet now the technology is available to turn much of this into reality, and decreasing costs may soon bring it within the reach of the average householder. Mini-calculators, which while they're partially curiosities, have eased some of the difficulties of household bookkeeping and even shopping. That is nothing compared with the potential for the computer. All sorts of information on consumer goods, ranging from price to construction specifications to testing results, could be stored in the memory of a large computer. Consumers, from their home terminals, could tie into the central unit to retrieve whatever information they wished. This sort of development would not totally replace shopping, but it would make the process cheaper and more efficient. The possibilities are almost limitless. Now, you may think this belongs in a science fiction magazine and it does have a sci-fi ring to it. However, it all represents possibilities that are well within current technological limits. We are not talking about a decade from now, nor are we speculating idly. We are talking about the present.

While such devices are not yet available to the average homeowner, computer terminals in the home are becoming increasingly common. If the pace of technological change in the computer industry keeps up at all with its past performance, reasonably priced units for the home should be available within five years. With such a system, you could shop for a new car from your living room. You could get immediate information on models and prices and also details on gas mileage, service, and upkeep, and the results of road tests. The applications go on and on. It would be possible to get a week's worth of nutritionally balanced menus from the computer by just typing in information on family size and income level. Or you might be able to get instant financial advice by putting in the details of your financial condition.

It may seem that there are big-brother overtones to having a computer in the home and feeding it personal data. The danger need not materialize, however; the individual's integrity and privacy could be maintained. The scope of individual action could be expanded because of the expanded amount of information. Persons would know more about the possibilities available to them and could thus take advantage of those they wished. Now it may be that things will not work out as pictured. The particular direction which technology will take is difficult to specify at this time. We have raised the issue merely to suggest the range of possibilities and indicate that we need not be hidebound in our thinking. While the pace of market developments accelerates, consumers are falling farther behind all the time. In making up for past mistakes, we must be aware of future possibilities.

While the computer has fascinating possibilities, it is not the only avenue available. The media, particularly the electronic media, offer opportunities that are nearly as great. Furthermore, they are already established, so the technological limitations would not be significant. Advertising in particular has great information potential, and we examine that next.

STUDY QUESTIONS

1. Explain why information costs are higher on less frequently purchased goods.

2. Would information costs be higher on a new appliance or a used one? Would they be higher on a used stove or a used refrigerator? Explain carefully, identifying the various kinds of information involved.

3. We mentioned in Chapter 4 that newcomers to an area find that shopping takes them longer than before. Explain the reasons, judged from the context of this chapter.

4. Why would information costs—the amount of shopping or search required—increase during periods of rising prices?

5. In some markets (like the automobile market), price is not set but is determined by bargaining. Do such procedures affect information costs? Explain.

6. Costs of search vary with the individual, the product, and the situation. Designate for the following examples whether costs would be relatively high or relatively low:
    a. Low-income person shopping for a refrigerator.
    b. Camera buff shopping for a new lens.
    c. Auto dealer buying a new car.
    d. Insurance salesman who has to take time off from work to shop for a new water heater.

7. Some consumers become fiercely loyal to a particular brand or make; if they have a Brand X refrigerator, they will buy another Brand X when a replacement is necessary. Does this approach make sense in light of information costs? What are the dangers of this strategy?

8. Product labels already contain a good deal of information on characteristics like ingredients and weight. Do you think this information is of much use to the typical consumer? Why or why not? If it is not, what improvements would you suggest?

9. The government sets standards on many different products, including peanut butter. Peanut butter must contain a given percentage of peanuts. Could the same result be achieved by replacing the standard with a requirement that the label clearly indicate the percentage of peanuts in the product? Are there any advantages to this approach?

10. What is the chief shortcoming of publications like *Consumer Research* and *Consumer Reports* as sources of information?

SUGGESTED PROJECTS

1. Pick a specific product, some appliance would probably be best, and make an in-depth search for information about it. Select two student groups from within the class:
   a. The first should study available literature on the product, including government publications, test results, material from extension services, and any other relevant information.
   b. The second group should go out and shop for the product, visiting different stores and collecting information on special features and price.

Both groups should keep careful records of how much time all of this takes as well as listing any other costs incurred (gasoline, and so on). Your purpose is to get as much information as possible. When it is all collected, decide how much you would have searched if you had really been buying the product. Include in your considerations the number of stores that had to be visited before a price range was defined and the number of publications studied before information became repetitious. Did these follow the pattern suggested in the text? What kinds of informational aids would have made the job easier?

2. Conduct a survey of information sources available in your area. In addition to those suggested under Project 1, include local consumer groups (public and private), Better Business Bureaus, and any other potential source of significant information to the consumer. Is adequate information available on most products? Does this information get to the people who need it?

3. Conduct a survey to find out what sources of information consumers actually use. You have to be careful here, for most people do not think in terms of information costs. Thus, you might ask something like: "When you go out to buy a product, how do you find out which one is best for you?"

or more simply, "How do you get your information on which you base your decision?" You might ask them to rank a series of alternatives (past experience, suggestions of friends, shopping around, test results, and so on) or merely let them suggest answers (see Appendix). What seems to be the most common source of information? Do the results suggest any possible ways to improve information flow?

4.   Gather a few samples of warranties or guarantees on different products. Did you find any that were actually misleading? How do they measure up in terms of the criteria listed in the text? Do you think they actually would affect your decision if you were buying?

5.   Examine samples of various product labels. Are they a fair representation of the product? Do they provide any significant information? What improvements would you suggest to make labels more useful?

6.   Pick a product like detergent or toothpaste that is available in many different-sized containers. Is there any relation between the sizes offered by one producer and another? How does the price per unit (per ounce, per pound, and so forth) vary among brands and among various sizes of the same brand? Be sure to check and see what company makes each brand; how many different companies did you find? What does this suggest? How can you evaluate all of this in terms of its impact on the consumer?

7.   You are probably aware that your local government (or state government) sets standards in many areas, including barber shops and restaurants. Make a comprehensive search for areas in which standards are imposed. Were you aware of all of them? How effective for the consumer, do you think, are these standards?

BIBLIOGRAPHY AND SUGGESTED READINGS

1. Better Business Bureau, *Editorial Research Reports*.
   These pamphlets are available through your local BBB and cover a whole range of consumer topics from buying meat to finding a mechanic. They are brief, to the point, and well worth picking up.

2. Boulding, Kenneth E. "The Household as Achilles' Heel." *Journal of Consumer Affairs*, Winter 1972, pp. 110–19.
   One of the elder statesmen of economics who is also one of America's outstanding social scientists, views the shortcomings of the family as a consumption unit. His analysis follows the lines of Professor Mitchell's observations.
      The *JCA* is a must for anyone interested in consumer affairs. It is currently the only publication of its kind and carries articles over the whole range of consumer affairs. American Council of Consumer Interests publishes this journal.

3. "A Close Look at Warranties and Guarantees." *Consumer Bulletin*, April and May 1971.

A guide to evaluating guarantees. *Consumer Bulletin* is no more. Its name was changed to *Consumer Research* in 1973.

4. "Consumer's Fighting Back via Better Business Bureaus." *U. S. News & World Report*, December 18, 1972, p. 58.

A review of recent activities of the BBB and their relation to consumerism.

5. *Consumer Reports*, Consumers Union, Mt. Vernon, N. Y.

CU's monthly publication containing testing information and consumer tidbits. A *bible* to some, a bore to others, *CR* is still the primary source of product-testing information in the United States.

6. "Economics of Information." *American Economic Review, Papers and Proceedings*, May 1973, pp. 31–51.

Articles by J. Hirshleifer and Lester Telser, with advanced discussion. Particularly Professor Telser's paper is not for the uninitiated. Papers suggest that because of information costs, consumer search will be very limited; also demonstrate that economists still are not quite sure how to handle the topic.

7. Friedman, Milton. *Capitalism and Freedom*. Chicago: University of Chicago Press, 1962.

See Chapter 9 for an introduction to the problems of occupational licensure. As a strong believer in free markets, Professor Friedman argues against licensure. You probably will not agree with him, but you will also probably admire his lucid analysis.

8. *Guide to Consumer Services*, U.S. Government Printing Office.

An index of federal agencies dealing with consumer affairs, including the organization's name, purposes, and legal duties. A good summary of where to find what in the federal bureaucracy.

Also of interest are *Consumer Information* and *Consumer News*, which contain a catalog of federal publications catering to consumers and notes of new developments.

9. Hawkins, M. H., and Devine, D. G. "Implications of Improved Information on Market Performance." *Journal of Consumer Affairs*, Winter 1972, pp. 184–97.

Documentation of a study showing that improved information also improves consumer performance.

10. Kemezis, Paul. "The Consumer and the Common Market." *European Community* 159 (October 1972), pp. 18–23.

A report on consumer-related developments in the nine Common Market countries, with special emphasis on information. A good summary on European attitudes that affect consumer affairs.

11. Lenhan, R. J., et al. "Consumer Reaction to Nutritional Labels on Food Products." *Journal of Consumer Affairs*, Spring 1973, pp. 1–12.

A study that shows some hope for informative labeling and notes that both more understandable labels and increased consumer awareness of them are needed.

12. Magnuson, Warren, and Carper, Jean. *The Dark Side of the Marketplace*, 2d ed. Englewood Cliffs, N. J.: Prentice-Hall, 1972.

13. Nourse, Hugh O. *Regional Economics*. New York: McGraw-Hill Book Co., 1968.

    A good introduction for those interested in the relations between information costs and location theory. See especially Part 1 on regional structure.

14. Scherhorn, Gerhard, and Wieken, Klaus. "On the Effect of Counter-Information on Consumers." In *Human Behavior in Economic Affairs*, ed. Burkhard Strumpel, et al. San Francisco: Jossey-Bass, 1972.

    A report of a West German experiment to provide consumers with additional information or gasoline prices and detergents. Indicates positive reaction of consumers to information that the marketplace would have denied them.

15. Stigler, George. "The Economics of Information." *Journal of Political Economy*, June 1961, pp. 213–25.

    The classic article on information costs. Despite analytics, most students will find it readable and useful. It forms the basis for the whole thrust of this chapter.

16. Stigler, George. *The Theory of Price*, 3d ed. New York: Macmillan Co., 1966.

    A very brief but highly instructive introduction to information costs.

17. Thorelli, Hans B. "Consumer Information in Sweden—What Can Be Learned?" *Journal of Marketing*, January 1971, pp. 50–55.

    An account of the Swedish experience with efforts to increase information flow. A good review, though judgments should be carefully considered.

18. Troelstrup, Arch W. *The Consumer in American Society*, 4th ed. New York: McGraw-Hill Book Co., 1970.

    See Chapter 19 for a good summary of consumer protection efforts in other countries.

19. Washington *Post*, Series of articles on Consumers Union, April 22–25, 1973.

    Four articles by *Post* staff writers on CU's current problems. Looks at the power plays within the organization and also differences in ideas concerning the organization's purpose, goals, and overall effectiveness.

20. *Weak Points of Cars*, A. B. Svensk Bilprovning, Swedish Vehicle Inspection Company, Vällingby 1, Stockholm, Sweden.

    The Swedish publication that tabulates the results of annual inspection. It illustrates some of the possibilities for distributing information. It may also be of use to car buyers in America, especially those who are thinking of a European car. Issued annually.

6

A Detour on Madison Avenue: Advertising and Information

SHOULD THE FOX GUARD THE CHICKENS?

A Matter of Perspective

Suppose we could bring in a couple from Mars and explain to them the consumer's need for information. Suppose further that we then tell them that American businesses spend billions of dollars a year to tell consumers about their products. What would they conclude? They would most certainly congratulate us on our imaginative and enlightened system. It would be reasonable to assume that if businesses make such an effort to get their message across to the public, the consumer's need to know about products must be more than fulfilled. They would be wrong, of course—remember, there is no intelligent life on Mars. Business does spend billions on advertising—$32 billion in 1972 according to the *Newsletter* of the American Council on Consumer Interests. However, despite such massive expenditures, advertising provides consumers with little useful information. That is the biggest paradox in the whole question of information costs. Despite tremendous advertising expenditures by business, the public's need to know about products remains largely unfulfilled. The situation resembles a doctor's prescribing sugar pills to cure a patient instead of available proper medication.

This situation can be traced to a basic difference in how advertising's function is perceived. Increasing numbers of consumers find advertising irritating, or at best silly. Not only does it tell little about the product, but

111

it often offends the sensibilities. The typical ad becomes something that is to be endured; it is nonfunctional, offering little of any practical value to the consumer. The best one can hope for is occasional entertainment. From the advertiser's perspective, however, such comments miss the point. He does not care about being informative, witty, or entertaining. What he does care about is increasing sales of the product. Ads that increase sales are by definition good; those that do not increase sales are not good. Thus, if an ad for Scrubbo Cleanser shows a celebrity extolling its virtues and that gimmick happens to sell Scrubbo, forget about anything else. The person may not use Scrubbo or even know how to open the can. That does not matter so long as the ad helps get Scrubbo off the shelf, into the grocery cart, and through the checkout counter.

There's the rub, the difference in perception we mentioned. The businessman wants to sell his product, while the consumer wants information. The two are not mutually exclusive—there are some very effective, highly informative ads—but they are not necessarily one and the same either. The advertiser asks, "Will it sell the product?" not, "Will it inform the public about the product?" That is why most of what is written about the subject is of little or no value to the student inquiring about advertising from the consumer's point of view. Advertising has been analyzed mainly from the seller's perspective, which views the consumer as someone to be attracted (some would say *manipulated*) rather than someone to be given information.

Would the Truth Hurt?

That raises an obvious question: Should advertising be asked to perform an information function? In answering that question, one important observation should be made. There is a need to improve the flow of information to consumers, but there are costs attached. Information can be gotten to the consumer more cheaply than it is now, but someone has to pay the costs of getting it there. Two possibilities suggest themselves: government and business. The government reduces information costs to consumers by forcing businesses to disclose key facts, establishing standards, or providing information directly. The costs are then either forced back on business or paid out of tax monies. Thus, if government bears the costs directly, it is ultimately the consumer as taxpayer who shoulders the burden. The government may be a more efficient approach, but even then, information costs have only been reduced, not escaped.

If business is forced to bear the cost of providing information to the consumer, this cost would be treated like any other cost of production. Thus, it would be reflected in the final price of the product. The degree to which this price increase would be passed along to the consumer depends on the degree of competition in the market.* In most cases, however, the consumer

* The less competition there is, the easier it is for firms to pass higher costs along to consumers. In more competitive markets, there are more firms, so consumers have more choices, and it is harder for a single firm to manipulate price.

will end up paying some, if not all, of the added costs through higher product prices. Again it is the consumer who ultimately pays the costs of information. If it has occurred to you that you are *already* paying higher prices to cover advertising and promotional costs, then you see the point. Look carefully at the data in Table 6.1. Since 1950, advertising has consistently accounted for between 2 and 3 percent of total income (gross national product) generated in the United States. When you think in terms of a trillion-dollar gross national product, that is a lot of money. Moreover, advertising expenditures equal between 3 and 4 percent of consumer expenditures. That is an average, including consumer expenditures in areas where advertising is insignificant (like health care). For consumer goods only, the percentage is even higher. Within the top 100 advertisers, for example, advertising expenditures run as high as one-third of sales. Few are that high, but figures over 20 percent are not uncommon, while most are around 10 percent [3, pp. 27–28]. It is clear, then, that a significant portion of the consumer's dollar goes to pay for advertising.

Earlier we compared advertising to a sugar pill provided by a doctor. To complete the analogy, we should add that the doctor charges the patient the full price of the true medication. Any doctor who practiced such quackery would be sued for malpractice, yet consumers find themselves in precisely the same position as the poor patient. They are paying the price for the medicine (advertising), but it does not help them recover from the

TABLE 6.1 Total Advertising Expenditures as a Percentage of Gross National Product and Consumer Expenditures. 1950–1972

	Advertising percentage *	
Year	GNP	Consumer expenditures
1950	2.00	2.92
1952	2.07	3.28
1954	2.26	3.45
1956	2.36	3.67
1958	2.32	3.51
1960	2.37	3.67
1962	2.23	3.47
1964	2.24	3.53
1966	2.22	3.57
1968	2.10	3.38
1970	2.01	3.18
1972	2.00	3.20

Source: Reprinted with permission from *Advertising Age*, Nov. 23, 1973, p. 5. Copyright 1973 by Crain Communications, Inc.
* Includes expenditures on television, radio, magazines, newspapers, and billboards.

sickness of insufficient information. That is precisely why advertising is so important. *If advertising efforts were channeled into providing information, there would be a net gain for consumers,* who would then be receiving something for the costs they are already paying. In that sense, informative advertising would be relatively cheap in that it would be available at little or no extra cost. Add to this the fact that the potential for advertising as a source of readily available information is difficult to overestimate. We have already noted that the consumer's problem is not information, but obtaining the information. That is the beauty of advertising; it is there. You do not have to seek it out; it seeks you out, coming into your home over the television and radio and in newspapers and magazines. Perhaps this is not such a desirable state of affairs under the present system but it does show the potential of advertising for providing information.

There is no better way to get so much information so effortlessly. Improving the information content of advertising may not solve the problem, but it is a first line of attack. If advertising really told consumers something about the product, consumers would have a much easier job. That is why it is so important to focus on advertising. We have looked into what advertising is capable of doing for the consumer; we now need to see what it is actually doing.

ADVERTISING AND INFORMATION CONTENT

A Standard for Judgment

It may appear that the analysis thus far has treated advertisements unfairly. Working from the assumption that advertising provides little information, we have explored the implications of that situation and the potential for improvement. There is justification for arguing that a general impression that ads are uninformative is not an adequate basis for making such an assumption. We need evidence beyond general impressions. Specific evaluation of the information that advertising currently provides is a starting place to look for such evidence. There are several ways to undertake such an evaluation. The most direct approach appears to be the most promising. It is quite simple and entails nothing more than looking at advertisements and then evaluating them on the information they provide.

As in any undertaking, the terms must be defined—in this case, standards, a basis for judging what is informative and what isn't. Happily, we do not need to improvise; there are established standards we can use. They are provided through the courtesy of the Federal Trade Commission (FTC), which is the agency within the federal government charged with overseeing advertisements. The FTC's efforts in this area are gaining more attention, and from time to time you will see that the agency has charged that a certain ad is misleading and must be removed. Such judgments are based on standards that the FTC has developed for evaluating advertising, standards that are available to us for our own evaluation [8 and 10].

The Federal Trade Commission classifies advertisements into three categories: *informative*, ads that provide significant information; *puffing*, ads that ballyhoo the product without really saying anything about it; and *misleading*, ads that either directly or implicitly misrepresent the product.* These are not necessarily mutually exclusive categories, but they do provide a structure for analyzing information content.

According to the FTC, informative ads provide information on price or relative price, functions of the product, construction specifications, and performance standards. I recall an ad for a chain saw that meets these criteria almost to the letter. The ad shows the saw in use, gives the price ("under $100"), details its features (metal body, self-oiling chain, automatic-recoil start, and so on), and tells something about what the saw will do ("cuts logs up to 20 inches in diameter"). If you were in the market for a chain saw, that ad would be helpful; it tells you enough about the saw for you to evaluate it.

Puffing ads, on the other hand, do not provide the consumer with that type of service. They substitute superlatives, endorsements by leading personalities, or claims of uniqueness for hard facts on price and performance. They are fluff (rhymes with puff) and while they may be entertaining, they are not very informative. Soft-drink commercials, which show happy, beautiful people downing gallons of a particular brand, fit into the puffing category. Magazine ads for liquor, which typically feature a close-up of the bottle, are another example. Puffing ads do not mislead, but they do not inform either; as their middle position suggests, they represent a sort of neutral territory.

That may be damning with faint praise, but it is more than can be said for misleading advertisements. Such ads feature unsupported—and often unsupportable—claims and rigged or irrelevant tests, and they portray the product in unnatural situations. These are typical traits of misleading advertisements, but since the range of possibilities is so broad, it is difficult to limit them. Ads may be misleading without resorting to outright lies, though that is not unknown. An advertisement is misleading if it portrays the product as something it is not. There are many examples of misleading advertisements in the history of television, including plastic placed over floors to show a "true wax shine" and shots apparently taken through an automobile window to demonstrate that the glass is distortion-free, when in fact the window had been wound down.

Before we evaluate advertising using these criteria, we should note that advertisements may not fit neatly into a single category. They may contain features of two or more types. Continually subdividing to accommodate these mixtures would destroy the classification system. We should, however, try to acknowledge this diversity, and we therefore introduce two intermediate

* The FTC uses *deceptive* instead of *misleading*.

categories: informative-puffing and puffing-misleading. That gives us something to do with ads that are largely puffing but do give some information, or ads that puff away to the point of becoming misleading.

Reliability also deserves mention. One can read, or view, between the lines of advertisements, but it is necessary ultimately either to accept or to reject what the advertisement says. An ad may appear to be quite informative, providing details about the product and demonstrating its effectiveness through different tests. *Appear* is the key word, for it is not always possible to trust what is being said. The track record of advertisers hardly inspires confidence. To deal with the problem, we shall apply a rule of reason, accepting what ads say at face value unless there is evidence to the contrary.

Finally, a warning is in order. Even with standards and a set of criteria for making evaluations, there is bound to be an element of personal judgment in their application. If the price of a product is $99.95, is it misleading to advertise it as "under $100"? Is it misleading to advertise soft drinks with those happy people and their beautiful smiles without mentioning that the drink promotes tooth decay? Most people would probably feel that to call these examples misleading would represent an overly strict application of the standards, but others might not agree. There is no easy way around this problem. For our purposes, however, it is sufficient to keep in mind that two people watching the same ad might evaluate it differently. That serves to qualify the results, but not invalidate them. We can reasonably assume that fair-minded observers working from the same set of standards will agree most of the time.*

A Very Expensive Wasteland

For our analysis, it would be helpful to distinguish among types of ads and the manner of their presentation. Thus far, we have talked about advertisements as a single group, when in fact there are important variations among them. There are differences first among the media. For that reason, we shall consider television, radio, magazine, and newspaper advertisements separately. That doesn't cover all the possibilities. There are also specialty or trade publications, billboards and other outdoor advertisements—currently under fire from environmentalists—flyers, loudspeakers, and other forms that attest to the ingenuity of individual advertisers. In some cases, particularly television advertising, a further breakdown is useful. Some ads run nationally, while some are local; others plug the station's own shows. To account for this, we shall distinguish four different types of ads: national (network), local, in-house (where the network or station advertises its own shows), and public service. These categories should give us further insight into how information patterns vary with different types of advertisements.

* As a check, students are urged to repeat the evaluations reported in the following sections. See Suggested Projects.

For several reasons, television is the logical place to begin our evaluation. First of all, television accounts for the greatest portion of advertising expenditures, so it is necessary to look to television to see where advertisers spend their money. Table 6.2 makes that point clear. Procter and Gamble, the nation's leading advertiser, spends over 95 percent of its regular advertising budget on television. For the top ten advertisers as a group, almost 75 percent of advertising expenditures goes to television. While smaller companies may spend less on television, it is the largest firms that represent the bulk of advertising expenditures. The top ten firms alone spent over one billion dollars on advertising in 1972. The breakdown between network television and spot advertisements is also significant. We shall see why when we consider the differences in information content between the two. While there are some exceptions, most of the large advertisers spend significantly more on network ads than spot ads. For the ten largest advertisers, almost one-half of their advertising expenditures go to network television.

Secondly, television is an integral part of the American lifestyle. The impact of television goes beyond the fact that most Americans depend on it for news and entertainment. Television affects the way we perceive the

TABLE 6.2   Advertising Expenditures by Types of Media: Top Ten Advertisers, 1972

Ad rank *	Company name	Total advertising expenditures (in millions)	General magazines	Spot TV	Network TV	Spot radio	Network radio	Other †
			Percentage of total					
1	Procter & Gamble	$197.3	4.0	36.7	58.8	0.1	...	0.4
2	American Home Products	116.3	5.5	30.1	52.6	9.6	1.4	0.8
3	General Foods	116.0	13.6	41.1	43.6	0.9	0.3	0.6
4	Ford Motor	115.4	21.0	14.6	42.8	14.9	1.9	4.8
5	General Motors	110.6	26.3	14.0	35.5	16.0	3.1	5.0
6	Bristol-Myers	107.7	19.5	16.5	51.9	5.0	0.4	6.8
7	Sears, Roebuck	92.0	25.1	21.9	39.5	12.4	0.9	0.2
8	Sterling Drug	83.9	10.5	12.5	67.2	4.3	4.3	1.2
9	Colgate-Palmolive	83.2	13.2	41.6	38.9	3.1	2.8	.3
10	Chrysler	63.4	17.4	16.6	38.4	23.3	2.0	2.2

Source: Reprinted by permission from *Advertising Age*, August 27, 1973, pp. 30–31. Copyright 1973 by Crain Communications, Inc.
* *In measured media only;* thus does not include all advertising and promotional expenditures.
† Includes farm publications, business publications, and outdoor advertising.

world and absorb its images. If, as Marshall McLuhan suggests, the medium
is the message, then the message is clear: television not only reflects modern
life, it is part of that life.

The results of the television survey are summarized in Table 6.3. The
figures represent averages for five hours' viewing based on six samples (two
for each principal network) taken by a group of students and myself. Each
sample was from 7 P.M. until midnight, Central Time. Thus the hours include prime-time and late-night programming. This is a limited sample
and cannot claim to be scientific, but it should be sufficient to indicate
overall trends.

Similar efforts at other times have provided similar results. Television
advertising, however, varies with the season. These surveys were taken
during the summer, which is a light time for advertising. This affects the
number of in-house and public-service ads, which also vary from station to
station. There are other questions about the treatment of these two categories, which will be explained as we go along.

In five hours of television, 50 minutes, or 16.6 percent of the time, was
taken up with advertisements. That means about one minute of ads for
every five minutes of shows. The survey results clearly indicate that whatever entertainment value the viewers may get from the shows is more than
the information they are likely to get from the ads.

Notice that in-house and public-service ads are included in the informative category. They do provide information about programming or
services, so they belong there. It is just as clear, however, that they are not
the type of ad we have been considering, since they do not provide information that is generally useful to the consumer in the marketplace. Leaving out
these two categories, only four minutes of purely informative ads remain.
That is only 8 percent of the total ad time, which in turn is barely more
than the percentage for misleading ads.

TABLE 6.3   Information Content of Television Advertisements

	I	IP	P	PM	M	Total
National	1:45	4:15	14:45	3:00	1:45	25:30
Local	2:15	6:45	3:45	2:30	1:30	16:45
In-house	3:00	0:15	3:15	....	....	6:30
Public service	0:30	....	0:15	0:30	....	1:15
Total	7:30	11:15	22:00	6:00	3:15	50:00
% Total	15	23	44	12	6	100

Source: See text.
NOTE: Time in minutes: seconds. Column heads stand for Informative, Informative-Puffing, Puffing, Puffing-Misleading, and Misleading. Based on average
viewing time of five hours.

That suggests that if viewers watched television the entire evening, they would be misled almost as much as they would be informed. If we add in the informative-puffing category, the scales tip towards information, but it is still not a very good record. The bulk of the ads are puffing, almost twice as many as any other category. As we noted, these are primarily brand-name identification, which do not say very much. If there is such a thing as a *typical* television ad, it is of the puffing type.

It might be heartening to note that there were so few ads judged to be actually misleading. It is possible, however, to argue that there should not be *any* misleading ads. In that context, 6 percent is hardly cause to rejoice. The puffing-misleading ads generally earned that designation by exaggeration, gross overstatement, or implications that misrepresented the product. These may be only venial sins, but they still have a negative impact on the viewer-consumer.

National advertising, while it made up just over half the total, tended to be the least informative. This is not too surprising; local ads provide information about specific stores where products and services are available and are more likely to have price information. On the other hand, national ads *could* provide information on product performance; instead, they tend to be little vignettes that do little more than glorify the product.

What sort of ads are in these different categories? While avoiding brand names, we can describe the characteristics of the different types in general terms. The national informative ads contained some price and performance information, or said something specific about the product and its functions. Local informative ads tended to be even more specific, giving information such as special prices (in a grocery ad), location, services, and interest rates (a savings and loan), or comparative price information. The misleading ads included pain relievers, all of which make claims that have not been supported. There was also an insurance ad that used scare techniques; and there were ads for household products in grossly unrealistic situations. You may have noticed a public-service ad in the puffing-misleading category. It was an ad for the armed services—a necessity with a volunteer army—that showed the happy serviceman running along sunny beaches with beautiful women.* It never mentioned the other duties of the service, which presumedly include the possibility of being shot at.

In summarizing this discussion, we must say that television advertising provides very little information; it is difficult to reach any other conclusion. There are some bright spots—nearly one-third of commercial ads contain some information. Some information, however, isn't a very good showing when you consider the amount of money spent on television advertising and the degree to which it saturates the country. Cost deserves a final comment. The most expensive national ads appear to provide the least information. A 30-second local grocery ad may provide much information,

* The U.S. government ranks among the nation's top 25 advertisers, spending over $65 million in 1972. Among the ads it sponsors are some that attempt to get information on government protection programs across to the public [3, p. 29].

but it is only an insignificant part of total advertising expenditures. Thus, while 15 percent of advertising time was rated informative, that does *not* mean that 15 percent of advertising expenditures resulted in informative ads. That percentage would be even lower. Therefore, while consumers pay for advertising through higher product costs, it is clear that they receive little information in return.

The Mobile Medium

The shift from television to radio advertisements presents us with a slightly different situation. These differences follow from the differences in the media, which in turn affect the pattern of radio broadcasting and advertising. This is reflected in the degree to which radio has become specialized; some stations broadcast only music—rock, country and western, or classical —while others specialize in news. In metropolitan centers, there are stations that serve particular ethnic groups, while in rural areas, there are farm-oriented stations. Some churches have their own stations, and so do some colleges and universities. With this diversity, it is difficult to generalize about radio advertising. A comprehensive survey would be necessary to account for the variation in the amount and types of advertising that different stations carry. Yet the nature of the medium itself forces certain constraints on radio advertising that limit all stations, regardless of orientation.

Radio is limiting; it is harder to talk about something than to show a picture of it. If advertisers are going to talk about the product anyway, there is a chance that they will say something informative. On the other hand, since it is possible to talk without saying anything substantive, that isn't always true. Most companies have a multimedia advertising package, so that their radio ads complement their television efforts; some companies even run the sound track from their television ads. Nevertheless, radio appears to have the edge in favor of more informative advertising. Survey results reported in Table 6.4 seem to support that contention. The manner of sampling was

TABLE 6.4   **Information Content of Radio Advertisements**

	I	IP	P	PM	M	Total
National	2:15	8:45	3:30	1:30	....	16:00
Local	3:30	4:30	3:15	....	1:00	12:15
In-house	1:15	1:00	....	....	....	2:15
Total	7:00	14:15	6:45	1:30	1:00	30:30
% Total	23	47	22	5	3	100

Source: See text.
NOTE: Time in minutes: seconds. Survey taken on three different stations at three different times of day. Total listening time slightly over four hours.

slightly different from that for the television survey; the results represent totals obtained by listening to different stations at different times of the day. Radio advertising varies with the time of day and is particularly heavy during morning and evening rush hours.

While puffing was the largest category under television advertising, informative-puffing emerges as the most important with radio; it accounts for over twice the time of the next category. Furthermore, slightly more advertising was judged to be purely informative, as opposed to puffing. To a degree, this reflects the importance of local advertising on radio. Note, however, that even national radio advertising ranks fairly high. Seventy percent of all the radio advertising carries some significant information, while only 8 percent contains misleading elements (versus 38 and 18 for similar categories on television).

Notice that there was less advertising on radio, compared with television; only about 12 percent of the time was taken up with ads, versus 16 percent on television. Radio ads are also cheaper than television. According to Table 6.2, radio represents only a small part of the overall advertising expenditures of the largest companies (although the automobile makers are an exception). Many of the companies spent more on outdoor advertising than they did on radio. The findings also indicate that small, local advertisers use radio more than the giant corporations in the top 100 advertisers. That reenforces the point we have already made—that expenditures on advertising do not correlate with information provided. Advertising may have the potential to be a significant source of information, but its performance in the electronic media belies that outlook.

Enough Light to Read By

The printed page, represented in our survey by newspapers and magazines, is the oldest form of modern communication. It was through the printed media that advertising got its start and took on its present form. Many newspapers and magazines are losing advertising revenue to such an extent that some well-known ones have ceased publication. At the same time, others are prospering because they fill a special need of advertisers. There are implications in this situation that directly affect the information that the ads pass along to consumers.

Newspapers contain a type of advertising that is purely informative—classified ads. These serve the consumer directly by locating items and in effect creating a market. These ads perform the classic function of bringing buyer and seller together. If you were interested in buying a used lawnmower, you might reasonably assume that someone in the area had one for sale; your problem would be finding that someone. It would be very difficult without classified advertising or something similar.

In its early form, most advertising was of the classified type. Other examples survive, such as the announcements on bulletin boards so common in neighborhood supermarkets. For the most part, however, advertising has gone beyond these elementary functions and now concerns itself with persuasion and advocacy. The summary of newspaper advertising in Table 6.5 does not include classified ads; it covers only commercial advertising. The figures in the table refer to the *number of ads and do not take size into account.* This obviously limits the survey, but if we assume that there is no relation between the size of the ad and the level of information, it is not a serious problem.

Newspaper advertising earns a rather good score on our information scale. While a quarter of the ads are puffing, over 60 percent contain some information. That is to be expected, since newspapers are an important means of local advertising. They afford local advertisers the chance to let consumers know what they have, what specials they are offering, and other information concerning hours and location. In this particular survey, the misleading ads were rather small, so that if some sort of space measurement were used, the percentage for the misleading category would be insignificant.

It is also worth noting that the particular issues included in this survey did not contain any grocery ads. That may seem like a minor point, but in most cities, such ads are a principal source of information and potential savings. Issues containing such ads would show an even higher level of information content. The same is true of big sales, none of which are reflected in these data.

Saying that newspapers are a primary source of information for consumers only confirms what most people already know. Newspapers are particularly good as a source of price information, which is obviously an important concern of consumers. Newspapers are of even greater value to consumers who already know what they want, for there is less information on product function and performance specifications. For day-to-day operations in the marketplace, the newspaper remains one of the consumer's main assets.

Magazines, as Table 6.5 shows, are also a good source of information, but here the picture is somewhat more complex. In the first place, the type of information is different. While newspapers contain information about local businesses, most magazine advertising does not. Furthermore, the type of measures we are using in this part of the survey—number of ads—is somewhat more biased with regard to magazines. That's because the puffing ads tend to be larger, like full-page cigarette and liquor ads. Thus, the number of ads in the puffing category probably understates the relative importance of puffing. Still, the results indicate that nearly one-third of all ads were highly informative, while well over half contained some information. While puffing was important, there was plenty of information too. You will notice that these results represent a compilation of the advertisements in four different magazines that represent three different types of publications. The type of magazine is an important determinant of the information content of the advertising.

TABLE 6.5 Information Content of Magazine and Newspaper Advertisements

	I	IP	P	PM	M	Total
Newspaper	5	27	13	5	2	52
% Total	10	52	25	10	3	100
Magazine	71	57	74	17	11	230
% Total	31	25	32	7	5	100

Source: See text.
NOTE: Figures indicate number of ads. Newspaper data represents
averages for a metropolitan daily during three weekdays in June 1973.
Classified ads are not included. Magazine data represent totals for
Time, Cosmopolitan, Playboy, and *Better Homes and Gardens* for
June 1973.

In recent years, mass-circulation magazines have fallen on hard times,
while specialty publications have fared much better. That is significant for
consumers, because the general circulation publications contain more general,
less informative ads. The specialty magazines, on the other hand, are aimed
at a particular audience. It can be assumed that persons reading one of
these publications has an interest in the particular topic and perhaps some
information about it. If you are not interested in home building, remodeling,
or furnishing, then a magazine devoted to those topics is not for you, but if
you are interested, you will find it useful.

This survey began with the disclaimer that it was not a scientific study,
and while that is true, some fairly clear trends have emerged. These trends
are strong enough that we may assume that a more systematic study would
tend to confirm them. When you consider the nature of the results, that
isn't a very encouraging thought. It does, however, provide a basis for our
further inquiry into advertising and information. From what we have
learned thus far, it is clear that improvement is needed; the problem now is
to translate that need into action and ultimately a program that will serve
consumers.

The notion that advertising should serve the consumer may itself sound
strange, which demonstrates how much has to be done towards this end.
Bringing about the necessary changes will be difficult and there may be disagreements about precisely what form the changes should take. There can,
however, be little debate about where the changes should begin. The survey
indicated that nearly 20 percent of the ads on television were in some way
misleading. Since there is no way that that figure, or anything near it, can
be justified, the first item on the agenda must be the elimination of misleading advertising.

GIVE TRUTH A CHANCE

Negative Information

It is not always possible to identify a misleading advertisement. If an ad features excessive claims or is patently unrealistic, then perhaps the consumer may realize that he should beware. More often, however, the misleading ad sounds quite reasonable, perhaps even informative. Independent tests, consumer surveys, or impressive demonstrations may be paraded forth to buttress the advertiser's argument. Such tests are easily abused, and what appears to be categorical evidence may actually be deception.

That appears to be what happened in an advertising campaign run by the Shell Oil Company several years ago. You may recall the ads that billed Shell's *Platformate* as an additive that added significantly to mileage. It showed car after car crashing through a paper barrier, having gone farther than cars using gasoline without Platformate. Thus, it appeared that Shell's gasoline delivered better mileage. Unfortunately, the campaign was as flimsy as the paper barrier. True, the cars using gasoline with Platformate did go farther, but as *Consumer Bulletin* was the first to point out, Platformate (or something like it) is found in nearly all gasoline meant for use in automobiles [12]. You could not buy the kind of gasoline Shell was using in the test. Any gasoline purchased from any pump would have Platformate in it and would go as far as Shell's.

Shell maintained that since the ad merely said that cars go farther on Platformate, there was no deception involved. No one bought that argument, however. *Advertising Age*, the trade journal for advertisers, sounded an "Amen" to a letter written by an agency executive that said:

> This is the kind of deception that gives all of advertising a black eye and makes the task of the honest practitioner of the craft just that much harder. It's also great fuel for those who promulgate government control of advertising. . . . [1]

There is no disputing that last sentence. If ads cannot be a minimum criterion of being dumb, but honest, then someone has to take the responsibility of keeping them off the air. In this case, it was a consumer group that exposed the hoax, but only after the ad had been running for some time.

Pain relievers represent another area of apparent deception and certain confusion. Aspirin is the main ingredient in such products, and aspirin, it turns out, is aspirin. A 1962 study published in the *Journal of the American Medical Association* indicated that statistically there is no significant difference in the performance of the five leading brands of pain relievers [7]. That was over ten years ago, yet producers still turn out advertisements that claim that their brand is superior, supporting their arguments with supposed *scientific tests*. Students who are familiar with statistical testing techniques know that such claims must be taken with a grain of salt (or perhaps aspirin). Their validity is at best questionable, for there is no evidence that if they were repeated on a larger population the results would be the same [11, p. 92]. Nevertheless, the claims continue unabated.

From the consumer's point of view, this is significant because of the variation in price among pain relievers. A student survey of prices of different brands, including various types of aspirin, so-called extra-strength varieties and buffered products, indicated that the price per tablet of a 100-tablet bottle ranged from over two cents to one-quarter of a cent. That means the most expensive brand was over eight times as expensive as the cheapest. Students may decide for themselves whether it is likely that the more expensive brand was eight times as effective.

There are significant medical questions attached to the use of aspirin. Some people cannot take it and must use substitutes. Others find that certain types contribute to digestive problems. Therefore, selecting the proper pain reliever is important. Unfortunately, none of these legitimate points are brought out in the typical advertisement for such products. There are broader questions too, such as whether these advertisements encourage consumers to take pills when they are not really necessary; there is the possibility, at least, that they contribute to drug abuse by developing a psychological dependency on pills.

The examples cited here are merely illustrative; similarly, the issues raised only suggest some of the more complex questions that lie beneath the surface of advertising. There is an obvious question of responsibility here, for with advertising so prevalent, the consumer must be protected from misleading advertisements. Since consumers are ill equipped to shoulder the burden and some advertisers seem unwilling, the responsibility falls to government.

Some New Directions

The job of policing advertisements falls to the Federal Trade Commission. The FTC was created in 1914, but not until 1938 was it given the specific authority to prosecute for misleading advertisements (see Chapter 8). The commission's performance has so far earned it few friends among consumer groups, but it has become more active in recent years and taken a tougher stand on misleading advertisements.

Public pressure has contributed to this renewed activity. In some cases, private groups have taken the initiative. One of the best examples of retaliation involves the so-called *countercommercials*. These are regular commercials, produced and paid for by consumer groups. They present the other side of the story, balancing the claims made in advertisements for products. Countercommercials have entered the pain-reliever debate, maintaining that aspirin by any other name or at any other price is still aspirin. Since television advertising time is expensive, few groups have been able to mount a comprehensive campaign of countercommercials. In light of this fact, an effort is under way to require television stations to provide free time for such ads. The argument is based on the FTC's *fairness doctrine*, which requires that both sides of any controversial topic be given equal airing. The fairness doctrine is meant to ensure that the public will be given a balanced view of any controversy.

Under this provision, television stations were earlier forced to give free time for antismoking commercials. The problem lies in deciding what constitutes a controversial issue. Consumer groups maintain that because of the doubt that surrounds many advertising claims, the claims qualify under that heading. Advertisers, understandably, take the opposite view, while television stations argue that such a ruling would bring them to financial ruin. At this time, the situation is still very confused, with suits and countersuits tied up in litigation. The confusion may be resolved fairly soon. In early 1973, the situation took a sharp turn when the FTC entered the picture and filed suit against the big pharmaceutical companies who make dubious claims. The companies must either provide acceptable scientific evidence to support the claims made for their pain relievers or take their ads off the air.

Perhaps more important, if the companies cannot support their claims, they will be forced to devote one-fourth of their future advertising to *corrective advertisements*. That means that they will be forced to atone for their past sins by admitting that all those claims they had been making for so many years are groundless. Corrective ads are actually a form of countercommercial given legal sanction by the FTC and paid for by the companies themselves. The concept of corrective advertising has been evolving since the 1960s. The FTC has already invoked the rule, forcing a fruit juice company to retract its earlier claims concerning the nutritional qualities of its product. The pain reliever case is clearly a landmark, and if the FTC wins, the decision will significantly affect other advertising.

If corrective advertising is established as a routine procedure, advertisers will be much more careful about what claims they make. A company forced to air corrective advertisements must bear a considerable expense. Not only are the ads themselves expensive, but the damage done to the firm's image and ultimately to the sales of the product in question could be significant. That possibility should encourage advertisers to police themselves more carefully. Even if the Federal Trade Commission does not act, however, firms that mislead the public will eventually pay the price. Most Americans still have a fairly favorable image of business, so when a company makes a claim about a product, consumers are predisposed to accept it. False claims represent a misuse of the trust placed in business by the public. They have already created disillusionment among some consumers, and if the situation is not altered drastically, the trend can only continue.

PROBLEMS AND POSSIBILITIES

Towards a New Perspective

Although the situation is still fluid, it appears that the future holds some promise for improvements in the quality of advertising. The obvious question is, Why has all this taken so long? Certainly the FTC must bear part of the blame, for at times the commission seemed to define its duties very narrowly and at others seemed to lack the will to act. It would be unfair, however, to place all the blame on the FTC. The commission's budget is inadequate. While it certainly could have done more with even its limited budget, the FTC was not in a position to undertake a thorough review of advertising. In effect, the FTC and the government itself reflected the prevailing public view of advertising. That is, no one took it seriously [6].

In general, there has been a failure to recognize advertising's tremendous potential as a source of information. Our argument so far has been developed in negative terms that emphasized the need to prevent misrepresentation. There is, however, an equally pressing need to look at the issue from a different point of view, stressing the positive aspects of the question. While getting rid of misleading ads would represent progress, it could still leave the overall level of information content very low. A positive program is needed that accords advertising its rightful position as an ideal source of information. Because it is relatively cheap and reaches all segments of the population, advertising has a potential informational and educational value beyond the capabilities of alternative sources. *It is nothing less than a resource*, a badly abused and misused one to be sure, but a resource nevertheless.

Putting advertising in that context serves another purpose; it helps us break out of the mental rut we are in when it comes to thinking about the question. Advertising is such a part of our lives that it is difficult to think of it except as it currently exists. Our thinking about advertising is badly out of date. Even when advertising has the potential to reach into every American home instantly, we still think of it in terms of the medicine show or the weekly newspaper. No doubt this has to do with the origin of present advertising methods and techniques. During the last century, advertising was unregulated and often outrageous, but it didn't matter in most cases. If the medicine show advertised a cure for fallen arches, heart attacks, and sore backs, it did so to a small group that could evaluate the product and the advertising. Even if someone was suckered into buying the product, the amounts involved were probably small.

Technological change, however, has altered the situation radically. Faster presses, the introduction of color, and widespread distribution improved the traditional media. Radio and television have spread the reach and potential effectiveness of advertising still further. Frederick Lewis Allen chronicled the changes that took place during the 1920s. The ads of fifty years ago make today's look like the picture of responsibility. For example, Allen tells of the unhappy people who had

> succumbed to pyorrhea, each of them with a white mask mercifully concealing his unhappy mouth. . . . The woman who would undoubtedly do something about B.O. if people only said to her what they really thought. . . . These men and women of the advertising

pages, suffering or triumphant, *became part of the folklore of the day*. [5, p. 73, emphasis added]

Those people, or their grandchildren, have become part of American culture and they are treated with a degree of nonchalance that masks their real importance. Consumers continue to treat advertising lightly even though increasing complexities in the market and technological change have left them behind, reducing their influence and their ability to counter the forces of advertising. If your grandparents didn't like the line the huckster on the back of the wagon was feeding them, they could at least yell, "That's a lie!" While you can do that to the person on the television screen, it isn't nearly so effective. You should recognize this argument as an aspect of the more general consumer problem—the consumer's inability to work in a changed environment. Consumers do not seem to have caught on to the fact that the environment has changed. The comment on horse-and-buggy thinking on space-age problems certainly applies here. Many consumers still have their blinders on. This has permitted the freewheeling and largely unchallenged development of the advertising establishment. The implications of advertising for consumers and its potential usefulness have not really been grasped.

Notice that we have come out in favor of advertising, not against it. Our criticism has to do with certain aspects of the way products are advertised, not with advertising itself. Unfortunately, even the mildest criticism of advertising tends to polarize opinions. Some groups seem to feel that there is something sacred about the current content and structure of advertising; they equate the status quo with what they call "our free enterprise system." Whatever that is, it is not a very good description of advertising and the American economy in the 1970s. Advertising expenditures are highly concentrated among a few firms. While there are millions of businesses in this country, the top 100 advertisers accounted for almost exactly half of all advertising expenditures in 1970. Over 80 percent of all network television advertising comes from those same 100 firms [2, p. 96]. That concentrates a tremendous amount of power in the hands of a few firms. It can be argued that, rather than support free enterprise, massive advertising expenditures actually promote monopoly elements by giving an extra advantage to certain firms. Advertising becomes a way of maintaining control of a market and forestalling competition. Thus, a doctrinaire approach only masks the real issues and confuses the question.

Run It up the Flagpole . . .

The clear need is to look at advertising in unemotional terms and devise a means by which it can serve the consumer better. The first step is to make consumers aware of what surrounds advertising. That means more than just exposing fraudulent claims and other misleading advertising. It means educating the public to what advertising *could* be. When that realization sinks in, the public pressure that is requisite for any meaningful change will be forthcoming. The idea is simple. It would involve nothing more than requiring that advertisers provide high-quality information about their products. The FTC's standards could be used; advertisements would be expected to contain information about price, performance standards, construction specifications, and anything else relevant to that particular product. The commandment to advertisers would become, Thou shalt be informative.

That proposal is straightforward, but its apparent simplicity masks many complexities. We have already touched on the first; it is necessary to specify precisely what *informative* means. There will have to be some latitude in the definition, for it is hard to provide much information about some products. Take coffee, for example. All coffees are not created equal; some are better than others, but how can that be put in an ad? The true test is in the drinking, and that cannot be accomplished on television or in a magazine. To accommodate this problem, it would be necessary to permit brand-name identification ads. They could simply say that the product is available and worth trying, although any ad agency worth its ulcers could think up a more glorious way of saying that. The only change would be that any claims of quality or public acceptance would have to be supported with hard evidence.

There might be a beneficial spinoff from such a policy. If businesses were forced to say something about their products, they might quit producing so many products about which there is nothing to say. This applies particularly to product differentiation—the practice of making a number of products that are only superficially different—which results in higher costs and confusion for the consumer. If businesses had to justify their products and explain how they were really different and better, they would certainly think more carefully before flooding the market with them.

The significant problem with this proposal is validating the information provided in advertisements. It is not enough simply to tell advertisers to go out and be informative; it is necessary to provide them with guidance and direction. Here is where a national information policy comes into the picture. Information provided through advertising would be an integral part of that overall policy.

Product testing is important in that policy. The results of such tests would be available to everyone, including advertisers. If the tests showed that the Clomp-Chomp lawnmower was the safest, most economical, and most dependable mower on the market, then Clomp-Chomp should be able to use those findings in their ads. The public would know that the company was not just making wild claims, since the information would have been validated. Thus, advertisements would be a way of getting quality information to the public.

Where does that leave companies whose products do not measure up well in such tests? They would not be forced to say that in their ads, but they would not be able to make any claims of performance or quality either. That would provide a powerful incentive to improve their product. Better information flow would therefore bring pressure on producers to offer quality products, which is precisely the way markets are supposed to work. Now producers can hide behind the consumer's lack of information and pass off inferior products on the public.

At this point you may be shuddering at the bureaucratic complications such a system could produce. There is no doubt that the FTC or a similar agency would have to increase its staff and budget to administer such a program. However, the very concentration of advertising expenditures that we mentioned above would simplify the process. The bulk of advertising could be covered by overseeing a relatively small number of advertisers. Furthermore, when advertisers become familiar with the new rules of the game, they would seek to comply out of necessity. A strict system of penalties would ensure that result.

Let us summarize how such a system would work. Firms would be free to advertise, but would be required to give definitive information about their products. Any claims made in the ads would have to be supportable and validated by an outside agency. On the assumption that if you don't have anything good to say, it is better to say nothing, this system would force advertisers either to provide information or to cut back on their advertising. There is one final ingredient that is essential for the success of such a system: *public awareness.* The public must be educated to the possibilities of advertising so that people will expect ads to provide information. That will be the ultimate pressure on advertisers. If public acceptance requires information, then information will be provided. That process will not be automatic until the public demands information, and educating them to awareness requires an extensive educational effort.

. . . and See if Anyone Salutes

We have treated advertising at great length simply because advertising has the potential to provide high-quality, low-cost information to all segments of the population. *Information* needs to be interpreted very broadly in this context. That is, it includes not only information about products per se but also about types of products and services. In short, advertising could perform a genuinely educational function.

Insurance advertisements, for example, could include detailed information about types of insurance, strengths of each type, and the best insurance package under different circumstances. Similarly, advertisements for banks or other financial institutions could include sound financial advice. By the ingenuity of advertisers, this information could be put across in an easily understandable fashion. It is difficult to think of a more effective way to get information to a broad cross section of the public. As people were continually exposed to this sort of advertising, they would gradually develop a more sophisticated understanding of these complex issues.

Citizens might decide that some percentage of total advertising time should be given over to such educational efforts. Such a proposal would be consistent with the overall thrust of this plan. The key word here, as we suggested earlier, is *responsibility*. This approach makes businesses responsible for providing quality information to consumers. That is a very conservative idea, for it assumes that if consumers have better information, the system will work better. It will also force businesses to be more responsive, for they will not be able to hide behind the wall of confusion that now separates them from consumers. Consumers, in turn, will be able to make more intelligent decisions, choosing those products best suited to their needs. This alone will force firms to respond to the challenge in an effort to increase sales and profits. In essence, we are merely trying to equalize the odds and give consumers enough power—through information— for them to exercise their function within the system.

In closing, one final question should be asked: Could such a policy be carried through? The answer depends on public pressure. Unless consumers demand something better from advertisers, they will fail to receive anything better. Recent developments within the FTC suggest that the public is waking up. As the consumer movement grows and extends its influence, changes should be accelerated. The changes we have outlined may seem like pipe dreams; remember that changes have already taken place in advertising, however. It was not too long ago that cigarette advertisements, now banned from television, were making health claims about their products. Similarly, the very idea of corrective advertising would have seemed radical a decade ago. Thus, it is not unrealistic to suppose that advertising over time can be made to convey information. The changes will not take place overnight and the program will not come in a single package. Progress generally comes in small steps. However, with each step, consumers will become better informed. In this case, the ultimate goal makes the journey worthwhile.

STUDY QUESTIONS

1. It is often argued that without advertising the economy would stagnate, since it is advertising that sell products. Evaluate that contention. Differentiate between a single firm's increasing its sales and increased sales of all products. That is, if one tire company advertises, will it necessarily increase the total number of tires sold throughout the economy?

2. In the case of new products, the argument presented in Question 1 has some validity. Is it, however, necessarily inconsistent with informative advertising? Why or why not?

3. Why is it that so little information is provided in advertisements? Evaluate the following explanations:
   a. Companies do not want consumers to know about their products.
   b. There is really nothing substantive to say about the products.

     c.   Puffing sells better than information.

     d.   Consumers do not care about information and perhaps do not even want it.

4.   We have stressed the need to educate consumers to the possibilities of advertising as a source of information. Why is that so important? How might such an educational program be carried out?

5.   You may have noted that for compact cars, particularly imports, price is usually given in the ads. For larger models, such information is much less common. What does that show about the approach used to sell different types of cars? If price information is given in some ads, is there any reason it cannot be in others?

6.   What types of products are likely to have the most informative ads? Does an examination of advertisements uncover any consistent pattern? Explain.

7.   In the United States, the air waves are public property that radio and television stations are licensed to use. What is the significance of this fact in relation to federal regulation of advertising?

8.   Television networks have departments that screen ads before they are aired. Remembering where networks get their money, how effective, do you think, is this process? Would it be reasonable to institute a policy that makes the networks (or local stations) responsible for any misleading advertisements they carry?

9.   Certain types of advertising, cigarettes and liquor, for example, are banned from television. What is the rationale for this policy? Could the same rationale support limitations on other types of advertising?

10.   If strict information standards were imposed on advertising, what would happen to the quantity of advertising, do you think? Would there be a difference between the immediate impact and the long-run impact of such a policy?

SUGGESTED PROJECTS

1.   Repeat the evaluation of the information content of advertising reported in the text; use the same categories, standards, and guidelines.

     a.   For television, one student can be assigned to time and classify the ads on each network. (More than one can be assigned if a double-check is desired.) If possible, surveys should be carried out simultaneously on all networks.

     b.   Radio can be done in the same way, although some effort should be made to get samples from different types of stations at different times of day.

c.   For printed media, be sure to review different types of publications. As a rule of thumb, ask this question about each ad: "Does it tell me anything that would really help me if I were buying the product?" How do the findings compare with those reported in the text? Make notes on ads that illustrate the various categories and discuss the ads.

2.   Prepare a report on the Federal Trade Commission's activities in regulating advertising. Explore the commission's legal status and authority. Has there been any change in the FTC's approach in recent years?

3.   If your local paper carries weekly grocery ads, calculate potential savings through the information they provide. Is the savings sufficient to cover the cost of the paper, the investment of time, and possible extra trips to different stores?

4.   Your library probably has microfilm copies of leading (and local) newspapers and magazines that go back several years. Beginning with the earliest copies available, compare advertisements from different periods. What changes are evident? Do you think these represent improvement?

5.   Survey consumers' attitudes towards advertisements. Try to find out if consumers actually use information from ads, and if so, what kind. Also, try to determine how much faith they put in ads.

BIBLIOGRAPHY AND SUGGESTED READINGS

The question of information and advertising is part of the larger problem of information costs. Students may therefore want to refer to the citations in the previous chapter. Many of them treat material in this chapter, even though they do not deal with advertising directly.

1. *Advertising Age*, February 28, 1969.
   Since this is the trade journal of advertisers, its perspective is pretty well defined. Nevertheless, it remains a good source for thoughtful consideration of advertising, and in particular, for statistical information on advertising expenditures.

2. *Advertising Age*, August 30, 1971.

3. *Advertising Age*, August 27, 1973.
   Annual statistical summary of advertising expenditures by the top hundred advertisers.

4. *Advertising Age*, November 21, 1973.
   Information on advertising, consumer expenditures, and gross national product.

5. Allen, Frederick Lewis. *Only Yesterday*. New York: Harper & Row, 1931.
   An informal, social history of the 1920s, full of vignettes about life during

America's first flirtation with mass consumption. Enjoyable reading and valuable in understanding present attitudes. Good section on advertising.

6. Cohen, Dorothy. "The Federal Trade Commission and the Regulation of Advertising in the Consumer Interest." *Journal of Marketing,* January 1969, pp. 40–44.
   A look at the FTC's role in this important field. Particularly good for its emphasis on behavioral aspects; that is, it considers how advertising fits into the complexities of consumer behavior.

7. DeKornfeld, Thomas. "A Comparative Study of Five Proprietary Analgesic Compounds." *Journal of the American Medical Association,* December 29, 1962.
   A landmark study showing that there is no significant difference in the effectiveness of leading pain relievers.

8. Federal Trade Commission. *Hearings on Advertising.* Hearings before the 92nd Congress, 1st session, 1971. S.1461 & S.1763. Washington, D.C.: U.S. Government Printing Office.
   Hearings on the FTC's role in regulating advertising. They offer a comprehensive review of the subject.

9. Federal Trade Commission. *News Summary.* Washington, D.C.: U.S. Government Printing Office.
   A weekly summary of FTC activities. An excellent and painless way to keep up with what is going on about the commission and advertising.

10. Federal Trade Commission. *Trade Practice and Rules.* Washington, D.C.: U.S. Government Printing Office.
    A guide to FTC regulations and rules on advertising standards.

11. Nader, Ralph. "Claims Without Substance." In *The Consumer and Corporate Accountability.* New York: Harcourt Brace Jovanovich, 1972, pp. 90–97.
    A look at the wild claims of advertisers. Includes a discussion of how advertisers responded (and in some cases did not respond) when asked to support their claims.

12. "The Platformate Illusion." *Consumer Bulletin,* January 1968.
    The original tipoff on Platformate. Illustrates how private consumer groups are important in providing information to consumers.

13. Scherhorn, Gerhard, and Wieken, Klaus. "On the Effect of Counter-Information on Consumers." In *Human Behavior in Economic Affairs,* ed. Burkhard Strumpel, et al. San Francisco: Jossey-Bass, 1972.
    Worth reviewing on the potential of corrective ads and counter commercials. Indicates that good results may be expected.

14. Stigler, George. "The Economics of Information." *Journal of Political Economy,* June 1961, pp. 213–15.
    Contains a section on advertising and a good treatment of classified ads.

7

The Consumer: Sovereign, Subject, or Sucker?

THE ATTACK ON CONSUMER SOVEREIGNTY

On "Monarchizing"

When Shakespeare's sovereign Richard II sat upon the ground "to tell sad stories of the death of kings," he might well have been speaking for today's American consumer. True, the textbooks say the consumer is sovereign, but the real power seems to lie elsewhere. While the marketplace may allow the consumer "to monarchize" from time to time, it is all a sham, merely "infusing him with self and vain conceit." Many are the consumers who might have asked the question with which Richard ends his lamentation: "How can you say to me, I am a king?" [*Richard II*, III, ii]

No such doubts are admitted into the secure world of economic theory. In that world, sovereign consumers direct the allocation of resources, and hence the productive process, by the pattern of their expenditures. The dollar vote emerges as the ultimate weapon in the consumer's arsenal, a means of rewarding favored producers and punishing others. It is the great equalizer, which ensures that the market will work as an instrument that serves consumer interests.

Outside of the textbooks, however, few observers see things working that way; most would argue that the consumer shares the gruesome fate that awaited Richard. Ralph Nader speaks of "the billions which consumers would not have paid if they knew or *could control* what they were getting [12, p. 5, emphasis added]. Others flatly assert that because of the "maldistribution of power and consequent abuse of the consumer . . . reduction in consumer power is almost complete" [19, p. 6]. This reduction in consumer power can be linked to increased specialization, which while increasing

135

efficiency, also broke the direct link between production and consumption. Once that link was broken, the individual's influence was further diluted by growth in market size, so that now the individual consumer is only a small cog in the giant market mechanism. Consumers are mastered by the very mechanism that is supposed to be their servant. This is the condition of consumer impotence—a chief source of consumer complaints.

The transition of consumers from active agents in the economic system to passive bystanders has done more than just erode their position in the marketplace. It has placed consumption in a new perspective. When the consumer no longer has a positive role to play, consumption becomes an end in itself for many people, seemingly based on nothing more than the gratification of every passing whim and fancy. It is in this context that the word *consumer* has become a pejorative term, meaning "one who takes but never gives."

If that is all consumption is and if consumers do not exercise control, then pretending that they do only serves the interests of producers. It gives them license, as John Kenneth Galbraith has argued, to manipulate the system to their own ends. "The fox," Galbraith noted, "is powerful in the management of the coop" [6, p. 10]. Under those conditions, consumers cannot operate effectively. Both the effective functioning of the market system and the consumers' own self-interest require that they have the power to protect themselves and influence events. Thus, the question of who has what kind of power may be the central question in all of consumer economics.

Power and the Useful Consumer

The heading for this section is a variation on Professor Galbraith's 1972 presidential address to the American Economics Association, which dealt with many of the issues we have raised [6]. Specifically, it pointed to the unpleasant fact that economic analysis is not well equipped to deal with power. A perfectly competitive economy is characterized by the diffusion of power, under which neither individual producers nor consumers can influence the market.

Economists' treatment of power as a nonconcept can be traced to Adam Smith's famous "invisible hand." He used that phrase to refer to the mechanism that ensured that the public good would be served if each individual sought only his or her personal goals. Thus, power made its debut in modern economics as an unseen, mystical force. Whatever force controlled the movements of Smith's invisible hand, it was not individual direction. The individual's role, in fact, was unconscious.

A closer look at the modern analysis of consumer sovereignty reveals a similar line of thought. Sovereignty implies power, but in this case it is a strange sort of power, held by consumers as a group rather than by the individual. Power is diffused and collective, expressed through the market as a collection of individual choices. This expression shapes the system, but it comes from consumers in the aggregate. The system works because no one has any real power. That last sentence might be rewritten to read "The system works *as long as* no one has any real power." From the consumer's point of view, that is why the system does not work very well. Consumers have upheld their end of the bargain, making decisions as individuals and thus diffusing their power. Producers, however, have accumulated sufficient power to influence the market. This imbalance in the system disadvantages the consumer. Consumers have no effective counterweight to the concentrated power of producers.

The restoration of the consumer's position requires, in the words used earlier, that consumers "have the power to protect themselves and influence events." That statement, however, covers a great deal of ground. It is one thing for consumers to protect their positions by insulating themselves against the vagaries of the marketplace. Influencing events is something else again, for it requires that consumers have an impact on the market. It is the difference between making peace with a hostile market and fashioning that market into a more congenial place. The consumer may have the power to attain one goal, but not the other. Thus, the phrase "consumer power" itself means very little as a general statement; such power exists at different levels. That realization holds the key to sorting out the confusion commonly associated with this topic. *It is not sufficient merely to speak of consumer power; to make any such statement meaningful, it is necessary to specify the degree and extent of such power.*

To cope with the day-to-day problems of the marketplace, consumers need some leverage simply to ensure that they are treated fairly. This is the first level of consumer power—the individual's ability to look after his or her own interests in the marketplace. The question is simply this, Does the consumer have enough power to ensure a fair shake from the system? That implies the absence of fraud, full and accurate representation of products, and prompt action on complaints. However, while individuals may wring fair treatment for themselves from the system, there is nothing to ensure that these benefits will be universally shared. That assurance, the extension of fair treatment to all consumers in the marketplace, is the second level of consumer power. Note the emphasis on all consumers and the fact that such benefits are enjoyed as a matter of course. Attaining that goal requires the transformation of the marketplace from a malevolent place to a benevolent one.

While such a change would represent a significant accomplishment, it should not be confused with consumer sovereignty. Sovereignty implies more than being treated well in a paternalistic system; it means that consumers actually direct the system. The consumer must have not only choices among goods and services but also choices among choices. Sovereign consumers decide what choices they are going to have in the marketplace. Thus, consumer power, which seems like such a harmless little phrase, actually covers a complex variety of topics. Not only can no simple analysis do justice to all the complexities involved, but no single analysis can cover the full range. To appreciate all the subtleties and interrelationships, it is therefore necessary to analyze each of the three levels of consumer power separately.

THE INDIVIDUAL IN THE MARKETPLACE

Sources of Consumer Leverage

It is clear that consumers are seriously disadvantaged in their individual confrontations with the market. That conclusion is inescapable. It is necessary to distinguish, however, between a difficult situation and a hopeless one. While the cards are stacked against consumers, that does not mean they are completely at the mercy of the market. Even though the marketplace is a hostile environment, the knowledgeable—or perhaps it is better to say *crafty*—consumer can still survive in it.*

Survive is the key word in that sentence. This discussion deals with the lowest level of consumer power. It is hardly a very sweeping assertion to say that consumers have some power with which to protect themselves. But while their position is not ideal, consumers can work to improve their positions with the power they do have.

It is certain that if consumers do not seek such improvement, no one else will. Even if the marketplace were well organized in terms of consumer's needs, consumer satisfaction would still hinge on individual transactions. The market, which we have been talking about in such abstract terms, ultimately comes down to a buyer and a seller. We want to balance the odds between the two. That is a large order, but as a beginning, it is necessary for consumers to assert themselves. That may sound simplistic, but there is no way around the fact that if consumers are to receive better treatment in the marketplace, they must demand it. Some effort is needed, to be sure, but the consumer who makes the effort and follows an aggressive strategy will be well served. On the other hand, consumers who act like sheep will be treated like sheep (except in states where such things are against the law).

An aggressive strategy begins before the consumer actually enters the market. Consumers who know what they want and know something about the products and services that will fulfill those wants are in a strong position. Once in the market, the consumer must demand explicit information. Being satisfied with ambiguities increases the probability of dissatisfaction later. When the consumer is dissatisfied, however, the need for an activist approach is the greatest. If a product is not performing adequately or a service is not rendered properly, then it is necessary to complain and to keep complaining until the deficiency is corrected [11].

---

* Low-income groups must be exempted from this analysis. Because they typically lack even minimal leverage, they do not have many of the options outlined here. Still, this discussion applies to something over 80 percent of the population. See Chapter 10.

Businesses are interested in profits, not consumers, but there is an obvious relation between the two. If businesses recognize that to secure their profit position consumer demands must be accommodated, they will respond to consumer pressure. Furthermore, businesses are notoriously squeamish about bad publicity. Businesses are concerned about their good name or image and the consumer can use this concern as a lever. This is particularly true now that the beginnings of the consumer movement have exposed the raw nerve of business to probing. Armed with a critical strategy that is liberally reenforced with persistence and imagination, the consumer should sooner or later be able to obtain satisfaction.

There certainly are limitations to this approach, the most obvious being the scope of its effectiveness. An individual cannot remake the market or rebuild the institutions of the economy. But particularly at the local level, where businesses are small and the individual's patronage is likely to be important, this action can strengthen the consumer's position. Drugstores are a good example. It is likely that you buy drugs and sundries at a fairly small store, where you have a chance to get to know the pharmacist. Such an environment is not overpowering, and it is possible to get answers to questions and consideration of special problems. The small drugstore illustrates why, in any intelligent argument about consumer activity, it is important to specify the level of consumer power. Finding a good drugstore will not allow you to do much about the policies of drug companies towards product pricing, testing, and distribution. These important problems represent a different level of power. Individuals can, however, minimize the impact of these problems on themselves and make their environment as congenial as possible.

Unfortunately, the consumer will not automatically enjoy these benefits. Quite the contrary, they are in no way guaranteed by the workings of the market. Consumers must work for whatever they get. It is impossible to condone businessmen who take advantage of the consumer, but it is possible to understand them. Typically, they will not do a great deal more than is required of them. If consumers demand very little, then that is what businessmen will provide. The implication here is that consumers have themselves to blame for many of their day-to-day problems. It is a sort of vacuum theory. If consumers abdicate their responsibilities, one can hardly expect businessmen to point that out to them. It would be a rare case indeed for a salesperson to berate a consumer for not demanding more specific information about a product. If the consumer is willing to accept vague generalities, the businessman is not going to offer more. Businesses will lower their sights accordingly, moving into the vacuum created by the consumer's abdication of rights. In this way, the minimum level of service or performance that the consumer can reasonably expect is systematically lowered.

The consumer has little direct control over the problems created by the growing complexity of the marketplace. It appears, however, that consumers have contributed to the deterioration of their own position by being satisfied with too little. It is tempting to characterize the consumer as one who has fought the good fight and lost, but too often, the consumer seems unwilling even to open hostilities. This is consistent with the well-known image of the apathetic consumer. It hardly fits, however, with either the portrait of the consumer developed in this book or the observed increase in consumer activism. A consistent and exact picture of the real consumer is therefore called for.

The Changing Face of Affluence

It should come as no surprise that the explanation of these divergent tendencies rests on the impact of affluence upon the consumer. Our theme has stressed that affluence is intimately bound up with consumer problems in general. To ignore the impact of affluence on consumer behavior is to miss the whole point. It may be true that the consumer is exploited, but it must be admitted that never have people been exploited in such comfort and style. While the fact of affluence is obvious enough, its consequences are much more difficult to trace. Notice the use of the plural—*consequences*; instead of a single line of causation, there are many forces at work, which may be pulling the consumer in different directions. Affluence has both an immediate impact and a more subtle effect that materializes over time. The latter may be ultimately more important and yet masked by more obvious short-run changes.

As consumer incomes rise, the composition of consumption changes. The difference relates to the concept of income elasticity—the rate at which the demand for a particular product changes as income changes.* The demand for foods prepared at home, for example, tends to have a fairly low income elasticity. Once people are adequately fed, additional increases in income will result in increased spending on things other than food or in a switch to prepared foods and restaurant meals.

This pattern was first identified about a century ago by the German statistician Ernst Engel [18]. Therefore, it is sometimes referred to as Engel's law, although Engel carried out studies on other products besides food. Economics students will recall that a graph showing the various amounts of a product consumed at different levels of income is called an Engel curve. While economists have understood the nature of this process for some time, it is only recently that they have been able to study how widespread affluence affects Engel curves. The effect is reflected in a broad definition of cost, which includes not just money outlay, but time and effort components as well. As incomes rise, the latter become increasingly important. Money cost remains a consideration, but the more affluent consumer is in the position to take other things into account [14].

---

* For our purposes, income elasticity can be defined as the percentage change in demand divided by the percentage change in income. Let Q_x stand for the quantity of good x and Y for income and we have $\%\Delta Q_x / \%\Delta Y$. Thus, if income goes up by 10 percent and the demand for x goes up 5 percent, the income elasticity would be 0.5; hence, the good is income-inelastic, for the increase in demand did not keep pace with the increase in income.

As incomes rise, those goods with a higher time-effort cost component will decline in relative importance in the consumer's budget. The consumer can now *afford* to express a preference for goods that save time and effort. To put it differently, the consumer is in a position to reduce the time-effort component of cost; minimizing *total* costs will therefore require that time-effort costs be reduced also. It is easy to see this tendency working itself out in the growth of demand for such things as automatic dishwashers, self-defrosting refrigerators, and garbage disposals. However, the same forces are at work in more subtle ways. Reducing time-effort costs means that the costs of operating, maintaining, and eventually replacing the product must be taken into account. In the case of automobiles, this accounting shifts demand towards compacts, which are cheap to operate and easy to maintain. For other consumer durables, it puts a premium on dependability and trouble-free operation.

Most of what has been said thus far refers to essential items, especially consumer durables. Affluence is also making itself felt in other areas. Because of the very nature of the items involved, the consumer is in a position to pick and choose, to be discriminating. This trend is evident in the fashion industry, particularly men's clothing; the fate of the white shirt is a good example. As a writer for *Fortune* noted:

> That homogeneous-looking middle class of the early 1960's has been increasingly fragmented in recent years . . . by an increasing insistence by the customers on using consumption to express themselves, to help in the fashioning of their own identities. [16, p. 94]

The net result of these changes is an increasingly demanding consumer. In essentials, consumers want products that function dependably, minimizing total costs. With nonessentials, the key word is individuality.* It is not inconsistent for both elements to come together in the same good. The consumer may want a refrigerator with decorator panels that can be changed with the decor in the kitchen, but only if the machine itself is mechanically sound.

At this point you should be bothered by the inconsistency between this portrait of the increasingly demanding consumer and the earlier contention that consumers have weakened their own positions by not being sufficiently demanding. This inconsistency indicates the difference between the short- and long-run effects of affluence. The process just described clearly belongs in the latter category. It has been countered, however, by short-run tendencies, which until recently have been more obvious. Resolving the dilemma calls for unraveling these various elements.

Timing is critical. While the mass consumption society has been emerging for most of this century, it has only recently reached maturity.

---

* Total cost considerations may enter here too. Professor Rosalind Schulman attributes the failure of the midiskirt to the fact that it represented a departure from simpler, easier-to-care-for styles. Higher initial and upkeep costs were particularly important in its rejection [14].

Development was interrupted by two world wars, the Great Depression, and several different minor disturbances. Mass consumption did not establish itself until after World War II, and in the sluggish economy of the 1950s, its growth was uneven. The years after World War II established a pattern that has been altered only slowly. After fifteen years of depression and war, years of shortages and rationing, consumers were eager to buy. Producers had the upper hand. While the circumstances that created this situation passed quickly, the mentality it created did not. The idea that consumers should appreciate the range of goods available to them lingered on. Consumers were in fact appreciative, and while the consumer indulgence so characteristic of the 1920s was lacking, most people were still preoccupied with their new-found affluence.

It was during the 1960s—the longest continuous economic expansion in the nation's history—that the situation began to change. As it did, however, a new set of forces came into play. When consumers began to look at their purchases with more critical eyes, they discovered that doing anything about their complaints was itself a very expensive proposition. There are costs attached to an activist strategy; these become apparent when you consider all that is involved. If you have a complaint, you must confront the seller, explain what is wrong, and justify your case. That is usually sufficient, but even if you meet with such early success, you have still invested a considerable amount of time, effort, and money. Time and effort costs become more important to consumers as incomes rise, but those are precisely the costs involved in this case. Consumers' costs of complaining increase with time and effort spent.

Costs are further increased by the fact that all of this is likely to be unpleasant. Only the most combative find this sort of undertaking enjoyable, which contrasts with what we said about searching for information. There is often consumption value in search, since many people enjoy shopping. In this case, the disutility of complaining must be added onto the other costs. If only a small purchase is involved, it may not be worthwhile to put yourself through a disagreeable experience. The costs involved would be more than the possible gain. With the many goods and services the typical consumer buys, pursuing all possible complaints would be an overwhelming task. It follows that the consumer is likely to follow through only on those complaints where significant amounts of money are involved.

The difference between the short-run and the long-run impact of affluence on the consumer should be clear. Short-run influences combined to promote the image of the passive, indifferent consumer, which to a degree is still with us. At the same time, however, the more subtle and ultimately more important long-run forces began to make themselves felt. It is not mere chance that consumerism first emerged as a significant force in the 1960s. It took that long for the process that was creating a more demanding consumer to make itself felt. That process also expressed itself through market forces. Previously, a consumer who had found a particular product unsatisfactory might not have complained, merely resolving not to buy it again. Several consumers complaining together could cause demand for a product ultimately to decline. Complaints became more common. Costs remained an inhibiting factor, but consumers developed a clearer perception of their own self-interest as their level of dissatisfaction rose. What has often been mistaken for militancy is nothing more than consumers reasserting themselves and demanding from the market the sort of performance they have a right to expect. As more consumers assumed this posture, it became socially acceptable, sanctioned as correct behavior. People who even a few years ago would have thought it bad form to complain now expertly follow up on their grievances. By its very nature, this process is slow and unspectacular. However, the ultimate impact of more discriminating consumers is of fundamental importance in the marketplace.

It would certainly facilitate this analysis if all of these developments had unfolded in a neat, sequential fashion. Unfortunately, that is not the case. Elements of consumer indifference coexist with consumer activism. Change has proceeded unevenly. The result is a confusing patchwork full of seeming inconsistencies and paradoxes. Despite the confusion, it is clear that consumerism is not a fad; it will not pass quietly away. Rather, it has become a permanent feature of society. The full impact of consumer activism has yet to be felt. Not only is the consumer reawakening as yet incomplete, but most activity to date has been directed at reclaiming lost ground. Consumers are paying for their earlier indifference. When this remedial action is complete, they will be able to direct their energies towards reshaping the system itself.

THE IMPERATIVES OF CONSUMER ORGANIZATION

Collective Security

The second level of consumer power consists of assuring all consumers not only fair treatment in the marketplace, but a voice in its operation as well. Those goals lie beyond the capabilities of the individual consumer. Both the size and complexity of the marketplace are important, the former because it dilutes the individual's influence and the latter because it makes figuring out the market's operation difficult.

Therein lies the rationale for consumer organization. It is blissfully simple. While the marketplace may overwhelm the individual, like-minded consumers should be able to organize themselves into groups of sufficient strength to assert their influence. In reaching that conclusion, consumers are following a well-worn path. Large corporations dominate the marketplace; their size gives them a degree of power well beyond that of a small firm. Similarly, giant unions can win concessions from management that would be impossible for individual workers.

You may recognize this as the idea of *countervailing power*, first articulated by John Kenneth Galbraith over twenty years ago [5]. In a competitive situation, power is diffused. However, as one group accumulates power, it assumes a dominant position. This naturally disadvantages others, who are thus encouraged to organize themselves to protect their own interests. They acquire power as a counterweight—hence, countervailing— to offset the original power center. This can be seen in the progression from big business to big government to big labor, each developing in response to earlier concentrations of power elsewhere. Consumer organization therefore follows as a logical step in the sequence.

A very useful analogy can be made here with the experience of workers. In the simple, preindustrial economy, labor-management relations were on a personal or even neighborly basis. The individual worker probably had a skill, and in the typical firm of small size, there was easy access to the employer in case of a complaint. All of that was changed with industrialization. The worker's position was weakened as skills became less important. Only basic skills were required and low-paid workers quickly replaced the more expensive craftsmen. With the advent of big business, the worker's position deteriorated still further. Management became more and more remote and the individual's influence was diluted as the number of workers grew. Those who objected quickly discovered that they were very small, and easily replaceable, parts of the operation.

The response of the workers was organization. Progress was slow and uneven at best, but despite numerous false starts, hostile public opinion, and an unsympathetic government, the rights of labor to organize and bargain collectively were finally recognized. Thus, workers as a group were able to assert themselves to a degree that would be impossible for the individual. Despite the obvious differences between the worker in the firm and the consumer in the marketplace, the principle of strength through organization applies in both cases.

Types of Consumer Organization

In one way or another, all consumer organizations are geared to helping the consumer come to grips with the problems of the marketplace. Under that general heading, however, it is possible to delineate four main types of organization. The first is direct market action, a pooling of dollar votes to give the real-world consumer the same sort of leverage his counterpart in theory enjoys. The second type provides information, as discussed in Chapter 5. Thirdly, there are organizations that focus on legal, administrative, and legislative goals. Finally, there are efforts towards cooperative purchases among consumers, offering the opportunity for greater specialization.

Direct market action applies to those groups that use purchasing power to affect the market; as such, it represents a logical extension of the theoretical apparatus discussed earlier. Boycotts are the best illustration of this process. If consumers feel that a particular store is unfair, they may direct their business elsewhere. If the boycott is effective, the store will be forced to come to terms. The punishment is administered through the market, using the conventional technique of the dollar vote.

In theory, the individual's dollar votes direct production. In the real-world marketplace, however, the individual's purchasing power is such an insignificant fraction of the total that except in localized circumstances, its influence is insignificant. It is therefore logical for individuals to unite and as a group direct their purchases. With blocs of dollar votes to shift around, the group has leverage that its individual members lack. The amounts of money involved are large enough to have an impact. Such groups are merely doing collectively what economic theory says the individual should do. This response is necessitated by the weakness of the individual consumer's position. The action-reaction sequence clearly illustrates countervailing power. The use of the market mechanism, however, marks such efforts as an extension of traditional techniques, not a departure from them.

Direct market action is therefore a very conservative response. That point is often missed in analyzing consumer organizations. Too often, the public image of consumer activists is one of militancy, suggesting a radical stance and vaguely subversive possibilities. This distortion is significant, for while such groups use classic market techniques, they are damned as threats to the market system. The truth is that such groups are working within the existing market system, using its mechanism to attain their goals. By creating new power centers to balance existing ones, consumer groups are merely equalizing the odds. The status quo clearly favors business interests; those who complain against consumer organization are simply bemoaning their loss of leverage against the consumer. What they are really saying is that it is unfair to deprive them of the unfair advantage they hold over the consumer.

Part of the hostility towards direct market action may be explained by the fact that such techniques are often used to attain noneconomic goals. Boycotts are commonly directed towards social or political ends. There is a rich tradition for such activities in the United States. Indeed, they lie at the very foundation of the American state. Recall that our colonial forefathers forced the repeal of the Stamp Acts by boycotting British goods and that the celebrated Tea Party in Boston was part of a later boycott of British tea.*

This is by no means an isolated example. Farmers in the nineteenth century attempted repeated boycotts of groups that they thought were unfair, just as their descendants in 1973 (somewhat more successfully) withheld livestock from the market in protest of the low prices they received. Boycotts also played an important part in the civil rights movement. The

---

* Although the word had not been invented yet. *Boycott* was the name of a 19th-century Irish landlord who was cruel, even by the standards of the time. His tenants refused to pay their rents, and soon any withholding action aimed at the redress of grievances came to be known as a *boycott*.

Reverend Martin Luther King, Jr., first gained national recognition with his Montgomery bus boycott. More recently, boycotts have been used to help other disadvantaged groups; witness the national boycotts of grapes and lettuce in support of unionization efforts among California farm workers.

It may seem strange to think that consumer groups have borrowed this technique from others, since what is involved is nothing less than consumption itself. Nevertheless, it is clear that the tactical use of consumer buying power was well developed before consumerism became a significant force. While consumers' efforts to reclaim this approach have encountered certain difficulties, it remains a logical and potentially effective means for consumers to reassert themselves.

Direct market action has been most successful at the local level, where it has been used against merchants who had previously taken advantage of their customers. Boycotts in ghetto areas have received the most attention, for it is there that the problems are usually most conspicuous. However, they are increasingly being used over a broader range of establishments. In a more positive vein, some organizations—church groups, for example—are using their purchasing power to reward businesses they feel are particularly worthy of support.

At the national level, boycotts have not been so effective. The long-run impact of the consumer beef boycotts of 1973 was minimal (although they may have been important as a gesture). Boycotts may serve, however, to reenforce tendencies already established. At a time when individual parents were becoming concerned with dangerous toys, small but vocal consumers' groups helped crystallize feeling and forced producers to face the problem. The boycotts may have lacked formal organization, but by making individuals more aware of the problem, they promoted a widespread consumer response.

As consumer awareness grows, it is certain that the collective use of dollar votes will become more common. Consumer organization, however, is by no means limited to that approach. The older, established organizations in the United States have concentrated their efforts elsewhere, trying to lower information costs to consumers. The best known of these organizations are Consumers' Research, founded in the 1920s, and Consumers Union, which followed a decade later. The operations of these groups were discussed in Chapter 5, so the whole analysis need not be repeated here. However, it is worth noting where they fit in the overall pattern of consumer organization. These groups, with their specialized facilities and larger resources, can undertake testing programs that individuals could not. Thus, they provide another example of how consumers, by pooling their resources, can improve their position in the marketplace.

It is interesting to note that both of these groups have broadened their perspective in recent years, interpreting information more liberally. Instead of just providing information about products, they have increasingly become clearinghouses for consumer information in a broad sense. Both groups keep a watchful eye on advertising and keep their readers posted about legal and institutional developments that affect the consumer. While it is still up to the consumer to make use of this information, the technique has been successful.

Even with information, however, consumers are still at a disadvantage. Legislation is complex, and a sustained lobbying effort is required to influence it. Lawsuits require specialized legal services and large amounts of money. The requirements in both cases are likely to be beyond the means of the individual. An aroused public can indeed have an impact, but there are so many things to get aroused about that public opinion alone cannot protect the consumer.

As a result, a different type of consumer organization has come to the fore in recent years. This type concentrates on protecting consumer interests through legal, legislative, and administrative actions. The legal and institutional framework within which consumption takes place is growing more and more complicated. Thousands of laws affect the consumer and a seemingly unlimited array of administrative agencies directly affect the consumer's day-to-day activities. It takes a professional merely to understand all of this; and to translate understanding into action requires a well-trained staff. In that simple marketplace we have referred to so often, the consumer could master the legal framework, but without effective organization, today's consumer finds that difficult.

There are two elements involved in the legal approach. The first has to do with influencing new legislation and administrative decisions, the second with ensuring that the protection the consumer already enjoys will be effective. (The former is covered in the next chapter.) Suffice it to say that legislative bodies respond to pressure, and unless a group is well organized and capable of applying sustained pressure, its chances for success are slight. Ensuring consumer's rights within the existing legal structure is hardly less of a problem. How many tenants know precisely what their rights and responsibilities are with regard to their landlords? Can consumers be sure that the agency in charge of regulating their local public utility is doing its job and protecting their interests? If they cannot get satisfaction on defective merchandise, do consumers know when they can take the seller to court? These questions are merely illustrative; they suggest something about the vulnerability of the typical consumer.

It should be useful at this point to subdivide the category by making a distinction between individual's rights and the rights of consumers as a group. To illustrate the former, consider a tenant who has been illegally evicted. The landlord may get away with breaking the law if the tenant is either unaware of his or her rights or cannot obtain legal help. Thus, the imbalance of power in the marketplace works against the rights of the individual.

A number of promising developments have taken place in this regard. Despite uncertain, and usually inadequate funding, legal aid societies have brought legal services to large numbers of people who might otherwise have been without them. Conventional law firms now allow their members a certain amount of free time to work on public-service cases, and a growing number of public-interest law firms devote their total energies towards such problems. In a related development, the advent of Public Interest Research Groups (PIRG) on many campuses has mobilized student resources to serve consumer needs.

The question of the consumer interest, in a collective sense, is somewhat more difficult. Rather than merely protecting the individual, the goal in this case, is extending consumers' rights by changing existing legal or administrative practices. With all its test cases and appeals to higher courts, this is an expensive and time-consuming process. The potential benefits, however, are great because the outcome affects not just the individual but all consumers. At the risk of sounding overblown, it can be said that eternal vigilance is needed in this area. Both legal and administrative decisions must be continually scrutinized. Indeed, the task amounts very nearly to being a watchdog on the system. The need for organization is clear, since individuals, with their own affairs to watch, cannot be expected to fulfill this function.

The final type of consumer organization constitutes a more direct attack on consumer problems. Consumers, rather than try to change the marketplace, may create an alternative to it by forming jointly owned and operated cooperatives [17]. Cooperatives are owned by their members, who are also customers; since profits are not involved, member-owners can enjoy improved service or lower prices. On many campuses, students have used this approach and formed cooperative student bookstores. Instead of trying to change existing campus or commercial bookstores—and the complaints against them are legion—students have devoted their energies to providing an alternative. Similarly, employee groups who feel that financial institutions are not serving their interests have joined to form credit unions. These are probably the most successful examples of cooperative efforts.

While cooperatives hold forth bright promise, their actual performance has been disappointing. The trouble is that if cooperatives are to operate on a large scale, they need not only formal organization but skilled management also. That requirement has been the bane of the cooperative movement since its beginnings over a century ago. Most cooperatives are short-lived because they suffer from inadequate capital and a lack of managerial talent. If a cooperative is to be successful, it requires the same sort of financial and managerial resources as any business venture. These are not likely to be forthcoming, particularly in so-called bootstrap operations. Unless the effort is backed by a sufficiently large organization that can command the necessary resources, its effectiveness will be limited. This suggests that cooperative developments might be more successful after viable consumer organizations have been formed.

Obstacles to Consumer Organization

It is now time to face an obvious question: If consumer organization is such a logical response to consumer problems, why haven't consumers organized more effectively? To provide an answer, let us return to our earlier analogy with the union movement. Workers were able to assert their influence through organization, which suggests that consumers should follow a similar course. The analogy, however, is imperfect; the differences between workers and consumers place the latter in a more difficult position and illustrate the problems associated with consumer organization. These difficulties arise from the differences in the common interests among workers and consumers. Workers had a most immediate issue to unite them: the prospect of economic betterment. Nevertheless, the triumph of the union movement took over three generations from its beginnings in the 1870s to the victories of the 1930s. During that time, the movement was so beset with factionalism that union solidarity was little more than a slogan.

Consumers can hardly be encouraged by this record. Unlike the workers, consumers have only weak common bonds. Everyone is a consumer, and therein lies the problem. Consumers may be united by the fact that they all buy things, but this is insufficient to offset the many forces that divide them. Since consumers represent the population as a whole, they reflect all the divisions common to the entire population. This lack of cohesion makes organization difficult. Common goals, specific and immediate, are needed to sustain an effective organization. In this case, there are so many issues, so many goals, and so many consumers that it is hard to imagine them all coalescing into a single movement, let alone a single organization. The very strength of consumers—their numbers—turns out to be their weakness. Common policies and common goals are difficult if not impossible to achieve. It may be possible to put together an alliance to fight for a particular goal, but once that goal is met, it is difficult to keep the group together. This helps explain the erratic performance of many consumer groups. An immediate goal can help overcome the diversity of interests by providing the group with a central focus, but the image becomes blurred by the demands of day-to-day business.

A second complication follows from the first. Organization is a means, not an end in itself. Even if a group organizes successfully, the broad range of consumer problems still creates serious difficulties. Again, the contrast with the labor movement is striking. While early union leaders had to work under adverse conditions, it was clear to them what they had to do. They could concentrate their efforts on improving pay and working conditions, focusing on individual firms or on legislative action.

Consumer groups enjoy no such luxury. Anthony Downs, who pioneered this type of analysis, illustrated the point using the tariff laws. A tariff is simply a tax on imports, and the typical citizen has no love for taxes. With higher tariffs, consumers are forced to pay higher prices, a pattern that is all too common. Tariff legislation regularly favors a few producers at the expense of millions of consumers. How can this imbalance be maintained? The answer lies in the consumer's old adversary, information costs. Downs notes that producers can afford to bring pressure on the parts of the tariff legislation that affect them. By contrast, few consumers can afford to bring any influence to bear on any parts of the law, since each consumer's interests are spread over so many products. In fact, most consumers cannot even afford to find out whether tariffs are raising the prices they pay for any given product. [3, p. 257]

Everything affects the consumer, so consumer groups must be concerned with everything. The wide range of interests means that resources will be spread impossibly thin.

Now it may not be too difficult to inform people about any particular issue, but when all of the other things about which people need to be informed are taken into account, the true proportions of the problem become apparent. The word *informed* here must be taken to mean more than just "know about." Knowledge per se is only the first step; effective action requires a familiarity with the legal and administrative structure and the ability to use it to bring about change. It should be clear then that merely asserting that consumers' problems will be solved through organization is naïve. The potential for improvement comes with organization, but forbidding problems must be overcome before that potential can be realized. Understanding the problems is the first step. The next step involves devising a strategy that accounts for these difficulties and can work around them.

The wide range of consumer problems is the main obstacle to consumer organization. This dispersion leads to a plurality of interests and means that consumer groups must be prepared to do battle on a thousand fronts. From this it follows that an organization with a limited, specific goal will have the best chance of success. Individuals attracted to the group can be expected to share a common interest; the energies of members can then be focused on the immediate problem. Information costs will also be reduced, for such a group will not have to be concerned about obtaining information on all aspects of consumer problems. Rather, it can concentrate on the particular element it has selected. This gives it a more realistic chance to obtain detailed information and to formulate workable strategies for dealing with the problem. This approach is no guarantee of success, but by withstanding the temptation to take on all comers and by concentrating instead on specific problems, chances of success should be improved.

The idea of specialization is implicit in this discussion. Groups like Consumers Union specialize in providing detailed information on a large scale. While there has been increasing debate over the aims of CU, its policy of limiting itself to a particular—though still very broad—area has enabled it to survive and to serve consumers over the years.

The setting of specific goals may at first limit the area in which consumer groups can operate. As noted, direct market action is likely to be most effective at the local level. If a local store has been taking advantage of customers, the need for action should be felt within the community. Available resources will be less, but demands on the group will be smaller also. Such efforts are aided by the fact that boycotts do not have to be absolute to be effective. The profit margins of most small stores are small enough that even a 10 percent change in sales can have an impact. In larger markets, the problems are magnified. It is one thing to boycott a local grocery store, but a boycott of General Motors is something else again. The necessary motivation may be lacking on the part of most consumers and it will take more people to create an effect. Furthermore, organizational problems will be significantly increased. Coupled with the mere size of the problem, this makes sustained action difficult.

There are examples of national boycotts, but their record of achievement has not been outstanding. The beef boycotts of 1973 were not supported by a highly organized effort, but rather sprang from growing frustration with rising meat prices. While there was coordination among local groups, the boycott itself was more of a spontaneous outpouring of resentment than a cohesive movement. Lacking an organizational structure, the boycott faded as quickly as it had developed. The boycotts of grapes and lettuce had a longer life span, but these were dominated by social concerns rather than consumer interests. Local groups have an additional advantage of being able to enlist community support for local problems more effectively than larger organizations. Such problems as the enforcement or revision of building and housing codes are essentially local; what is appropriate in one area may not be in another. In the area of legislative action, the point is equally clear. It is easier to bring pressure on a city council than the United States Congress.

This does not mean that all groups must be local. In the area of information, for example, a larger audience may be a necessity. Groups like Consumers Union could not function effectively if restricted to the local level. Large groups (with local chapters) can still specialize on particular problems. If consumers organize, as they actually have organized, to promote safe toys, they might embrace a variety of approaches. Though they may provide information, boycott offenders, or seek legislation on safety standards, their overall goal is still specific. In this case, parents who feel strongly about the problem can identify with the aims of the group and support its efforts. Expecting people who are concerned about toy safety to be equally concerned about other problems will only dilute their influence and ultimately their effort and effectiveness. Other groups can take up other causes—there are certainly enough to go around—so that each group will have its own focus.

If consumers concentrate on specialized objectives, some of the benefits of organization will be lost. Although the suggestion of organization was developed emphasizing the benefits of numbers, the present argument suggests that numbers should be limited. Numbers, however, are not the only measure of an organization's effectiveness. A group that enjoys broadly based support will have more resources, but a large membership is in itself no guarantee of such support. Consider the large number of people who are nominal churchgoers but neither support nor attend any church. The effectiveness of the church depends on a smaller number of active participants. Most movements owe their success to the initial dedication of small groups. It is doubtful if most Americans favored independence in 1776, just as most Russians did not support Lenin in 1917. Success in both cases depended less on mass support than on the efforts of a very small number of people.

Because everyone qualifies for membership, consumerism may aspire to be a mass movement. Nevertheless, mass support must be organized. The key here is not numbers; it is hard work by small groups. The short history of the consumer movement shows this to be true. Ralph Nader started out almost alone. He was considered an upstart and was not taken seriously, a mistake which his opponents were later to regret. Gradually, Nader and other consumer advocates built up small organizations that had an impact much greater than their numbers would suggest. At this writing, consumerism cannot be considered a mass movement. Many consumers are still apathetic, and a few are openly hostile to any organized movements. That does not mean that consumerism is not a potent force; it means that its effectiveness rests on the efforts of small numbers of people who have worked hard to expose consumer problems and seek reforms.

It appears that the consumer movement has turned a corner in this regard and has entered a transitional phase. Consumer consciousness has been raised to the point that individuals are more aware of their problems and more willing to do something about them. Such structure as exists within the movement provides a channel for complaints and direction for dissatisfaction. Thus, while consumerism may not yet be able to claim that it is a mass movement, it is clearly working in that direction. Concentrating on smaller groups may at first deprive consumers of some of the benefits of organization, but development in this area must be looked at in evolutionary terms. As an emerging force, consumer groups are not yet in a position to tap all their potential support. Until they can, they will not be able to realize the full benefit of organization. In view of the magnitude of the problem, that is hardly a damning comment. The consumer movement has come a long way in the span of a single decade. Building on foundations that reach back even further, the movement can claim solid accomplishments. It is unrealistic to assume that any movement could be born full-grown and enjoy immediate successes everywhere. The potential for improvement has been demonstrated to consumers; as the movement matures, this potential will be more fully realized.

This analysis suggests a final question: Granted that there is a need for a large number of small groups to accommodate the plural interests of consumers, is there a role for larger groups? The answer is yes, if for no other reason than that they are needed to perform a coordinating function. What has been suggested thus far is a constellation of consumer groups, each concentrating on its own area, but functioning in cooperation with each other. As any stargazer knows, a constellation implies order and position; without it, there is confusion. Thus, it would be a serious blow to the consumer movement if the various small groups took to petty bickering and in-fighting rather than cooperation.* The danger of duplication of effort also exists.

* However, some competition may be beneficial. It is likely, for example, that old consumer organizations have been revitalized by the development of newer, activist groups.

Some duplication is unavoidable, but if it becomes significant, a great deal of effort will be wasted. The larger group can help ensure that the various organizations are aware of each other and what they are doing. Furthermore, it may exercise some control or at least provide direction to minimize squabbles.

The larger consumer group may also be necessary to carry through on pressing problems—organizing support for national legislation, for example—which cannot be handled efficiently at the local level. Where extensive litigation is involved, resources may be needed beyond the capabilities of a small group. As in the case of providing information, larger groups are essential for such undertakings. The strategy that large, activist groups follow is the key factor in determining their success. By limiting themselves to a relatively restricted range of undertakings and concentrating on them, they may be very effective. If they fail in this regard and spread themselves too thin, a sort of helterskelter superficiality results. However, public-interest lobbies, like Ralph Nader's Public Citizen, Inc., and especially John Gardner's Common Cause, have proven themselves capable of dealing effectively with big problems [2]. These groups and others like them are still relatively new, so it would be premature to attempt an overall assessment of their activities. They have made some encouraging beginnings, however, and have attracted national attention to consumer-related problems. Publicity should not be overlooked. This is the age of the media, and the group that can attract the attention of the media and maintain its interest over time will find its task made easier.

Individuals like Ralph Nader attract extensive coverage, but most people lack the set of qualities that make Ralph Nader an event. It is hard to think of anyone else in the consumer movement who matches him.* Yet attention from the media is vitally important. It helps explain, for example, the success that the beef boycotts enjoyed for a time in 1973. Not only did the boycotts make the news, they also made it into regular programming and for a time were a feature of every late-night talk show. That kind of exposure drives the point home and forces people to recognize what is happening. There is a danger that various groups will engage in grandstanding to attract attention. Groups that jump from cause to cause, throwing out sweeping allegations along the way, may attract attention for a time, but their efforts at sensationalism will quickly wear thin. When the consumer movement was new, this approach had something to recommend it. At least it got people's attention. Now, however, such hit-and-run tactics are counterproductive. What is needed instead is a sustained campaign in the media to focus interest on key problems and maintain that interest until the movement towards a solution is well under way.

While organizational efforts have already paid dividends, the real effect of consumer organization is still to be felt. The path-breaking work is done; consumer groups are now taken seriously, and many have the clout

* A few, like John Gardner or Bess Myerson, come close. Others, like the presidential advisor on consumer affairs, Virginia Knauer, may enjoy coverage because of their positions.

to ensure that their views will be aired. As consumer awareness grows and organizational problems are overcome, such organizations will become increasingly significant. That may be the outstanding development to look for as the consumer movement moves through its second decade.

IN SEARCH OF THE SOVEREIGN CONSUMER

Who Pulls the Strings?

Thus far consumer power has been examined in terms of giving the consumer more leverage in the marketplace. That leverage is obviously necessary if the marketplace is to become a more congenial place for consumers. Congeniality, however, should not be confused with sovereignty. Consumers could obtain the power to ensure that they would be treated fairly and yet still not be sovereign. Sovereignty means that consumers decide how the society is going to use its resources.

That fact suggests the distinction between consumer choice and consumer sovereignty. The consumer today has choices, and if the improvements looked forward to are realized, these choices would become more meaningful. The question is: Who decides what those choices are? Consumer choice means that the consumer is presented with a series of options. Sovereignty implies that consumers themselves determine what those options are [13].

The phrase "directing production" therefore means that the sovereign consumer has choices among choices. To illustrate this point, Abba Lerner harkens back to a simple economy organized around family production. He says:

> Every family had its own house and garden where it produced everything it needed. It alone decided what to grow or to make and how to divide its time between work and play. No other family was concerned with how it made its choices, and it was not concerned with how other families made their choices. [10, p. 258]

Such families were sovereign because they had direct control over their resources, made their own decisions on how those resources were to be used, and hence determined what goods would be available. Poverty, however, went along with sovereignty, for the range of possible production (and therefore consumption) was extremely limited. Today's consumers, while they are not sovereign in the earlier sense, enjoy a level of affluence undreamed of by the frontier family. Consumers' problems spring from the specialization and division between production and consumption that make their affluence possible.

If consumers do not determine what their choices will be, who does? The answer is producers. The real world emerges as a mirror-image of the textbook; in the real world, producers are sovereign and consumers respond to them. Professor Galbraith has championed this view for nearly a quarter of a century. Whereas at first he was a voice crying in the Massachusetts wilderness, he has become the spokesman for a significant body of thought. The outlines of the Galbraithian position have already been suggested. Galbraith's view is based on an observation that John Maynard Keynes originally made that human wants may be classified as either absolute or relative. Absolute wants are independent of other's consumption, while relative wants are not. Thus, Keynes felt that while relative wants might be limitless, he believed it should be possible to satisfy all absolute wants [4, p. 122]. Professor Galbraith concludes that if relative wants do not originate with the individual, they cannot be very urgent. Rather, they are contrived by producers who convince consumers of what they want. Thus, in Galbraith's words: "One cannot defend production as satisfying wants if that production creates the wants" [4, p. 124]. Therefore, to understand how the system works requires the recognition

> that wants are dependent upon production. It accords to the producer the function both of making the goods and of making the desires for them . . . [production] . . . through advertising and related activities, creates the wants it seeks to satisfy. [4, p. 127]

The implications of this argument are far-reaching. Our concern here is with what it does to the consumer's position. Certainly, the idea of consumer sovereignty has gone out the window; the consumer is less than ineffectual in this schema. In Galbraith's revised sequence, it is the producer who is sovereign, dictating responses to the consumer who has no real voice in the system. If this picture is drawn correctly, consumers are merely puppets dangling on corporate strings. That is hardly a very flattering characterization, but it isn't an impossible position either. Consumers still have their affluence to enjoy, and there remains the possibility that they may obtain some lower level of market power. If it could be assumed that producers were benign, consumers could settle back in comfortable resignation and accept the inevitable reduction in their status.

A Closer Look

Presented with an either/or choice between the Galbraithian position and the classical doctrine of consumer sovereignty, most would admit that the former is closer to the reality of the modern marketplace. Yet casting the question in such terms is itself unrealistic, for the consumer's position does not submit to such easy categorization. The truth is most likely to be found in the murky gray area that lies between the bits of clarity provided by well-formulated positions.

The logical place to begin sorting all of this out is Galbraith's analysis of relative, or culturally determined, wants. This point has raised a great deal of controversy. The outstanding conservative thinker Friedrich Hayek seized on it in identifying what he saw as the *non sequitur* of Galbraith's position. The fact that wants may be culturally determined did not, to Hayek, prove that they are unimportant. He maintained that in the arts, for example,

> Professor Galbraith's argument could be easily employed without any change of the essential terms to demonstrate the worthlessness of literature or any other form of art. Surely, an individual's want for literature is not original with himself in the sense that he would experience it if literature were not produced. [8, p. 347]

Hayek was arguing against what he saw as the collectivist tendencies in Galbraith's argument; one need not agree with his overall view to see that he has a point. To amplify it, let us go back once more to our frontier family living in their newly constructed log cabin. Since the cabin meets the family's immediate need for shelter, it could be classified as an absolute want. It is likely, however, that the cabin is also cold, drafty, and dreary. Isn't it logical to assume that the family, of its own accord, would think of improving the quality of its shelter as soon as possible?

Most people wouldn't classify improved insulation, a better fireplace, and a few coats of whitewash as relative wants. Such desires could originate with the individuals involved. If that is true, then what about adding a recreation room or installing central air conditioning? In the latter case, the desire to avoid summer heat is a natural tendency; air conditioning is merely an improvement on the shade of the nearest tree. The differences here are in degree rather than kind; as a result, the level of comfort at which wants become secondary is not at all clear.

Since it is obvious that many wants are culturally determined, the distinction itself is almost superfluous. With affluence, people seldom buy goods for the intrinsic value anyway; they buy a whole series of characteristics that the good has. Since the valuation of those characteristics is highly individual, it would not be very productive to try to distinguish among them, even if it were possible.

Let us accept that most wants are culturally determined, then, and try a slightly different approach. The question should not be what determines wants, but rather, what determines the culture? That may seem like a strange question, but it moves us closer to the heart of the matter. Consumers are conditioned by their social setting; thus, the question of who determines what that setting is directly influences consumer wants and ultimately consumption itself. If this premise is accepted, it appears that many of those who object to culturally determined wants are in reality objecting to the culture itself. Their real complaint is with the value system that produces a particular set of wants. Were consumers to express more of a preference for better social services and improved educational and health facilities, those too would be culturally determined wants. The difference between wanting such things and wanting a second car lies in the character of the culture.

A number of radical writers have clearly identified this point. Paul Baran, the Marxist theoretician, makes it quite clear. He indicates that he, like other Marxists, has never "advocated the abolition of consumer sovereignty and its replacement by the orders of a commissar" [1, p. xvii]. Baran maintains that the real point is:

> whether an economic and social order should be tolerated in which the individual, from the very cradle on, is so shaped, molded, and "adjusted" as to become an easy prey of profit-greedy capitalist enterprise and a smoothly functioning object of capitalist exploitation and degradation. The Marxian socialist . . . believes that a society can be developed in which the individual would be formed, influenced and educated not by the "values" of corporate presidents and the outpourings of their hired scribes, but by a system of rationally planned production for use, by a universe of human relations determined by and oriented toward solidarity, cooperation and freedom. [1, p. xvii]

Even if you don't think that consumers are merely "objects of capitalist exploitation," you should appreciate that the passage was worth quoting at length. Baran makes it clear that he feels that the present system works to the advantage of the capitalist and that consequently the consumer is abused. Whether that is true or not, the individual certainly responds to the system and its values.

The subject of consumer sovereignty has become even broader. With affluence, consumption becomes intimately bound up with the culture itself; sovereignty in one requires sovereignty in the other. If it is true that consumers have lost the ability to direct production, it is also true that consumers have lost control over their culture. To understand that statement, it is necessary to inquire into how the present system evolved.

A Process of Evolution

While affluence has profoundly affected consumers, the changes it brought about were gradual, representing an evolution. We have been speaking in terms of quantum leaps, comparing how things began with how they are now. It is a long way, after all, from the frontier cabin to central air conditioning, but it is the events of in-between that are important. Those things were tied together and represented only small changes. So we must, instead of thinking of a movement from the horse and buggy to the modern automobile, think of the change from the horse to a Model A, from there to a Model T, from crank to electric starters, and so on. Taken alone, none of these changes are particularly startling; their cumulative effect, however, has been monumental. The point is that there were no clear breaks with the past. To be sure, there was much talk of new eras and bright tomorrows, but most of it was verbiage and things were never much different from what they had been immediately before.

That helps explain why the fundamental changes that took place *over time* were not perceived as such; they crept up on people. Since there was continuity to the pattern of change, there appeared to be no reason to change basic ways of thinking. Methods from the past were merely extended into the future. If it was logical for the frontier family to want to improve its cabin, is it not equally logical for a family today to want to improve its house? Anyone who has walked through the cold to an outdoor privy knows the value of indoor plumbing. If having a bath inside is an improvement, doesn't a second bath represent even more improvement?

In short, the consumer continued to think in terms of gradual change, perceived as improvement. The economic system obliged by turning out more and apparently better things. The system was responding to the basic desires of consumers. Particulars are not especially important. Few consumers yearned for electric can openers before they were available, but saying that such gadgets were therefore passed off on the public misses the point. Consumers were conditioned to think in terms of continued improvements, so there was nothing surprising about electric can openers. It was a natural development, even if that specific product was not developed in response to a particular need. What consumers did, in effect, was to indicate to producers that they wanted more of the same. That meant continued refinement and more convenience. Since the system seemed capable of turning out an endless supply of goods and services, there was no real need to specify what form these changes would take. The particulars would take care of themselves. With more of everything, whatever one wanted would turn up sooner or later.

This raises a rather disturbing possibility: *consumers may be much more sovereign than most people think.* That point is easily missed because sovereignty applies not to particular goods and services, but to the general form and direction of the system. Consumer sovereignty, which seems so unrealistic when presented as an abstraction, actually emerges as a workable concept. The form that consumer sovereignty takes may not follow the textbook version, but the process is indeed similar. Were that the whole story, we might be able to leave the question at this point. While one might not like the results that consumer sovereignty has produced, it would have to be admitted that at least the consumer has had a hand in shaping the marketplace.

To end the discussion here, however, would be to leave before the story is complete. The overall process has been identified, but its ramifications have not been considered. To complete the picture, it is necessary to remember that while the series of gradual changes that took place over time were themselves insignificant, taken together, they represent a significant development. Affluence has influenced both producers and consumers so that neither group is the same as it was before. Yet until recently, the consumer's approach to the market was fundamentally unchanged. That is the crux of the matter.

On the producers' side, the changes are obvious. Small firms grew into giant corporations, competition was reduced, and the surviving giants acquired not only market power, but enormous advertising and merchandising capabilities also. This concentration is particularly significant because consumers had given producers carte blanche as far as the specifics of increased production and new products were concerned. It meant that a few firms had a lot of power in deciding what goods would be available to consumers. However, as long as producers were fulfilling the general requirements that consumers set down, the problem did not appear to be serious. Producers were thus able to consolidate their positions; they behaved more and more as if they directed the system, which in effect they did. What developed was a sort of uneasy truce, broken only when consumers became concerned about the basic direction of the market system. That concern was itself a product of affluence.

Consumers finally awoke to the fact that conditions had changed. Affluence made consumers more demanding; they expected products to perform better and to fit their personal preferences exactly. The idea that consumers should be grateful or that producers are somehow doing them a favor has gone forever. While these changes have been uneven, they have combined to break down the consensus that had previously existed about the form and direction of the system.

This time it was producers who were caught unawares. Accustomed as they were to directing the market, they chose to ignore the increasingly assertive spirit the consumers showed. Thus, when the flood of foreign cars inundated the American market in the late 1950s, automobile makers chose to treat it as a fad rather than as an expression of a preference for smaller, less expensive, and more economical cars. As a result, despite Detroit's belated response, the share of the American market taken up by imports grew from an insignificant 4 percent to over 30 percent. In some cases the changes were subtle, as in fashion, where individualization gradually replaced standardization. In other instances, the changes were dramatic. Consumer complaints began to make the headlines, and company after company felt the wrath of hostile consumers. These changes can be interpreted as an effort by consumers to reassert their control over the marketplace.

That is about where things now stand. The picture is confused by the complexity of the changes under way and the interaction of forces in the marketplace. It is therefore not easy to tell exactly what is going to happen. Consumers themselves are not sure; they reflect different motivations. Some still do not care, while others are demanding radical changes. Some of those in between merely want higher-quality products, while others are not sure whether products inherently warrant the fuss. At the same time, consumers are finding that reasserting their influence over the total operation of the marketplace is not very easy. Producers are entrenched in their positions and not easily dislodged. They are not about to give up the privileges they have accumulated, and their power enables them to resist effectively. This is true both in the marketplace—where large firms are invulnerable in the short run—and in the political arena. Producers have political as well as economic power and are adept at using it.

It is possible to make several observations. Evidence to date suggests that fundamental change is under way. The word *fundamental* is critical, for nothing short of control of the system is at stake. Given America's demonstrated pragmatism and willingness to experiment, it is unlikely that any radical change will emerge. Some accommodation will be reached so that both producers and consumers can claim a measure of victory. The best guess about the future is that present trends will continue, giving consumers more of a voice in operating the marketplace. Producers will have to become more carefully attuned to consumers' wishes and more responsive to them. George Katona feels that this process is already well along. In a comparative study of consumption in the United States and Europe, he observed that there is

> a two-way process of influence, from consumers to business as well
> as from business to consumers. . . . Interaction prevails in this re-
> spect as in all forms of learning. Both the traditional doctrine of
> consumer sovereignty and the thesis of Galbraith that large producers
> control and manage their customers' presume a unidirectional process
> of influence, which in fact represents the exception rather than the
> rule. [9, pp. 115–16]

Judged from past experience, Katona's scenario represents the most likely pattern of development. It is possible, however, that past experience may not be a very good guide. If producers have become so inflexible that they cannot adapt, if consumers demand truly radical change, if the society's value system is undergoing a profound alteration, then the outcome could be quite different. At this point, it is possible only to speculate.

There is another term in the equation that will surely be involved in the solution. Political power is an important element in the confrontation between producer and consumer. Both sides are anxious to enlist the support of government to their respective causes. The success of one or the other in doing so may determine the outcome. Thus, the question of consumer power leads ultimately to the relation between the consumer and government.

STUDY QUESTIONS

1. Improvements in communications and transportation have tended to produce big market areas. This is particularly noticeable with large suburban shopping centers, which draw customers from a wide area. Explain how these developments have weakened the consumer's position. What effect have they had on the cost of complaining?

2. Self-service discount stores are now common throughout the country. Is the consumer's position in such stores stronger or weaker than it would be in a conventional department store? in a neighborhood store?

3. Apply the concept of income elasticity in the following cases:

a. While food generally has a low income elasticity, why is this less true in ghetto areas?

b. Potatoes are a classic example of a good with a low—or even negative—income elasticity. Explain why.

c. While meat is obviously a food, what would you predict about its income elasticity? Explain.

4. For people in the middle-income ranges (and above), a great many goods are technically affordable. That is, they have the money to buy if they are so inclined. Why are such people likely to be concerned with factors beyond the initial price of the produce? What are the implications for the consumer movement as more and more consumers are in this position?

5. Inflation has been a continuing problem in recent years. Do you feel that it has helped promote consumer activism? Explain.

6. Labor unions were used in the text as an example of effective organization. In fact, most groups within the economy are organized, including medical doctors, teachers, farmers, and nearly all business and industrial groups. What advantages do these groups have that consumers lack? Can consumers learn anything from them?

7. Political parties require mass support, in the form of votes, to win elections. Can the principal parties therefore be considered mass movements? If not, what determines the success of a political party? Can an analogy be made with the consumer movement? Explain.

8. While there are numerous exceptions, consumer organization has generally been strongest among the relatively affluent and the relatively poor. Why should the consumer movement draw its strength from these two groups, which seemingly have so little in common?

9. Because of product differentiation, you can walk into any grocery and find a stunning array of different brands of many products. Explain how this illustrates the difference between consumer choice and consumer sovereignty.

10. Is consumer sovereignty, as it is presented in textbooks, possible in a modern, technological economy? If not, does that mean that the consumer has no hope of reasserting control over the economic system?

11. If consumers were actually sovereign, would that mean that every consumer would be able to find the products he or she wanted in the market? Discuss.

SUGGESTED PROJECTS

1. Consumer organization, like many of the topics in the chapters that follow, provides ample opportunity to draw on the experience of actual

practitioners in the area. Invite representatives of local consumer organizations to discuss their group's operation with the class. How well do the goals, activities, and problems of these groups follow the pattern laid out in the text?

2.   Make a survey of consumer organizations in your area. How would you classify them according to the four types examined in the text? Do you feel that they have developed to the point that they are viable organizations that contribute to the consumer's welfare? Do you see a need for developing a new type of organization in your area? Discuss.

3.   Beyond private law firms, what sort of legal services are available to consumers in your area? Is there a legal aid society or a law firm that specializes in consumer problems? Do you feel that consumers in need of legal advice are adequately served?

4.   Try to estimate the cost of pursuing a complaint about a product or service. Consider the costs of gasoline, time, and the like as in Project 1, Chapter 5. Do you feel it is these costs that limit consumer complaints, or is it that many people find complaining distasteful?

5.   Are there any consumer cooperatives in your area? If there are, meet with their managers and find out about their activities. What are the main problems these organizations face?

6.   Review the operation over the past year of some large public interest organization, like Common Cause; you can use the *Reader's Guide* or some other index for this purpose. Is any pattern evident? How well do you think such groups have come to grips with the problems outlined in the text?

7.   It was argued in the text that consumers are demanding higher quality and more dependable products. If that is true, producers should be aware of it; this awareness should in turn be reflected in their advertising. Make a spot check of advertising to find out to what degree these qualities are stressed.

8.   Is there a Public Interest Research Group on your campus? If so, how successful has the group been in its efforts? Has it been able to sustain its momentum? What are the main problems it has faced?

9.   See also Suggested Project 2, Chapter 8.

BIBLIOGRAPHY AND SUGGESTED READINGS

1. Baran, Paul. "A Marxist View of Consumer Sovereignty." In *The Political Economy of Growth*. New York: Monthly Review Press, 1957.
A noted Marxist examines capitalist production, providing a penetrating and often disquieting analysis of the consumer.

2. "Common Cause." *New Republic*, March 20, 1971. See also *Time*, August 16, 1971, and *Business Week*, October 23, 1971.

   News reports and analysis on the organization and operation of Common Cause. As a public-interest lobby, Common Cause became involved in litigation concerning the 1972 presidential election.

3. Downs, Anthony. *An Economic Theory of Democracy*. New York: Harper & Row, 1957.

   The classic analysis of political activity in a democracy using the outline of economic theory. We have already seen how Downs's conclusions help explain the difficulties involved in consumer organization. We shall make further use of his work over the next two chapters.

4. Galbraith, John Kenneth. *The Affluent Society*. Boston: Houghton Mifflin Co., 1958.

   Especially Chapters 9–11. Though modified somewhat by Professor Galbraith's later writings, this remains a complete statement of his *revised sequence* and producer's sovereignty.

5. Galbraith, John Kenneth. *American Capitalism*. Boston: Houghton Mifflin Co., 1952.

   Professor Galbraith's first big work. It contains his statement of countervailing power and identifies the main themes that dominate his later books.

6. Galbraith, John Kenneth. "Power and the Useful Economist." *American Economic Review* 63 (March 1973): 1–11.

   Professor Galbraith's presidential address to the American Economics Association. It represents something of a break with his earlier work by dwelling on the possibility of conflicting power relationships. In doing so, it foreshadows his most recent work.

7. Gintis, Herbert. "Consumer Behavior and the Concept of Sovereignty: Explanations of Social Decay." *American Economic Review, Papers and Proceedings* 62 (May 1972): 267–78.

   A radical critique contrasting classical, Galbraithian, and radical views on consumer sovereignty. In the last of these, the author stresses the consumer's alienation.

8. Hayek, Frederick. "The Non Sequitur of the Dependence Effect." *Southern Economic Journal*, April 1961, pp. 346–48.

   A famous assault on Professor Galbraith's contention about the urgency of different levels of wants.

9. Katona, George, Strumpel, B., and Zahn, D. *Aspirations and Affluence*. New York: McGraw-Hill Book Co., 1971.

   A comparative study of consumption patterns and consumer attitudes in Western Europe and the United States. An important effort to study consumer behavior across national and cultural boundaries. We shall use this work further in Chapter 11.

10. Lerner, Abba. "The Economics and Politics of Consumer Sovereignty." *American Economic Review, Papers and Proceedings* 62 (May 1972): 258–66.

A leading American economist's consideration of consumer sovereignty. He associates the free market with Western liberal democracy and also treats the relation of competition and consumer sovereignty in economic theory.

11. Lewis, James. *The Consumer Fight-Back Book.* New York: Award Books, 1972.

    The subtitle of this delightful little book summarizes its thrust—"Guerrilla Guide to Buyer Protection." The author offers timely warnings about the pitfalls of the marketplace and useful advice on how to avoid them. A "how to" book on surviving in today's market. Irreverent and enjoyable.

12. Nader, Ralph. "A Citizen's Guide to the American Economy." In *The Consumer and Corporate Accountability.* New York: Harcourt Brace Jovanovich, 1972.

13. Rothenberg, Jerome. "Consumers' Sovereignty Revisited and the Hospitality of Freedom of Choice." *American Economic Review, Papers and Proceedings* 52 (May 1962): 260–68.

    The author contrasts consumer sovereignty with consumer choice and concludes that the latter may be preferable. A thoughtful consideration of the complexities involved. Recommended for anyone interested in exploring the topic.

14. Schulman, Rosalind. "Communication and Feedback in the Technology of Consumption." Paper presented at the VII International Congress on Cybernetics and Human Sciences, Namur, Belgium, September 1973.

    Professor Schulman develops a forceful argument to support emergence of more demanding consumers. Excellent summary of the impact of affluence.

15. Schulman, Rosalind. *The Economics of Consumption for a Changing Society.* Philadelphia: Drexel University Press, 1972.

    A fuller exploration of the forces at work on the consumer. Contains useful empirical analysis of changing consumption patterns over time.

16. Silberman, Charles E. "Identity Crisis in the Consumer Markets." *Fortune,* March 1971, pp. 92–95.

    A look at how new consumer demands affect traditional production and marketing techniques.

17. Staples, Ralph. "Direct Charge Cooperatives." *International Journal of Cooperative Development* 5, no. 4: 11–13.

    Recounts the Canadian experience with consumer cooperatives, indicating that they have the potential for offering consumers significant savings.

18. Stigler, George J. "The Early History of Empirical Studies of Consumer Behavior." *Journal of Political Economy* 62 (April 1954): 98–100.

    A review of early budget studies, including the work of Engel. Provides a perspective on income elasticity.

19. Troelstrup, Arch W. *The Consumer in American Society,* 4th ed. New York: McGraw-Hill Book Co., 1970.

8

Government and Consumer Protection: The Uncertain Ally

THE SETTING FOR GOVERNMENT PROTECTION

The Pendulum Swings

The idea of government protection, which today seems like such a natural response to consumer problems, is very much a product of the times. Consumers a century ago would not have found it at all natural. Since they had just freed themselves from what they saw as unfair restrictions, they thought in terms of government interference, not protection. The idea would not even have occurred to consumers in earlier periods because they functioned in a closed system, which made additional protection unnecessary. Over a relatively short period, the relation between government and consumer has been subject to repeated changes. Pendulumlike, the weight of opinion has swung from active government policies to a more passive approach and back again. Speaking of a norm or a typical relation between government and the consumer can only be done in terms of a specific period. The relation has been too fluid to permit any such designation that applies over a long time.

Throughout the Middle Ages, buyer-seller relations were carefully prescribed. Convention, supported by the church as well as the government, weighed heavily in all transactions. Custom regulated commercial activity, and both buyers and sellers played well-defined, carefully specified roles. It was a restrictive system for consumers, but a comfortable one that offered both security and protection [28]. With the emergence of modern nation states and markets, this paternalism began to break down. However, another restrictive system replaced it. The economy was considered too important to be left alone and was manipulated to serve the interests of the state. Instead of free exchange in open markets, consumers had to contend with monopolies, elaborate controls on commercial activity, and limitations on their choice of jobs. The interests of consumers, to the extent that they were recognized, were considered secondary to the interests of the nation. It was this system, commonly called mercantilism, that so offended Adam Smith. By the eighteenth century when Smith wrote, its power had already begun to ebb, but Smith sealed its fate. He popularized the notion that both private and public interests are best served if economic activity is unfettered; without interference, buyers and sellers should be left to confront each other in free markets.

Thus, it was not until *laissez-faire* began to dominate public thinking that consumers emerged as independent agents in the economic system. For the first time, they were on their own, making their own decisions according to their own preferences. While consumption is as old as mankind, the characteristics we associate with present-day consumers are a much more recent development. As consumers gained their independence, they had to look after themselves, but they were equipped to do so through the market mechanism. If a product was overpriced, unsafe, or otherwise undesirable, consumers merely rejected it in favor of one that was more suitable. There was consumer protection, but the consumers provided it themselves. You will recognize this as very similar to the world described in economic theory.

Even from this brief historical sketch, it is clear that the consumer's position has changed radically in recent centuries. Consumers were transformed as they passed from the controlled economy of medieval times through a period of transition under mercantilism into the freer markets of more recent years. Changes currently under way should therefore be seen as part of a continuous process, not as unique developments that threaten long-established patterns. Just as the consumer's position changed with the initial appearance of markets, it must continue to change with changes in those markets.

The Rationale for Consumer Protection

As markets have grown progressively larger and more specialized, the consumer's position has grown correspondingly weaker. The same rationale that applies to consumer organization can therefore be applied with equal force to government protection. In terms of countervailing power, the consumer is using the power of government to offset the power of sellers in the marketplace. Therefore while it is useful to distinguish between government protection and consumer organization, they are really alternative responses to the same problems. Both represent consumers' efforts to come to grips with the realities of the modern marketplace.

There is another aspect of this question that deserves attention. It begins with the status of everyone as a consumer. In a political sense, the words *consumer, citizen,* and *voter* can be used interchangeably. Thus, when consumers seek protection, they are in effect seeking it from themselves, assuming that political power in a democracy rests with the people and that the government exists as their instrument. Since consumers are citizens and citizens elect the government, it should follow that effective consumer protection is easy to achieve. However, the same obstacles that hinder consumer organization, particularly the pluralism of consumer interests, also make effective political action difficult for consumers. The votes are there, but consumers do not have the means to focus their efforts in such a way as to guarantee results.

At the same time, the government—the citizen-consumer's own government—responds to business interests. The reason is simple; it is implicit in the very name *special* interest group. Such groups are able to focus on a single issue and to bring pressure on government to ensure that public policy reflects their views. The consumer lacks both organization and a single-minded goal and is therefore in a much more difficult position. Governments respond to pressure, not to vague, diffuse feelings. If consumers are to get their point across, they must be organized. It is true that government will respond to public opinion, but it is most unusual for that opinion to coalesce of its own accord. It takes organization to bring problems to the public's attention and to keep them there until something is done. That cannot be fitted into a single category. The problem in discussing government protection.

Defining Consumer Protection

Government intervention in the economy is so widespread that it cannot be fitted into a single category. The problem in discussing government intervention or protection from the consumer's perspective is to decide which sorts of government actions should be counted. Since everyone is a consumer, anything the government does affects consumers. Even if we limit ourselves to policies that affect consumers as consumers—that is, actions that directly affect consumption—the possibilities are still extensive. Tax policies clearly affect consumers, and so do agricultural, energy, and banking policies. Foreign policy is no exception. The sale of wheat to the Soviet Union in 1972–73 was primarily motivated by international political considerations. Yet it was so massive that it helped create rising prices and actual shortages in the United States. Consumer interests, although seriously harmed, did not weigh heavily in the decision.

Energy is another example. American consumers have shivered through the past few winters as oil supplies shrank. With imports in short supply and boycotts a constant threat, it is hard to remember that until 1973, oil imports were limited on national security grounds. The threat to national security now comes from a reduction in imports of crude oil, not an increase. However insecure the limitation of imports may have left the country, it did wonders for the security of giant oil companies and domestic oil producers. Alas, consumers lost all the way around. Not only did consumers have to subsidize domestic producers; they had to bear the brunt of the eventual dislocations and rapid price increases. Those who recall spending winter mornings in line for gasoline hardly need that pointed out to them.

Unfortunately, these examples are merely illustrative. They do little more than suggest the extent and the degree to which consumer interests are disregarded. In doing so, they underscore the need for consumer groups to serve as active agents for consumer interests. This need in turn demonstrates that the field of consumer affairs, policies that directly affect consumers and consumption, is much broader than consumer protection.* How then can any limits be set for investigating these questions? The easiest way is to reemploy the concept of countervailing power. We only need ask this question: Does a particular policy tend to sustain consumers in the marketplace by helping them to cope with its size and complexity? The policies that qualify under this rule are those that bring to the consumer the advantages that other groups in the economy enjoy.

In this regard, there is no question about the recent development of specific consumer protection legislation. Such things as safety standards, truth-in-lending laws, and prohibition of misleading advertising clearly meet this requirement. Similarly, the activities of independent regulatory agencies qualify as consumer protection. These agencies are specifically charged with maintaining the public interest in the operation of particular industries. They have broad-ranging powers over key sectors of the economy. Some deal with specific fields like drugs, communications, and transportation. Others, like the Federal Trade Commission, cross industry lines. In each case, there is the recognition that normal market forces would be insufficient to protect the public interest. The agencies or commissions are supposed to act as the public's representatives, ensuring that operations will be conducted in the best interests of all consumers. They represent not only a classic American response to the problem, but in historical terms are among the most important forms of consumer protection.

Consumer protection takes other, less obvious, forms too. Antitrust legislation is one notable example. Here the effect on the consumer is less direct, but no less important. The government, by curbing monopoly elements in business, attempts to promote competition. This in turn should benefit the consumer through lower prices and increased business responsiveness to consumer needs.

In the United States, these responsibilities are divided among various governmental units. Under the structure of the American government, which in lofty prose is described as the American federal system, citizens are affected by various levels of government. There is a tendency to think of the federal government as *the* government, but from the consumer's point of view, developments at the state or local level may be equally important.

---

* Even this does not exhaust all possibilities. Governments also supply goods and services to consumers—police protection, roads, education, and the like. The next chapter analyzes these problems.

GOVERNMENT AND THE PUBLIC INTEREST

The Critical Decades: 1870–1900

It may seem strange to begin analyzing modern consumer protection by reviewing developments of a century ago, but for the United States, these were critically important years. Not only did the economy take on many of the features that still characterize it, but the response to those changes was institutionalized and repeated again and again in the years that followed. The United States developed both a modern economy and the means of dealing with it during the last third of the nineteenth century. During those years, the economy can be characterized by one word: *change*. While industrialization had been proceeding since before the Civil War, the process accelerated after 1870. Manufacturing output increased by over 400 percent between 1870 and 1900. Technological breakthroughs enabled steel production to grow from 19 *thousand* tons in 1867 to 100 *million* tons in 1900. By the beginning of the new century, the United States was the world's leading industrial nation, accounting for over one-third of world output [21, pp. 149–55].

This growth in output was accompanied, and to a degree made possible, by rapid technological change. The new technology required huge investments that were economical only if output was correspondingly large.* Heavy manufacturing came to be dominated by a few firms, and in some cases by a few individuals. In steel, it was Andrew Carnegie who dominated the industry until J. P. Morgan bought him out in 1901. The financier Morgan combined various steel interests into the United States Steel Corporation, the nation's first billion-dollar business. In oil, it was John D. Rockefeller, whose name became synonymous with petroleum—and wealth. Rapid development was not confined to manufacturing. Investment in railroads grew fourfold between 1870 and 1890, as track mileage increased by nearly as much [21, pp. 112–13]. Improvements were also being made in water transport and in overland transport. As a result, new areas, particularly in the West, were opened up to economic activity and became part of the market for the first time.

Producing goods and services is not an end in itself. This increased output had to be sold, and to sell it, increasingly large firms came into being. A national market emerged for the first time. Commerce expanded beyond a single region, crossing state boundaries in the process. With increased output (which generally meant lower prices) and improvements in transportation, goods were distributed nationwide. The pace of change continued and eventually outstripped the economy's ability to deal with it. Institutions that had been developed in an earlier period were inadequate to cope with the newly developed concentrations of economic and political power. Self

---

* North notes that an oil refinery of the optimal size could be built in the 1850s for $400; by 1900, the price was $1.3 million. [21, p. 151.]

restraint was not a notable feature of the period, and there appeared to be no other power, public or private, capable of restraining the giants.

The facts of this economic transformation are widely accepted. It is generally agreed that there were abuses of power and that the institutional structure of the economy could not cope with the new order. The disagreement arises over the nature of the response to the problem. There are two contrasting views, which may be described as *traditional* and *revisionist*, offering radically different perspectives on the question of government protection of the consumer. Their relevance to current developments will be obvious.

The traditional view is that while the changes in the economy caught the public unaware, there was eventually an awakening to the need for reform. During the last part of the century, reform movements developed in both major political parties and outside them in a series of splinter groups. These forces culminated in the Progressive Era during the first years of the twentieth century, a period characterized by widespread reform and institutional change [29, Chaps. 12 and 14]. The thrust of the reformers was to impose controls on the new economic giants and secure a place for the public interest in their operation. The two most important means of achieving these goals were antitrust legislation and independent regulatory agencies. These still form the core of government policy in this area.

The independent regulatory agencies, the members of which are appointed by the President and confirmed by the Senate, are specifically charged with maintaining the public interest. Firms involved are not free to do as they wish, but rather must accommodate the agency's perception of the public interest in their operations. In this way, the public is protected from the abuses of private power [29, Chap. 1]. The various agencies fall into two general categories. The first deals with public utilities in the broad sense, such as transportation (Interstate Commerce Commission, ICC) and communication (Federal Communications Commission, FCC). Firms in these areas are in essence granted a monopoly under the condition that they accept regulation. The other type operates within the private sector, overseeing general business practices or specific aspects of operations in key industries. These agencies, like the Federal Trade Commission (FTC) and the Food and Drug Administration (FDA), are more closely associated with consumer protection.

Business, by and large, has been hostile towards these efforts. The possibility that such hostility is more apparent than real is raised by the alternative explanation of these developments. Popularized by Gabriel Kolko, this view maintains that businesses used regulation and government intervention as tools to serve their own ends [18]. The key to this view is again the changes that took place in the economy at the end of the last century. To the earlier observation that economic institutions were unable to cope with that change must now be added a second: Business interests were not able to cope with it either. New products and new techniques meant that existing firms were continually vulnerable. Established patterns of behavior broke down as firms grew larger; as a result, there were no real rules of the game, and individual firms were left to their own devices. In short, the situation was chaotic and the businessman's position became untenable. Regulation offered a way around the problem; to see how, one must consider the actual impact of such policies.

Federal regulation of passenger and freight rates, for example, spares the carriers the dangers of possibly harmful competition. Anyone who has ever observed a gasoline price war knows what competitive price cutting can do. Rate regulation makes that nearly impossible in transportation. Furthermore, by guaranteeing the carrier its routes and limiting the number of competitors, regulation secures the fiefdom of each firm. Similarly, the government defines what constitutes unfair business practices (through the FTC). A limit on business practices can easily be extended into a limit on competition. If a few firms dominate an industry, there is always a tension between the good of the industry as a whole and the good of the individual firms. The latter is likely to win out, even if there is a gentlemen's agreement among producers. Thus, regulation serves to keep potentially maverick firms in line.

The consumer in this situation is in the same position as the family that finds that its cat has been protecting the mice. Institutions that are meant to protect the consumer in fact serve the interest of business. Government regulation becomes a means of stabilizing or cartelizing industries, with consumer protection relegated to secondary importance.* Once more, since this is done in the name of the public interest, it can all be accomplished with a progressive spirit of high-minded liberality.

It is probable that neither of these views is entirely correct; evidence can be found to support both of them. For our purposes, it is the contrast that is useful. It provides perspective. There is a genuine need for government regulation. Yet a sophisticated view requires the recognition that such regulation carries with it certain dangers and does not in itself always ensure the public interest. Regulation is a mixed blessing, and while its advantages probably outweigh its shortcomings, that comment misses the point. The real need is to make government intervention more effective so that it truly serves the consumer. While it may be impossible to design a perfect system, it is certainly possible to improve on the one we have. To see what is required, it is necessary for us to take a closer look at how the system functions.

Regulation—Problems and Portents

While it is often said that people are known by the company they keep, the company they do not keep may be a better basis for judgment. If you know who a person's enemies are, you know a lot about the person. If regulatory agencies are judged on that basis, their list of enemies is impressive

---

* Cartels, which are illegal in the United States, are organizations within an industry that set rules for members, often including price setting, production quotas, or market limitations. Regulatory agencies, however, commonly carry on at least some of these functions.

indeed. They have succeeded in bringing together in opposition individuals who otherwise have very little in common. They have, for example, provoked hostility from Ralph Nader, the action-interventionist, and Milton Friedman, the leading advocate of free markets. The prescriptions differ in that Mr. Nader would strengthen and regenerate the agencies, while Professor Friedman would abolish them, but both agree that such agencies are not now serving the public as they should. Groups like the American Bar Association and Consumers Union have expressed similar reservations.

Detailing all the complaints against all the agencies would require volumes in itself. There is a common pattern to such complaints, however, so problems may be identified by looking at selected agencies. While the specifics may differ, the overall situation does not change much from agency to agency. Indeed, only a cursory review is needed to conclude that there is a consensus among observers that the regulatory agencies simply are not doing their job. The American Bar Association, for example, concluded after an investigation of the Federal Trade Commission that it suffered from a "serious misallocation of resources and a confusion of priorities." To solve this problem, the report suggested that the FTC should

> set up its own apparatus to define and to keep current a unified plan in the consumer area. Past efforts to do this have produced no effective results. The primary requisite for planning is adequate information about what consumer problems are. . . . [1, p. 54]

To appreciate those comments, you have to remember that the FTC has been in operation for well over fifty years.

The same picture emerges if we look at the Food and Drug Administration, which, because of its broad powers in the inspection of food and the regulation of drugs, is among the most important of all the agencies to the consumer. It is a very telling commentary that when the FDA forces a drug off the market—because it is either unsafe or worthless—the news makes the front pages. If firemen do *not* put out fires or postmen do *not* deliver the mail, it makes news; with the FDA, it is the other way around. The agency is merely doing its job, but that fact alone is newsworthy.

It would be unfair to be critical of the Food and Drug Administration without noting that its record of consumer-mindedness compares favorably with other agencies [27, p. 581]. The problem is typical of many other agencies; that is, its performance is uneven. The typical pattern has been for the FDA to get an energetic new director and to vigorously carry out its responsibilities. This burst of activity is seldom sustained. Because of personnel changes, lack of resources, or political pressure, the agency lapses again into inactivity. How critical that inactivity can be was pointed out by an investigation by the government's own General Accounting Office. The GAO double-checked the FDA's inspection of some 97 food plants; of that number, only 30 met the FDA's minimal sanitation standards. The problem is not so much that the FDA does not do its job, but that it can't. During a recent year, its 210 inspectors were charged with covering over 60,000 establishments; they were able to inspect only 7,500 [7, p. 154].

The FDA is also responsible for monitoring the drug industry (both prescription and nonprescription drugs). There are really three issues here: price, effectiveness, and safety. Since research and development costs are high, drug companies have a considerable investment in any drug that reaches the market. This encourages them to follow a pricing policy that will allow them to recover their investment as rapidly as possible. The result is commonly inflated drug prices. It is one thing for consumers to pay too much for a worthwhile drug, but often they derive very little benefit from their purchases. This is particularly true of nonprescription, or patent, medicines. Despite lavish advertising claims, which the FTC is now moving to curb, these remedies are often a waste of money. Yet consumers spend billions of dollars on them every year to combat coughs, colds, runny noses, and assorted ailments.

Safety is the most serious problem. In 1962, the law was revised to give the FDA specific power to provide safety clearance on all new drugs [27, p. 578]. Such clearance is to be given only when scientific tests—at least two—provide evidence that the drug is both safe and effective. Yet because of economic pressure on the drug companies that encourages them to get new products on the market as soon as possible, these provisions are sometimes not enforced [7, p. 155]. This is all the more harmful because consumers think they are being protected and thus may literally be the victims of a false sense of security.

In evaluating this situation, the institutional framework of regulation must be considered. While the various commissions have professional staffs, commissioners themselves are usually not professionals; they are lawyers, politicians, or industry experts who are appointed for a specific term. Since reappointment is uncertain, a short-run perspective is encouraged. This in turn leads to what one analyst calls a "minimum squawk" strategy, in which various interests are balanced in an effort to avoid upsetting anyone. The particular strategy that any commission follows depends on how it perceives its responsibilities and who it thinks its clients are. That point is particularly important because agencies often behave as if their first responsibility were to the industries they are supposed to regulate instead of to the public. In what seems to be a switch of roles, the commissions become spokesmen for the industries.

Some would argue that the agencies have simply been bought off, and there have been instances when that has happened. Out-and-out graft, however, is an inadequate explanation; the situation is more complex than that. It arises from the complex and technical job that the agencies must perform. Suppose the telephone company requests an increase in rates; the request will be accompanied by a battery of supporting documents covering technical and financial questions. Since the telephone company has an obvious interest in the case, it will be able to focus all of its very considerable resources on seeing that the request is approved. The regulatory commissions are rather small, after all, so that the commission members are the focal point of intense lobbying. Even if the commissioners are fair minded and honest, most of the information they receive will come from the company.

Furthermore, there are natural ties between the regulatory agency and the industry. Staff members of each are likely to have similar backgrounds, read similar trade publications, and deal with similar problems. In short, they speak the same language, and this is bound to carry over even when they are in adversary positions. This is all the more true because movement between the agencies and industry is common, so each is likely to be, or have been, in the other's position. This is something of a problem. Promising staff members of a regulatory agency may be hired away by the industry to a job with a much more attractive salary. Thus, it is difficult for the agency to keep its most qualified people. This practice may also affect the direction the agency takes. One expert noted:

> Since employment in the regulated industry is one of the most obvious opportunities after a regulator's term in office, alienating members of the regulated industry may prove very costly. . . . Some regulators may behave without regard to this consideration. . . . Most regulators in ordinary consideration of self-interest, however, must be expected to weigh this calculation heavily. [15, p. 48]

The problem of inadequate resources was dramatically demonstrated a few years ago when the Federal Communications Commission announced that it was dropping its investigation of the American Telephone and Telegraph Company. The company was so big that the Commission simply did not have the resources to carry off such an investigation. There was a touch of pathos in the Department of Defense's offer (eventually rejected), to lend the FCC some cost accountants so that they might continue the probe.

This discussion has centered on the consumer interest, with little to say about the consumer. Suppose now that consumers are moved to action by the proposed increase in telephone rates. That in itself is quite a supposition, for while consumers may be annoyed by the increase, it will still amount to only a small fraction of their total budgets. Thus, while the telephone company has a clear view of its own self-interest, it is much less likely that the consumer will. If consumers pursue the case, they are immediately confronted by the complex legal and administrative structure of the regulatory system. Next, they must master a tangle of administrative decisions and court rulings full of unfamiliar phrases like *rate base* and *fair rate of return*. All of this requires time, money, and effort beyond the capabilities of most individuals. It is beyond the capabilities of most consumer groups too. After all, if the FCC could not take on AT&T, it is unlikely that a consumer group can. As a result, the consumer's influence is likely to be small. The combination of plural interests and information costs is difficult to overcome. Traditionally this has meant that the *public interest* is whatever the regulators say it is. They may keep the faith, but every pressure on them is pushing in the other direction.

If this summary is not sufficiently pessimistic, there is one more note that should be added. Most of what has been said thus far applies by implication to federal regulation. Regulation, however, goes on at the state and local level also, where the problems are even more severe. Regulation must be carried out with even fewer resources than at the federal level. This is a genuine concern to consumers because many key industries are regulated at the state level. Public utilities, for example, are generally regulated within the states they serve. The same is true of insurance companies, resulting in particularly weak regulation of that industry. When the Pennsylvania Insurance Department assumed a more activist position, an uproar resulted. In Iowa, the Commerce Commission has recently been revitalized and despite minimal resources, works actively in support of the public. Over its first five years, however, the commission prosecuted just one case.

Regulation at the local level is even more of a problem. There is often no professional body to carry on the regulatory function, so it falls to the city council. That such groups are not equipped to deal with the problem goes without saying. Yet local transportation companies (like taxis) are usually regulated in this way. At present, cable television is also regulated at the local level. Since the potential for growth in that industry is so large, a disaster awaits the consumer interest if the situation is not changed.

Some may feel that the picture presented above is drawn in overly harsh tones. The consumer certainly has benefited from aspects of the regulatory system; but isn't that the way it is supposed to be? However praiseworthy those benefits may be, there is no denying the fact that too often the consumer is served poorly, if at all. Anyone who is satisfied with a system that is not all bad might well be content with things as they are, but those who feel that all of us deserve something better, must conclude that there is a real need for improvement.

There is, however, no simple way for improvement to be realized. Pretending otherwise is a good way to ensure that no real change takes place. To appreciate that fact, you need only recall why there is a problem in the first place. It is because plural interests and information costs prevent consumers from exerting a direct influence. Unless those conditions change, it is hard to imagine how the consumer's direct influence can increase. That is why talk about increased consumer awareness and participation in the regulatory process qualifies as wishful thinking. It simply is not going to happen. There is an alternative approach, however, that is more promising. It carries no guarantees and certainly cannot be expected to provide quick results, but over time it holds out the possibility that consumers may be able to direct the system towards its stated goals. It begins with the recognition that effective government protection requires consumer organization. Individuals can make a difference, but to mount an effective overall campaign, consumers must be organized. The problems may be too great for even a well-organized consumer group to handle directly, but such a group (or groups) would be in a position to take the first steps towards a solution.

There are three steps involved. The first has to do with providing information. A well-financed consumer group could serve as a watchdog. To do this effectively, however, requires full-time professionals who are experts in the field. The mere existence of such a group would put pressure on the various regulatory agencies. The group's real value, however, would be in publicizing its findings. That does not mean a press release or two, but a well-organized campaign in the media. Business, after all, has no monopoly on the tools of Madison Avenue. There are some hopeful signs. Ralph Nader's research teams have worked in this area [4]. Organizations like Consumers Union and Common Cause have also publicized the neglect of the public interest. Despite their considerable efforts, much remains to be done.

The second function of consumer groups in this regard is direct involvement in the regulatory process. This too is under way. Various groups have brought suits against different regulatory agencies to challenge their decisions. This should not be thought of as providing an ultimate solution, but it can still be a useful tactic. Dramatic change is possible, but it is much more likely to come step by step. Each case, each small victory, is important.

Over time, it is possible that such pressure could bring real change. Prospects, however, are not bright. To improve them, it is necessary to include the third aspect of organized consumer action. The problem has been framed in political terms, which suggests a political solution. Consumer groups must get the message across to the typical consumer. That message is simple: You're being taken. It is not necessary that consumers know all the detailed operations of the regulatory system. The odds are against this being possible. They do need to know what is going on and that what is going on is not to their advantage. Once they are aware, consumers need to be directed towards a political solution, which means pressure on elected officials.

Here is where consumer organization is needed again. Consumer anger needs organization and direction. Given that, political pressure can be applied. Note that the regulatory system is being reached indirectly through the political system. That roundabout way may seem inefficient, but it stands a better chance of success—it does not require that individuals become experts on regulation; it merely requires that elected representatives understand that unless they use their power to bring about effective regulation, their tenure in office will be short.

The regulatory mechanism is there, like a ship that has been pirated. What is needed is for consumers to recapture it. Regulation is complex, and even if it were properly directed, some problems would remain. Regulation will not offer an instant solution in all cases; and in some cases, less regulation may be called for. New solutions need to be tried, but until consumers have reasserted themselves politically, it is unlikely that any innovative approaches will be forthcoming from government. The real question is, then: Can consumers assert themselves through the political system? Some observers, Professor Galbraith among them, feel this is already happening. He perceives a growing public awareness of the inconsistencies in the system. This he describes as "public cognizance," a necessary precondition for effective change. He maintains:

> There is a divergence, a conflict between the purpose of economic institutions, the large corporations in particular, and the public need. This means there will be an increasingly visible struggle for the government. . . . The first struggle will be to recapture the legislature for the public interest. [13, p. 73]

If that is an accurate observation, then the future holds the prospect not just for improvements, but ultimately for final recognition of consumers' interests.

Trust and Antitrust

At about the same time that America developed its penchant for creating independent regulatory agencies, it also began to face the related problem of concentrated economic power. The development of monopolies or trusts concentrated vast amounts of power in the hands of a few firms. It is natural that reformers should have focused on combating these developments. Out of their efforts grew the American tradition of antitrust. From the consumer's point of view, the problems involved in antitrust are similar to those related to regulation. Like regulation, antitrust is complex and if anything, even more legalistic. Plural interests and information costs again combine to reduce the consumer's effectiveness. Thus, if the consumer's interests are to be safeguarded, political pressure is required to ensure that the law is vigorously enforced.

Since consumers' strategies are essentially the same in both cases, the analysis of antitrust can be developed quite briefly. Every introductory economics textbook contains a section on the evils of monopoly. Given the firm's goals and cost structure, it can be demonstrated that monopoly results in higher prices and lower output, hardly a solution that consumers are likely to favor. This provides the basic rationale for antitrust activities. If monopoly is bad, then fighting it is good. The public interest is obvious. The situation is not really quite that simple, however. Pure monopoly—one firm in an industry—is relatively rare in industry. Thus, it is necessary to speak of monopoly elements or actions in restraint of trade. The courts decided rather early that bigness was not the same as badness, so that a firm could not be considered a monopoly just because it was large. Thus, General Motors survives with over half of American automobile production despite repeated antitrust threats.

Antitrust efforts begin with the Sherman Antitrust Act of 1890. The act makes "contract, combination, or conspiracy in restraint of trade" illegal, and further stipulates that efforts to monopolize trade are also illegal [27, pp. 54–55]. A law is useless unless it is enforced, and the Sherman Act was not vigorously enforced for over a decade. The first serious prosecution under the act had to wait until 1903, when Theodore Roosevelt brought suit in the Northern Securities case (a transportation monopoly in the Northwest). Despite Roosevelt's reputation as a trust-buster, monopoly power continued to accumulate. In response to public pressure, the Clayton Act was passed in 1914; it forbade unfair pricing practices, restrictive contracts, and non-competitive mergers. Along with the Federal Trade Commission, which is charged with enforcement, these acts remain the foundation for American antitrust activities.

A distinction is necessary between the general effect of monopoly and specific instances of monopolistic behavior. The latter is much more clear-cut. If two firms in an industry get together and set prices or rig contract bids, that is clearly "in restraint of trade," and the consumer suffers. Such was the case when General Electric and Westinghouse conspired to set prices on electrical goods in the 1960s and when big oil companies later rigged asphalt bids on public contracts.

The general effect of monopoly cannot be dealt with in simple terms. The automobile industry is an example. That industry is obviously concentrated; there are four domestic producers, one of which (American Motors) is very small. General Motors clearly dominates the industry. Its Chevrolet Division, for example, typically accounts for more sales than any of the other three companies. Is the consumer hurt by this concentration? To answer that, it is necessary to remember that the companies, because of their size, not only control price but also can dictate to the consumer (in the short run) what sorts of automobiles will be produced. Detroit at first failed to respond to pressures for smaller cars. Significantly, only American Motors made serious moves in that direction, a policy that paid off as demand for small cars continued to rise. Furthermore, the industry's record of innovation is much better with frills than with substantive improvements. Safety features were not incorporated until federal pressure was applied. Similarly, foreign producers took the lead in such innovations as safer body construction, dual braking systems, cleaner engines, and other minor yet very helpful touches like rear-window defrosters.

Detroit remained wedded to the idea of annual model changes. These changes, while largely stylistic, took attention from more significant refinements and cost a lot of money. One study estimates that between 1956 and 1960, annual model changes cost car buyers $5 billion a year, and if the declining gasoline mileage that accompanied those changes is taken into account, the cost goes up another $7 billion [9]. In just four years, that is $48 billion that model changes cost American consumers. Yet consumers had no real choice aside from turning to imports, which they did in increasing numbers. If the industry had been more competitive, consumers would have had a greater opportunity to express their preferences. Choices would have been broader and more meaningful, and it would have been easier to bring pressure on producers.

This, remember, is only one example. Others might be drawn from any other big manufacturing industry. The problem is that the policy implications of all of this are not clear. Bringing about increased competition in the automobile industry is easier said than done. Because of capital requirements and economies of scale, it is impossible to return to the large number of small companies that characterized the industry in its earlier days. Furthermore, the courts have tended to make good conduct the most important criterion in antitrust deliberations.* The structure of the industry, the number and size of the firms, have received much less attention. The conduct

---

* Except under Section 7 of the Clayton Act. I am indebted to Professor David H. Ciscel for these points.

of an industry is obviously important to consumers, but so too is structure. It is structure that finally relates to consumer power, for with a larger number of smaller firms, consumer leverage will be increased. Thus, antitrust is not always enforced in the manner best calculated to serve consumer interests.

There is a final point that should be made about the underlying assumptions of antitrust. It is assumed that competition is healthful and should therefore be encouraged. Some observers feel that such efforts run counter to the realities of the situation. They maintain that economic concentration is a fact of modern economic life and that efforts to restore competition are likely to be ineffective. Facing large corporations realistically means accepting them for what they are. Professor Galbraith and others who advocate this point of view would not, however, suggest that the economic giants be given free reign. They argue that the public should come to grips with the large companies and control them. The word *control* is used here in a more general sense than it has hitherto been used. It means that the public should be represented in the operation of these firms, which is a more active concept than regulation.

Those who feel that this violates the principles of the market system should take a close look at how things work now. It is argued that large parts of the economy are characterized by a private planning system rather than markets. Since firms plan their own output, profits, and so on, the system obviously works to their advantage. Dealing with this reality requires bringing this planning system under public control and directing it in the public interest [14]. Such efforts might require developing new economic forms. This development would be consistent with the continual evolution of economic organization, which never fits easily into static categories. It is necessary for consumers to acknowledge this evolution; indeed, their self-interest demands it. With that recognition goes the ability to treat problems in a straightforward way, seeking the best solution possible. Again, consumer awareness emerges as the prerequisite for effective action. As we have suggested, consumers can mobilize support for their position, but only if they are aware of what is involved and organized to press their point of view. They may want to search for new solutions or to increase pressure on the Antitrust Division of the Justice Department for more vigorous prosecution under existing laws. Neither alternative is viable in the absence of awareness.

PATTERNS OF CONSUMER PROTECTION

The Legislative Record

The modern history of government efforts to protect consumers began after the Civil War. The federal government passed the first specific consumer protection legislation over a century ago with the Mail Fraud Act of 1872. That ought to suggest the effectiveness of such legislation, since mail fraud remains a serious problem today. Early consumer protection legislation can be summarized quickly; there wasn't much. In the 65 years that followed the enactment of the first legislation, only two new laws were passed. Both were important and remain today the cornerstone of an effective consumer policy; they are the Pure Food and Drug Act of 1906 and the Federal Trade Commission Act of 1914. Yet their effectiveness at the time was limited.

For example, it was not until 1938 that the FTC was empowered to prosecute cases of deceptive advertising. That same year, the FDA was strengthened by laws requiring that new drugs be cleared with the agency, and its powers were extended to cover cosmetics. Still, these provisions lacked teeth. It was a quarter-century later before the FDA's drug-clearing powers were extended sufficiently to make them effective.

Since 1960, some twenty-five bills have been passed that can be identified clearly as consumer protection legislation. That is over twice as many as were passed in the years from 1872 to 1960 [12, pp. 373–75]. Bills are now being introduced at an even faster rate. If all the consumer protection bills currently before Congress were to pass, the amount of legislation would increase fourfold. It is clear that despite its long history, consumer protection has not received serious attention until quite recently. This fits remarkably well with the general analytical pattern we have laid down, which maintains that consumer problems are a function of the sophistication and development of the economy. It was not until the economy reached this relatively high level that the problems could or would emerge as significant concerns. As that process has accelerated in recent years, there has been a corresponding increase in efforts to promote consumer protection.

The accelerated pace of consumer protection legislation did not represent a clean breakthrough. The legislative pattern is full of cutbacks and changes. The ultimate goal seems vague and only dimly understood. Legislation covers the safety of children, boats, toys, automobiles, and pipelines. Additional legislation ranges over problems in food quality (an effort begun six decades earlier), lending controls, packaging and labeling and drug quality, to touch on only the less esoteric efforts. These are, by and large, significant issues, though some are less pressing than others.* It is their very diversity, however, that is significant, for it underscores the *lack of a coordinated policy*. Recent consumer protection legislation has been specific instead of attacking the problem as a whole. While this has brought about some genuine improvements in the consumer's position, the effort has been a hit-or-miss affair.

There are so many problems that Congress could spend all of its time passing laws to cover them and still not keep up. Dealing with specifics is a never-ending process. What is needed is a systematic program that would deal with fundamentals. The random approach means not only that important problems may be missed but that it will be more difficult to maintain

* Boat safety, for example, is important, but how many consumers does it affect? Ghetto residents are hardly likely to give it very high priority.

momentum and direction. This failure to develop a systematic approach can be explained by our earlier analysis. Effective protection will be forthcoming only when public pressure is organized and directed. Pressure has not been lacking, but until very recently, it has not been sustained. Issues crop up, often in response to some disaster, that attract attention and result in pressure for legislative action. Thus, much legislation is the result of short-run influences and chance developments. When these pressures have passed, they leave their legislative remains much as a seashell is left after the animal inhabiting it dies.

This problem is complicated by the fact that something is not always better than nothing. The laws passed to deal with these problems are often less than adequate and sometimes even harmful themselves. The hurried nature of the effort works against thoughtful consideration of the problem. The result is an improvisation that, while it may not provide adequate shelter, is sufficient to reduce public pressure and hence the probability of more meaningful reform.

Sustained pressure is necessary to bring about a comprehensive program to deal with consumer problems. *Sustained* is the key word; periodic outbursts of activity must be integrated and maintained over time. That is no easy task, but there is evidence that things may be moving in that direction. While the full impact of consumer efforts has yet to be felt, some groups have succeeded in focusing attention on key problems.

Consumerism as a movement is still very new. Where the problems are so serious, it is easy to become overanxious. Although our analysis has emphasized problems, progress has been made. It is difficult to maintain perspective, but if one looks for beginnings rather than completed structures, there is reason to be hopeful. It is possible to identify the foundations of a comprehensive policy, particularly involving information. The truth-in-lending law not only has provided more information, but has forced people to think about interest charges. Movements towards more informative labeling also represent steps in the right direction, however faltering. While this is a long way from a comprehensive information program (Chapter 5), it nevertheless represents progress. The clear need now is to build on these foundations, integrate the bits of consumer protection that are floating around, and develop an overall program. There is an additional facet to such efforts. To be effective, they require not only consumer pressure, but leadership and direction from within the government itself. It appears now that consumer pressure must seek this also.

At present, existing consumer protection programs are scattered throughout the government. Regulatory agencies and existing departments are responsible for many of them. There are consumer protection activities within the Department of Agriculture, the Department of Health, Education, and Welfare, the Justice Department, and so on. Similarly, government activities that relate to the consumer, such as product testing, are carried on in many agencies, including the Department of Defense and the General Services Administration. Reorganization would be difficult, and it might be impossible or even undesirable to centralize all of these functions. Nevertheless, the important ones could be brought together and the remainder coordinated. When the Department of Transportation was created, it drew together transportation programs previously handled in other agencies, just as the Department of Health, Education, and Welfare had done earlier with programs under its jurisdiction.

These needs have been recognized for some time. As early as 1959, Senator Estes Kefauver called for creating a department of the consumer with cabinet rank [27, p. 584]. In 1972, Congress was on the verge of creating such a department. Majorities in both houses favored the proposal, which enjoyed bipartisan support. The bill, however, was caught in the crush of activity immediately before Congress recessed, which in combination with pressure from the administration resulted in its defeat.

Some progress can be reported. In 1969, the office of Special Assistant to the President for Consumer Affairs was created within the executive branch. While a special assistant's status is nebulous, usually fulfilling only an advisory capacity, the office did provide a focal point for the emerging debate on consumer affairs. The office had only a brief tenure in the executive branch before it was shifted to Health, Education, and Welfare, where it is now known as the Office of Consumer Affairs. How effective the office will be in its new setting is a matter of conjecture. It appears certain, however, that pressure for a cabinet-level department will continue. It is difficult to make predictions under such fluid conditions, but there is every reason to hope that such a department will be created within the next few years.

The creation of such a post would not represent any panacea, any more than the creation of the Department of Transportation took care of all transportation problems. Indeed, some consumer advocates oppose the move because they fear it would fall under business domination. A similar fear is expressed about an alternative proposal to create an independent agency with responsibilities for consumer affairs. Evidence from the state and local level supports the idea that a consumer affairs office can be effective in advancing consumer interests. While some offices of this kind are little more than window dressing, others have successfully championed the consumer's cause. The successful ones reflect not only consumer support and strong leadership, but also a desire on the part of the governmental unit involved to meet the problem. There is no reason to suspect that things would be any different at the federal level. Properly supported, a department of consumer affairs would enable the government to begin to develop the kind of comprehensive program that is needed. As such, it emerges as a necessary first step in meeting consumers' needs.

Hold the Standard High

Much of the recent government activity in consumer protection has involved setting minimal standards for consumer products. Such standards are meant as a guarantee to the consumer that these products or services meet specific requirements for safety, performance, or cleanliness. The individual is freed of the need to collect specific information. Either legislation or administrative agencies may set the standards. In some cases, private and public efforts combine, as in licensing medical doctors and lawyers and to a lesser extent teachers. In these instances, private professional bodies and state licensing agencies cooperate in certifying individuals within the profession.

There is certainly no question about the widespread use of standards. In addition to the FDA's efforts, there are local health departments that inspect establishments serving food. Banks, barber shops, builders, taxicabs, and teachers all must meet standards. Recently, the automobile has been singled out for attention, first on safety and then on pollution control. One of the problems with standards is that such efforts are generally under-financed. Without adequate enforcement, standards are meaningless. They may even harm the consumer by creating a feeling of security when in fact none exists. Yet far too often, an illusion of protection has been considered sufficient, as if merely passing a law and imposing a standard could somehow benefit the consumer.

There are numerous illustrations of serious problems associated with standards. Electrical wiring offers one example. On-site inspection of wiring is required in most places, which makes sense if the wiring itself is being done on the site. With new developments in preconstructed, modular housing, however, the wiring is done in a factory; the entire unit is then moved to the site. If the wiring has to be torn out and inspected again, the cost savings of factory production are lost. Yet this type of wasted effort has happened in many areas. Standards meant to protect the consumer are used to preserve special-interest groups, thus preventing innovations from taking place in home-building. This contributes to spiraling housing costs and has created actual housing shortages in some localities.

Occupational licensure can work in the same way. Licensing may be a way to assure minimal standards, but it also keeps some people out of a profession. This gives a degree of monopoly power to those already in a profession and secures their control over price and output. The important question is, Who does the licensing? If the profession licenses its own members, there is a greater likelihood that it will work to limit entry. Even if a state board is responsible for licensing, there still may be a problem. That is because such boards are typically filled with appointees from the industry; while they represent the public, their perspectives are necessarily tied to their professions. To offset this tendency, some states require that such boards contain a reasonable percentage of qualified persons who represent consumers, not the profession. The American Medical Association, which licenses medical doctors, has come under repeated attack for limiting entry into the profession [10, pp. 137–60]. Similarly, in many states there is an ongoing dispute between barbers and the state licensing agency over who should hold licensing power for the profession. Even schoolteachers are not exempt. Many critics maintain that complex certification procedures serve the interests of state educational bureaucracies and colleges of education rather than student interests.

Seemingly helpful regulations may hurt the consumer in other ways. Limitations on interest rates, for example, are intended to prevent exploitation of the borrower. If the limitations are set low enough to have an effect, however, some borrowers will be closed out of the market. Poor credit risks are thus denied access to conventional credit and forced to turn to alternative, more expensive sources of credit. There is at least a suggestion that some money lenders and legislators collaborate to ensure that result.

One of the basic problems with standards is implied by the name itself. Imposing standards means *standardization*, which in turn means that products will share similar qualities. This is a particular problem for product safety, which is compounded by the need to decide where the standards should be set. A chain saw, for example, is a potentially lethal weapon. If the operator is careless, no amount of refinement or built-in safety is going to overcome that fact. On the other hand, a skilled, careful operator might safely use a saw that would be dangerous for someone else. Can the same standard serve in both cases?

The National Commission on Product Safety recommended that producers of hazardous products be made liable for damages they inflict [8]. Professor Walter Oi has demonstrated, however, that shifting liability of accidents from consumers to producers "can lead to the increased production of the riskier grade" [24, p. 5]. That surprising conclusion rests on some rather complex economic analysis, but it deserves mention here to illustrate that complications can arise. Seemingly obvious solutions need to be analyzed carefully before they are accepted. That same comment applies to standards generally. There has been a sort of knee-jerk reaction in favor of standards, with too little thought given to their implications. Careful consideration of what is involved, including exploring alternative approaches, would represent an improvement. Effective consumer protection is too important a goal to jeopardize it with inadequate solutions.

Here we have another need for improved information flow. This is essentially an information problem. Imposing standards implies that the consumer cannot make an individual decision, a conclusion that may be warranted when information is difficult to obtain. Combining improvements in information flows and standards should therefore provide a flexible approach. Several possibilities suggest themselves. One is that products might be ranked according to some safety scale; this certification would provide the consumer with additional information but would not keep products off the market. A related, perhaps complementary approach, would be to force producers to provide detailed, easily understandable information on all products. In each case, the consumer's need to know is satisfied, while individual choice is maintained [24, pp. 23 and 26].

Balancing the rights of the individual and the need to protect the community as a whole becomes the issue. Should consumers be allowed to buy dangerous products if they do so with full knowledge of the hazards involved? What is the degree to which consumers need to be protected from themselves? These questions extend beyond product safety. Standards are set for products like peanut butter, for example, which specify the percentage of peanuts that must be included. A strong argument can be made that consumers who are so inclined should be able to buy a poor-quality and presumably cheaper brand provided they do so with the full understanding that the product is of low quality. Consumer education would be required for such a system to work, but its potential benefits suggest that the effort would be worthwhile.

Unfortunately, this alternative will not work in all cases. The problem of wiring inspection cited above, for example, would not submit easily to such a solution. That is because such cases are essentially political problems; legal instruments have been captured by special interest groups to serve their purposes. The only solution is effective political action by consumers to win back their rights. If standards are to serve the purpose for which they are intended, continual pressure is required to ensure that they are relevant to current problems and needs.

Related Developments—A Survey

It is difficult to summarize all the different aspects of consumer protection and treat in detail the host of different current developments. To the student of consumer affairs, this is a happy problem, for it reflects the strength and vitality of the response to consumer problems. This response reflects rising consumer consciousness, which is necessary before substantive improvement can be expected. Many of the developments are concentrated at the state and local level. The federal system has its drawbacks, often representing duplication of effort and inadequate protection; at the same time, it has advantages. It allows a flexible response and enables consumers to pursue their goals by varied routes.

State and local governments took the lead in consumer protection, responding substantially in advance of the federal government. In both New York State and New York City, for example, early efforts at consumer protection were among the first to gain national attention. Statistics are misleading because some agencies are much more active than others, but in 1972, over half the states had consumer protection offices and over three-fourths had agencies to handle consumer fraud [3]. While many agencies work with inadequate funding, they have nevertheless proved their value to the consumer. Active prosecution of consumer fraud is a very effective way of protecting the consumer. Not all problems indicate fraud, but those that do can be numbered among the most serious, especially for human suffering. Progress has been significant, including new weapons against such practices as:

Pyramiding, a sales technique in which consumers are told they will get a product free if they can get just ten (the number varies) of their friends to buy it. Since the rate of increase is exponential, few consumers will be able to convince enough friends to buy the product. Just as someone always gets stuck with a chain letter, so some buyer will be stuck with the merchandise, usually at inflated prices.

Sale of distributorships, which is related to pyramiding. In this approach, the consumer becomes a distributor, buying a supply of the product. Again, however, the supply is "free" if he or she can get ten friends to become distributors. The result is the same.

High-pressure sales, especially in the home. Many states have enacted *cooling-off* laws, so that the consumer may negate any contract signed under such conditions within a specified period. This protects the consumer from momentary lapses and reduces the impact of con men.

Fraudulent land sales. There are new federal laws that protect the consumer from high-pressure sales of vacation land.

Signing a contract on a long-term credit purchase and then selling it to a finance company. If fraud is involved, the consumer might not be bound to the original contract, but once it is sold, the company can collect. The finance company becomes a *holder in due course.* This provides the fraudulent operator with capital and enables him to skip town easily. New laws would make such contracts void even after they have been purchased by another company.

This is merely a sample; much still needs to be done. State and local efforts can be models for federal action, although some problems can be handled most effectively at the local level. It is easier for consumers to find out if a particular offer is legitimate if they can simply call a local law enforcement officer. In an active sense, such officers can publicize warnings when they find a fraud being carried out in their domains. Local enforcement is needed for other reasons too. Many technical legal questions confront consumers; the laws that cover them vary from state to state. Laws governing bankruptcy, liens against property, repossession, and garnishment show this kind of variation. These are technical areas, but they can be vitally important to the consumer. Developing the kind of laws that adequately protect consumers should have a high priority with state and local groups.

There is a problem in the variation that exists among the states. While citizens in some states enjoy benefits of progressive legislation and active enforcement, others must do with little of either. States without adequate protection often harbor fraudulent operators. This shows the need for both more aggressive state action and federal legislation covering national concerns.

While legal action is an effective tool for consumer protection, it need not wait on vigorous public action. If the legal structure is there, consumers can use it themselves. Since consumers typically lack the resources to do this effectively, there is a need to lower the costs of action to consumers and expand their access to legal means. Developments are promising. Key individuals have shown that existing laws can aid the consumer, even if no one is currently investigating their use. A knowledge of the law is required, and it is encouraging to note that the law itself is responsive. One man, a law professor, moved the Federal Communications Commission to allow antismoking advertisements on television under the FCC's equal-time doctrine. That was a significant decision, for it began the movement that finally removed cigarette advertising from television [11]. A Boston lawyer, Edward Swartz, grew so upset with unsafe toys that he carried his campaign all the way to the federal government. He was a prime mover in the eventual passage of the Child Protection and Toy Safety Act [25].

Since the typical consumer is not a lawyer, he does not have such techniques available. Other techniques exist, however, as new developments are bringing legal instruments to more and more consumers. One is the increased use of small claims courts. Plaintiff and defendant act as their own lawyers in these courts, reducing the costs to consumers and offsetting the advantages that would otherwise go to firms with large legal staffs. Bringing suit, under such conditions, is within the reach of most consumers. One of the drawbacks is that in many states, small claims means just that. In some states, claims involving as little as $250 are denied access to these courts. A more reasonable figure—*Consumer Reports* suggests $1,000—would open these courts to a wider range of consumer complaints. Furthermore the knowledge that such recourse was available to the consumer would not be lost on businesses; there would be an added incentive to reach a mutually satisfactory settlement [6].

The class-action suit is another device that has recently proved effective in supporting consumer interests. Legal action may be too expensive for the individual, but if he or she can join others who have been harmed, they may bring suit as a group or a class. Similarly, a government agency may not prosecute for one person, unless damages are excessive, but would for a group. This brings legal action within the reach of many more people and allows for a more efficient attack on the problem [12, pp. 134–43]. In short, the class-action suit allows consumers to overcome many of the difficulties confronting individuals. With its organization, it allows consumers to offset bigness in other parts of the economy. Class actions are a check against fraud in the marketplace. If an individual sues a firm that is selling overpriced merchandise and wins the case, the firm can pay damages without really being hurt; it will more than recover its loss on other sales. However,

> the impact of having to make restitution in a class action, if judgement is rendered against the seller, may force the firm out of business or induce it to change its practices, preventing damages to others. [19, p. 15]

Since the potential loss is greater, class actions encourage responsible actions among sellers.

Despite the potential of class actions, there is some question about their future. Traditionally, the courts have taken a rather narrow view on class-action suits, maintaining that individuals each had to be able to show that they had suffered significant loss before they could undertake action. There was then some relaxation of this view, during which time class actions assumed more importance. By 1974, the courts seemed to be reverting to their early pattern, limiting the use of this approach. Whatever its immediate prospects, it is difficult to imagine that the class action will not emerge again as a significant force. It should be seen as only one aspect of consumers' overall efforts to mobilize the legal system to meet their needs. That effort itself is part of the still larger movement towards reestablishing the consumer's position in the market. As that movement gains momentum, consumers will be able to take a more active part in shaping their environment, thus ensuring that future developments in the market will be consistent with their interests.

STUDY QUESTIONS

1.   Identify the consumer's interests in each of the following government policies. Which of them would you classify under consumer protection?
   a.   Expanded trade relations with the People's Republic of China.
   b.   The requirement that nutritional values be clearly stated on all breakfast cereals.
   c.   A vote on a bond issue for school construction.
   d.   Legislation to allow no-fault insurance.
   e.   The law that requires that consumers be given access to their files at credit bureaus.

2.   Retail price maintenance schemes (also called fair-trade laws) enforce pricing policies on merchants and prevent discounting. What is the rationale for these laws, which obviously favor small retail stores? Since these laws result in higher prices for consumers, why do consumers allow such legislation to be passed?

3.   Some utilities—power companies, for example—are privately owned and subject to government regulation, while others are publicly owned. Explain how these two approaches represent alternative responses to the same problem. Is it possible to generalize and say which one best serves consumer interests?

4.   Many early regulatory efforts at the state level were declared unconstitutional. On what basis could such a judgment be made? How can you explain the rapid change in attitudes that accompanied the growth of regulation?

5.   If you buy a drug, do you have any way of knowing whether it is safe, effective, and reasonably priced? Would you know how to go about finding out? How does this illustrate the big problem of consumers with regulatory agencies?

6. In most cases, consumers do not buy their telephones; they rent them from the telephone company instead. What impact does this have on what customers actually pay for their phones? Is there any other significance to the fact that the company retains ownership of the phone?

7. Most observers agree that despite problems involved, there is a need for building codes:
   a. What arguments can you give to support the need for such regulations?
   b. Explain how they can be subverted to serve the interests of special-interest groups.
   c. Can you think of another way to protect the consumer, thereby avoiding these problems?

8. What segment of the population gains the most from imposed standards? Since standards usually result in higher-priced products, which segment of the population bears the heaviest cost?

9. Safety standards on automobiles have resulted in significant improvements. Evidence on impact-absorbing steering columns and seat belts, for example, show that they have reduced traffic fatalities. Why did it take so long for these improvements to be incorporated into automobile design? Do you think most consumers were aware of the needs in this area?

10. Why do you think consumer fraud is a more serious problem now than it was fifty years ago? What, do you feel, is the best way to combat it? Why is consumer education the ultimate solution to the problem?

11. It may be argued that most consumer protection legislation benefits middle- and upper-income groups rather than low-income groups. This appears to be true with such things as boat and toy safety and controls on land sales. Considering the process by which legislation is enacted, explain why this result is predictable. What can be done to offset this trend?

SUGGESTED PROJECTS

1. If your local government has a consumer protection agency, invite a representative to speak to the class. Does the agency have the power and resources to protect the consumer adequately?

2. Consumer protection cannot be effective if consumers are not aware of it. Conduct a survey to find out how much consumers actually know about the protection to which they are entitled. You will want to explore different aspects, including the following:
   a. Pick out some recently enacted consumer legislation and see whether people are aware of it.

b.   Set up a hypothetical situation between buyer and seller (mis-representation of the product, complaints, and so on) and see whether consumers would be aware of their rights under such circumstances.

c.   Find out what people do when they have a complaint about a product or service.

d.   Find out whether consumers are aware of local consumer protection agencies and private consumer groups.

e.   See how many regulatory agencies consumers can name. Do the consumers know how these agencies are supposed to protect them?

Can you conclude from your survey that consumers are generally well aware of available protection? Did you notice any pattern to their responses? Are there particular areas that need to be strengthened? What proposals would you make to improve consumer awareness?

3.   Survey the consumer protection agencies in your area. Is there a single agency, or is responsibility shared among various units?

4.   In conjunction with Project 3, list items for action on consumer protection, including what you see as the most pressing needs in your area.

5.   In your area, what industries are regulated at the local level? at the state level? Research the activities of these regulatory bodies. How would you evaluate their effectiveness in protecting consumer interests?

6.   Look into the history of consumer protection in your state or locality. When were the first efforts made? Do they follow the pattern discussed in the text?

7.   Investigate the position that the chief political parties take on consumer protection. Does it receive much attention in their literature? Is there a significant difference between the parties?

BIBLIOGRAPHY AND SUGGESTED READINGS

1. American Bar Association. *Report of the ABA Commission to Study the Federal Trade Commission.* Washington, D.C.: Bureau of National Affairs, 1969.
The ABA took a close look at the FTC and found it wanting. This report represents a thoughtful consideration of the problems with the Commission and also its potential for serving the public better.

2. Bain, Joe. *Industrial Organization.* New York: John Wiley & Sons, 1962.
A standard reference work on industrial organization. Chapters 13, 14, and 15 deal with the problems of government regulation.

3. "Consumers Battle at Grass Roots." *Business Week*, February 26, 1972, p. 86.
A summary of consumer protection activity at the state and local level.

4. Cox, Edward F., et al. *The Nader Report on the Federal Trade Commission.* New York: Grove Press, 1969.

Another look at the FTC, this time by Nader's Raiders. The report called for modernization of procedures, more open operation, and most of all, a more aggressive attitude.

5. Consumer Protection Division, Iowa Attorney General's Office. Des Moines, Iowa.

Like other states, Iowa has greatly expanded its consumer protection activities. Materials concerning cases referred to in the text were supplied by this office, although they refer to activities in various states.

6. "Buyer vs. Seller in Small Claims Courts." *Consumer Reports,* October 1971, pp. 624–31.

An exploration of how small claims courts operate and how they can help the consumer. Contains a survey of such courts and suggestions for making them more effective.

7. "The FDA." *Consumer Reports,* March 1973, pp. 152–56.

A two-article series covering the FDA's activities in food inspection and drug licensing. The articles from these two issues reflect *CR*'s expanded position in consumer affairs.

8. *Final Report of the National Commission on Product Safety.* Washington, D.C.: U.S. Government Printing Office, 1970.

A review of hazardous products and problems they cause. While some of the economic analysis has been criticized [see 24], the report represents a serious effort to deal with a serious problem. It is the Commission's "final report," but represents only the beginnings of government activity in the area.

9. Fisher, Franklin, and Griliches, Zvi. "Abstract of the Costs of Automobile Model Changes since 1949." *American Economic Review, Papers and Proceedings,* May 1962, p. 259.

An estimation of the cost of model changeover to the American consumer, showing the significance of such changes.

10. Friedman, Milton. *Capitalism and Freedom.* Chicago: University of Chicago Press, 1962.

Chapter 9 presents Professor Friedman's analysis of occupational licensure. An excellent summary of the pitfalls involved in licensing.

11. Fritschler, A. Lee. *Smoking and Politics: Policymaking and the Federal Bureaucracy.* New York: Appleton-Century-Crofts, 1969.

A good case study of how the federal bureaucracy responds to pressure. As the subtitle indicates, this is an analysis of policymaking and as such offers valuable insights to consumers.

12. Gaedeke, Ralph M., and Etcheson, Warren W. *Consumerism.* San Francisco: Canfield Press, 1972.

A good collection of readings on consumerism. See section 16 for statements giving differing views on consumer class actions. Appendix 1 also reviews consumer protection legislation.

13. Galbraith, John Kenneth. As interviewed in *Forces*, no. 22, 1973, pp. 71–75. Thoughtful reflections by Professor Galbraith in this Canadian journal.

14. Galbraith, John Kenneth. *The New Industrial State*. Boston: Houghton Mifflin Co., 1967.

    A fully developed statement of Professor Galbraith's views, particularly on the firm as a planning system. He develops his idea of the "technostructure," a word that has since entered the language in reference to the technicians who actually run the big institutions in the economy.

15. Hilton, George W. "The Basic Behavior of Regulatory Commissions." *American Economic Review, Papers and Proceedings* 62 (May 1972): 47–54.

    An excellent summary of many forces that affect regulatory agencies. A good introduction for those who are interested in material not generally contained in texts, yet still written in an understandable fashion.

16. Hofstadter, Richard. *The Age of Reform*. New York: Alfred A. Knopf, 1955. Classic study of the Progressive Era by a leading American historian.

17. Keeton, P., and Shapo, M. *Products and the Consumer: Deceptive Practices*. Foundation Press, 1972.

    Organized along casebook lines, this study focuses on primary problems of consumer protection. A good reference.

18. Kolko, Gabriel. *The Triumph of Conservatism*. New York: Quadrangle Books, 1965.

    The revisionist view of American reform. Kolko's arguments, while often polemical, have been supported by more detached scholars in individual studies.

19. Lane, Sylvia. "Economics of Consumer Class Actions." *Journal of Consumer Affairs*, Summer 1973, pp. 13–22.

    A good review of class-action suits, including an economic analysis of their impact. The analysis shows that the effect of class action on consumer welfare may vary; the author concludes that they are still an important instrument in building an equitable economy.

20. Magnuson, Warren. *The Dark Side of the Marketplace*, 2d ed. Englewood Cliffs, N. J.: Prentice-Hall, 1972.

    A graphic description of the suffering that attends so much consumer fraud and a call for more effective laws and better enforcement.

21. North, Douglass C. *Growth and Welfare in the American Past*. Englewood Cliffs, N. J.: Prentice-Hall, 1966.

    Excellent in applying economic theory to U.S. economic history. Chapter 12 on growth in the post–Civil War period is of special interest.

22. Office of Consumer Affairs, Executive Office of the President. *Consumer Offices in State, County and City Governments*. Washington, D.C.: U.S. Government Printing Office, 1971.

23. Office of Consumer Affairs, Executive Office of the President. *State Consumer Action Summary*, 1971.

This publication and no. 22 review consumer protection agencies at the state and local level. The Office of Consumer Affairs is now in the Department of Health, Education, and Welfare.

24. Oi, Walter Y. "The Economics of Product Safety." *Bell Journal of Economics and Management Science*, Spring 1973, pp. 3–28.

    A disturbing analysis, which concludes that certain approaches meant to ensure safer products may have the opposite effect. Highly analytical, but anyone interested in this topic might do well to read at least pages 23–27.

25. Phillips, Charles F., Jr. *The Economics of Regulation.* Homewood, Ill.: Richard D. Irwin, 1965.

    For those interested in regulation, this is one of the standard sources.

26. Robertson, Wyndham. "Tempest in Toyland." *Fortune*, February 1972, pp. 115–17.

    Another review of consumer action, this time concerning the battle for safer toys. Also covers the National Commission on Product Safety.

27. Troelstrup, Arch W. *The Consumer in American Society.* New York: McGraw-Hill Book Co., 1970.

    See especially Chapters 12–13 for a summary of consumer protection.

28. Tuma, Elias H. *European Economic History.* New York: Harper & Row, 1971.

    See Parts 2 and 3 about the changing role of the consumer in economic modernization. This is an interesting question which merits additional attention.

29. Wilcox, Clair. *Public Policies Toward Business*, 3d ed. Homewood, Ill.: Richard D. Irwin, 1966.

    Good summary of government activities in regulation and antitrust.

9

Consumption
and the Public Sector:
Making Taxes Pay

"ON YOUR WAY HOME, PICK UP A DOLLAR'S WORTH OF DEFENSE"

Consuming Public Goods?

The next time you are with a group of friends, ask them to list the things they have used, or consumed, that day. The chances are that they will mention things like food, soap, books, gasoline, beer, and clothing. Maybe someone will even think of housing, electricity, and insurance. The odds are, however, that they will not mention police or fire protection, national defense, education, highways, sewage disposal, or street lights. And therein lies the paradox. The second grouping is made up of *public*, or *collective*, goods; these are consumed just as surely as the goods in the first group and make an easily perceived contribution to consumers' welfare. Anyone who has endured the chaos of a sanitation workers' strike or the fear that goes with a firemen's strike can appreciate how important the public services are. Yet consumers still tend to think of consumption as limited to those goods and services purchased directly for themselves, omitting such items purchased through taxes.

The oversight persists even though control of public goods is the subject of an ongoing political debate. While such matters as the level of defense spending are clearly political, it should be just as clear that they affect the consumer directly. An increase in defense spending means either higher taxes or cuts in other areas of government spending like education, highway construction, and medical research. The consumer is affected either way.

The point is clear when we consider the importance of public goods in the individual's budget. Americans purchased almost $116 billion worth of

195

TABLE 9.1   Total Personal Taxes and Selected Consumption Expenditures in the United States: 1960–71
(In billions of dollars)

	Personal taxes *	Automobiles	Home furnishings	Food	Clothing	Housing	Personal savings
1960	50.9	20.1	18.9	80.5	27.3	46.3	17.0
1961	52.4	18.4	19.3	82.9	27.9	48.7	21.2
1962	57.4	22.0	20.5	85.7	29.6	52.0	21.6
1963	60.9	24.3	22.2	88.2	30.6	55.4	19.9
1964	59.4	25.8	25.0	92.9	33.5	59.3	26.2
1965	65.7	30.3	26.9	98.8	35.9	63.5	28.4
1966	75.4	30.3	29.9	105.8	40.3	67.5	32.5
1967	83.0	30.5	31.4	108.5	42.3	71.8	40.4
1968	97.9	37.5	34.3	115.3	46.3	77.3	39.8
1969	116.2	40.4	36.3	122.5	50.3	84.0	37.9
1970	115.9	37.1	37.4	131.8	52.6	91.2	54.1
1971 †	115.8	46.2	39.5	136.6	57.0	99.7	60.4

Source: Economic Report of the President, 1972, Tables B-10 and B-15, pp. 207 and 212.
* Includes all federal, state, and local taxes paid by individuals, but not social security payments.
† Data for 1971 are provisional.

public goods in 1971 by paying that amount in personal taxes. Even an individual's personal tax bill understates the consumption of public goods, since personal taxes amount to only about half of all government revenues. The rest comes from other tax sources and borrowing. Some of this may properly be classified as investment, but distinctions are unclear.

What is clear is that consumers *spend* a great deal of money through taxes. Table 9.1 shows that Americans spent more on taxes than they did on housing and twice what they spent on clothing. Despite our well-publicized, and often lamented, love affair for the automobile, we spent $2.50 on public goods for every dollar we spent on automobiles; and for every dollar the American consumer managed to save, almost two dollars went to the government in taxes. Among the principal expenditure categories, only food accounts for more than taxes. At least it still costs more to feed ourselves than it does to feed the government. Yet the care and feeding of governments is still a primary expenditure for Americans; as such, it merits the same kind of attention given to private spending.

The Special Problem of Public Goods

Clearly, no treatment of consumer economics that failed to consider public goods would be complete. But if it is proper to speak of consuming public goods in the same way as consuming private goods, why not treat them together? The answer is that while both represent consumption, there is an important distinction between the two. With private goods you can purchase or not, and hence pay or not, according to your own individual taste. With public goods, you have no such option. They are supplied collectively, to the community as a whole, and the community as a whole pays. This follows from the fact that public goods are by nature indivisible; they cannot be supplied to one person without supplying them to everyone. If you live in an apartment, your unit cannot very well be supplied with fire protection without the whole building's being supplied [3, pp. 23–24]. Thus everyone benefits, whether you pay for the protection alone or whether everyone in the building pays. Similarly, if you pay to have a street light installed in front of your house, your neighbors will benefit from the light, even though you are paying for it.

When everyone benefits (potentially, at least), there is a strong argument for having everyone pay. This suggests an alternative statement of the same point. It is often said that there are *externalities* involved in the consumption of certain goods, which means that the benefit is external to (or goes beyond) the individual. Such is the case in both examples above, fire protection and street lighting. Education also involves externalities, for while it benefits the individual, it benefits the society as a whole too. Thus, all taxpayers pay for education, whether or not they (or a member of their family) are actually in school.

These examples are reasonable enough, but the issue is not always so simple. Problems arise because not everyone benefits to the same degree from public goods. Individual consumption is based on individual preferences, whereas public goods are collective. Therefore, individuals cannot adjust the consumption of public goods to meet their own tastes. Suppose, for example, that you do not wish to consume so much national defense. You could write the secretary of defense and ask that your name be scratched from the next heat of the arms race, but that would only ensure that you would make it into some FBI file. You cannot even risk jail by not paying your taxes to support the military—in the manner of Henry David Thoreau —because the most important taxes are withheld before you ever receive your income.

Decisions about consuming public goods are made collectively. The entire community decides on the level of taxation and the pattern of expenditures. To illustrate this point, Douglass North commented that

> the Seattle City Council voted to permit 21 murders, 104 rapes, 962 robberies and 417 assaults, as well as various numbers of lesser crimes, in the first half of 1970. [13, pp. 114–20]

The city council, of course, did not vote on rape and murder, but it did allocate a specific sum to law enforcement. The level of crime followed from the level of enforcement. Some citizens might have wanted more enforcement, others less. Once a particular level was chosen, however, everyone had to accept it as an expression of the community's preferences.

Does this mean that it is necessary to build an entirely new analysis for public goods? Emphatically, and happily, no. Our conclusions about consumer strategies apply equally well to public goods. A change is called for, however, in that our analysis so far must be amplified and extended to account for the fact that the direct link between cost and benefit (or taste and consumption) is broken with public goods.

For the consumer, the problem is still maximization of satisfaction on a given income. Since consumers lack *direct* decision-making power over the portion of their income that goes to public goods, they must exercise what power they have to ensure that public expenditures generally reflect their own preferences. In a small community made up of similar types of people, this may not be too serious a problem (illustrated by the way in which suburbs generally support their schools). In a larger community like the nation, consensus is likely to be lacking; that leads to extended, often bitter, debates, as reflected in all the recent talk about "reordering national priorities."

Those who favor such a reordering are really saying that they do not like the way public goods are currently being allocated. To bring about a change, it is necessary for them to win over the majority within the community. As the range of problems that the country faces becomes broader and as more and more individuals develop their own perceptions of these problems, the public debate on such questions can only increase. We can predict, therefore, that the debate on priorities, goals, the allocation of public goods, or whatever name you choose to call it, will continue into the future.

Although there is a considerable literature on these topics in public finance, political science, and public administration, it is usually not written from the consumer's point of view. The need is to analyze these ideas from the consumer's perspective, developing the notion of public goods as an extension of private consumption. Having said that, however, it is necessary to add that consumers themselves often act as if they do not see things in that light. Because this point colors the whole analysis and therefore the consumer's perception of public goods, it must be explored before the specifics of the problem are considered.

The Underlying Bias

While public goods and services are purchased through tax payments, there is evidence that most people do not see it that way. Their attitude is reflected in everyday manners of speech. The typical consumer would say that he "bought a vacuum cleaner" or "bought a garbage-disposal." When similar services—such as street cleaning or trash collection—are publicly supplied, however, those same people would not speak of *buying* them, only of *paying* the taxes. This demonstrates a fundamental bias; with private goods, the focus is on the benefit, while with public goods, it is on the cost [8, p. 110].

Again it is John Kenneth Galbraith who has served as the public's conscience in publicizing this double standard. He was among the first to note that we view even frivolous private goods with pride, but look at the most significant public goods with regret [8, 109–10]. Thus, the parent who grumbles about higher taxes for education will in the next sentence extol the virtues of his new electric can opener. There is an obvious inconsistency here; on the one hand, there is our infatuation with gadgets, on the other the view that

> public services . . . are a burden which must, in effect, be carried by private production . . .
>
> At best, public services are a necessary evil; at worst they are a malign tendency against which an alert community must exercise eternal vigilance. [8, pp. 109–10]

If it is not immediately clear to you why eternal vigilance should be required against such things as education, community health services, or public recreational facilities, you are beginning to see the point. Public goods are *different* from private goods because of the externalities involved, but they are *not* by nature *inferior*. They are provided, as private goods are, to satisfy particular wants. The fact that so many people miss this point and view government production as sterile may stem from simple shortsightedness, or it may reflect a reverence for the rugged individualist and the free enterprise system. Yet the need for government services is so inescapable that it seems obvious to ask Professor Galbraith's question: How can "a system which still rejoices in the name of free enterprise in truth be so dependent on government?" [9, p. 296].

These ideas were organized earlier into one of the fundamental precepts of the Galbraithian system—the theory of *social balance*. It is generally recognized that most production is complementary, if there are to be more automobiles, there must be more steel, more rubber, more gasoline, and more junkyards. Since these are largely private goods, the market maintains a balance. However, more automobiles also require more roads, more traffic control equipment, more police, and more attention to the problems of congestion. These are public goods and their growth has generally not kept up with developments in the private sector.

In the extreme, this "private opulence and public squalor" leads to impaired economic performance (ask a business person how many important appointments he or she missed because of planes circling over crowded airports). In a positive sense, it can be said:

> By failing to exploit the opportunity to expand public production, we are missing opportunities for enjoyment we might otherwise have had. Presumably, a community can be as well rewarded by buying better schools or better parks as buying bigger automobiles. By concentrating on the latter rather than the former, *it is failing to maximize its satisfactions.* [8, p. 204, emphasis added]

That is an important observation about citizen-consumers. It suggests that their *perception of government may be inconsistent with their own self-interest.* The reason should be clear. Citizen-consumers use government services, paying for them with income they would otherwise have spent themselves to improve their well-being. Public goods thus emerge as an alternative to private consumption. Using opportunity costs as a measure, the benefit from public goods should equal the benefit from private expenditures.

In fairness to the consumer, it should be noted that the link between public goods and satisfaction often seems remote. Education, for example, bestows long-term benefits, which may not be immediately apparent. Other public services, like police protection, are most effective when they are least obvious. A crime wave brings criticism of police and charges that they aren't doing their job. However, when peace and quiet prevails, police receive less attention and are seldom credited with promoting tranquillity.

This in itself underscores the importance of public goods. If citizen-consumers view public services as inferior or fail to recognize the contribution they make to individual welfare, their perception gets in the way of their own self-interest. It follows that if consumers actually want to maximize satisfaction, they must develop a strategy to deal with the consumption of public goods.

CONTROLLING PUBLIC GOODS

A Strategy for Public Consumption

Citizen-consumers cannot say they want to consume this much education or that many highways, the way they would if they were buying breakfast cereal or clothing. Decisions about collective goods are not made by individuals, but by the officials they elect to represent them. Even if the citizen-consumer is asked to express an opinion on a specific question, as in the case of a referendum on a school levy, the electoral process is still involved. This suggests that if the citizen-consumer is to have any hopes of maximizing satisfaction, it will be necessary to duck into the nearest phone booth and emerge as that mythical character known as the informed voter. You know how the script runs. Voters must take an interest in campaigns, learn the issues, identify the position of the candidates, and develop their own opinions so that (if they are not too exhausted) they can vote intelligently. Anyone who does less is automatically suspect and probably un-American.

Even with the dimensions of the problem only vaguely defined, it is clear that this view is naive. The citizen-consumer is expected to vote for candidates who, if elected, will make decisions about the public goods the consumer receives. But when you consider all that is involved, the prospect is appalling. There is such a wide range of public goods that it is almost impossible for the voter to know what they are, let alone the candidate's position on all of them.

A voter in South Dakota, for example, can hardly be expected to know where his or her congressman stands on the question of subsidies to the United States merchant marine. Yet these subsidies represented a direct cost to the taxpayers of $750 million in 1971, and indirectly contributed to high prices through high transportation costs [15, p. 174]. That is almost $10 for every American taxpayer, and while that may not seem like much, there are probably a lot of things our friend in South Dakota would rather have done with the $10.

The magnitude of the problem facing citizen-consumers is now apparent. How can they hope to unravel all the issues involved in a vote on municipal bonds or annexation, let alone such things as agricultural price supports, tariff policy, or the merchant marine. They can't. Having been told all their lives that it is their duty to be well informed, when they find this to be an almost impossible task, they are likely to be filled with self-recrimination about their failure. The voter ends up as a frustrated non-participant, not the well-informed supercitizen of the textbooks.

The emphasis on the costs of information about public issues echoes the consideration of information costs related to private consumption. Is it valid to compare them? Consider the question for a moment. Consumers need information before they buy and will continue to seek it as long as the expected savings is greater than the cost of the search (Chapter 5, pp. 86–89). Similarly, voters must seek information, and if this analogy is correct, they should seek it only as long as the expected return is greater than the cost of obtaining the information. This leads to the surprising conclusion that it may be rational for the voter to be uninformed on at least some issues.

Anthony Downs, who helped pioneer this line of analysis, reaches a similar conclusion. He emphasizes that the political system, like the economic system, features specialization and the division of labor. Information gathering is among these specialities. As a result, large quantities of information are available if the individual voter seeks them out. Downs concludes that to reduce the costs of information "it may be rational for a man to delegate part or all of his political decision making to others . . ." [6, p. 233]. To delegate decision making, voters take the word of a trusted friend, or an independent research group or newspaper, rather than investigate all the issues themselves.* It is still the citizen who votes, but his or her ballot is cast according to the direction of others in the sense that the responsibility for making the decision has been delegated. Most people behave in this fashion, since few make up their minds completely independently.

An election for judges will illustrate this theme. It is difficult to get

* Many people follow this practice in a negative fashion. If, for example, they consistently disagree with a particular newspaper, they define their position by taking the exact opposite view to the view the paper takes. This is a rational approach, as long as one's enemies are chosen carefully.

enough information to make an intelligent decision in such cases. However, the local bar association or some other citizens' group usually makes endorsements. The voter who delegates responsibility to such groups has a sound basis for judgment. Those who do not will most likely have to vote randomly or according to whim.

Voters must exercise great caution in delegating responsibility. It is obvious that such responsibility can only be given to an individual or group that the voter has come to respect and that reflects the voter's own goals and aspirations. The selection process may be difficult, but it is rational so long as the cost of an incorrect decision is less than the costs of obtaining the information individually.

Political parties may seem an obvious source of direction, but Downs issues a warning in that regard. Parties, Downs argues, are interested in maximizing votes, which is to say winning elections. They are not interested in a particular social state per se. Therefore, a rational voter

> cannot assume members of any party have goals similar to his own. But without this assumption, delegation of all political decisions to someone else is irrational—hence political parties can never be the agents of rational delegation. [6, p. 234]

This process of delegation helps explain the common phenomenon of seemingly indifferent citizens who suddenly become active when an issue touches them directly. The individual who never thought much about freeways becomes the bane of the city council when someone proposes a freeway through his backyard. It is common to criticize such people, charging them with indifference to all problems but their own. Yet they may be acting quite rationally if they feel that such decisions are too important to delegate, despite the high costs of information, communication, and action. At the national level, these costs are correspondingly higher, and such examples are less common.

It may seem that the preceding analysis does not fit with the earlier contention that the citizen-consumer needs to recognize the importance of public goods as consumption. The two are consistent, however, if the voter is delegating the right decisions to the right groups. Remember that we have held only that citizen-consumers should develop a strategy to deal with the issues that affect them, not that they should be informed on everything. Consumers who delegate some decision making have evolved a rational strategy to serve their self-interest at the least cost to themselves. Control and consumption of public goods, then, finally emerges as something quite like control and consumption of private goods. The difference is that with private goods, these principles are applied to the goods themselves, while with public goods, the application is a step removed. Citizen-consumers control public goods through the political process, but this added difficulty changes neither the basic problem facing consumers nor their approach.

The Level of Government—A Fable

In the American system, thinking about government in the singular is usually inappropriate. Citizens confront governments at all levels, so that while the Department of Defense is government, so are the New York Port Authority, the State of Washington, the Cleveland Public School District, and the Omaha Public Power District—and that is just a sample. Some people see this smorgasbord of governments as the real solution to the problem of citizen control. They feel that big government is too remote to reach the people it is supposed to be serving. If citizens cannot control government because it has grown so far removed from their day-to-day lives, then the obvious solution is to bring government "back to the people."

There is certainly nothing new about the suggestion that individuals are best served by the governments closest to them. Its current popularity, however, can be traced to the tremendous growth in the federal establishment over the past generation. Since the country's problems have grown at least as fast as the government, there are grounds for maintaining that big government is not the answer. This view has recently emerged from within the federal government and is reflected in the program of federal revenue sharing with state and local governments.

There is something to this idea. In terms of our earlier analysis, it is possible to contend that state and local governments can better serve the people. It does stand to reason that the voter should be able to exercise more effective control over local officials. Individual voters may not feel they have much impact in a national election, but locally their votes, and those of friends, are very important. This is analogous to our earlier argument that consumers can be more effective in smaller markets; the logic is the same in both cases.

Furthermore, while issues may still be complex, they are likely to be less complicated than those at the national level; as a result, information costs are lower. This also relates to citizen-consumers' view of their self-interest, which should be clearer in local elections. Urban voters may be forgiven if they do not know where they stand on agricultural price supports, but they should certainly know what they think about the schools their children attend and the streets they travel to work.

Citizen-consumers have another element of control at the local level that they cannot exercise in national politics. If they really are opposed to policies in a particular area, they can "vote with their feet," and leave. True, a person can leave the country too, and some do, but this is an extreme step. It is not so extreme, however, to move from one area to another if you do not like the way things are going. Thus, those who feel that education should be well financed can congregate in areas where it is, and those who like low taxes can move to low-service areas.

Table 9.2 is only a sample of states in different parts of the country, but it clearly shows the marked variation that exists in both taxation and

TABLE 9.2   **Property Taxes and Expenditures Per Capita: Selected States, by Region—1962**

State	Property taxes	Expenditures*
Massachusetts	$167	$215
New York	226	414
Illinois	130	175
Minnesota	132	205
South Carolina	33	91
Alabama	23	105
Texas	83	144
Colorado	125	224
California	155	269

Source: *County & City Data* [4, Table 1]
* Total expenditures, excluding capital outlay.

public expenditures (and hence the level of services). Some care must be taken in interpreting these statistics; if population is relatively sparse, services are going to be more expensive to provide on a per capita basis (as in Colorado). On the other hand, concentrations of population create new problems, and costs rise (as in New York).

Nevertheless, the variation is still marked. For every public dollar spent in South Carolina, $4.54 is spent in New York, and even if costs are higher in New York, that still reflects a marked difference in public goods supplied. There are two ways to look at these differences. One is to assume that they reflect actual community tastes; in that case, they represent the level of public goods actually demanded in different states. The other is to conclude that the variation shows that some areas are undersupplied with public goods, a situation that reduces individuals' level of satisfaction and impairs economic performance.

Elements of both explanations are involved. To explain these disparities fully, it is necessary to explore economic organization, social structure, and historical development. It is logical to assume that the demand for public services will be higher in some areas than in others, but the extreme inequalities that exist clearly work to the disadvantage of some citizen-consumers. Balancing these needs will remain important in the years to come.

The state-to-state variation in expenditures is not the only problem in this area. While the theory says that government closer to the people should be more effective, it doesn't always work that way. To illustrate, consider the tragicomic experience of a group of Long Island citizens who tried to have a traffic light installed. Now installation of a traffic signal may seem like an insignificant undertaking, but you would have a hard time making that point with the parents from Port Washington, New York, who felt that such a signal was needed between their library and elementary school.

The area around Port Washington consists of four incorporated villages and several square miles of unincorporated area. It also includes seven special districts for such things as school, police, and sewer services. When the parents went forth in search of the traffic signal, they found that the school was in the township, but the library was in the village. As if that were not complicated enough, they discovered that the street that ran between the two

> was a county road, but located in and patrolled by the Port Washington Police District, which is independent of the village, town and county. [10, p. 73]

If you are keeping score, that is four different jurisdictions within a matter of a couple of hundred feet. The parents found that while the county controlled traffic lights on county roads, the town controlled parking on the street. Not surprisingly, the parents felt the whole venture was an exercise in windmill tilting as their request was passed from one jurisdiction to another.

A year after they had begun, the parents still had nothing to show for their efforts but a "No Parking" sign, which was recommended to the county "on the spurious theory that speeding drivers and anxious children would have a better view of each other" after the police rejected the request for a light [10, p. 274]. They had found that the fragmentation of responsibility among the different jurisdictions made it practically impossible to find out who had final authority. This in turn sheltered those with authority from public pressure, for they were able to hide among the many boards, commissions, and councils.

That is not to say, however, that groups in authority are immune from pressure. Well-organized citizens with specific goals operate among them effectively. The problem is that the goals of these citizen organizations often bear only faint resemblance to anything that can be identified as the public interest. If the special-interest groups are concerned about the general public interest, it is merely as a means to advance their own aims. Recent developments in New Orleans illustrate the point. The case revolves around that most American of monuments, the football stadium. Glittering new stadia —domed, of course—are supposed to be a symbol of civic pride and accomplishment. At least that is what the people of New Orleans were told when they were asked to approve a $35 million stadium. They were also told, it is worth pointing out, that the stadium complex would be financially self-supporting and that no public funds would be involved in its operation [4, p. 178].

Only after the issue had been approved did anyone bother to point out that the referendum gave the Louisiana Stadium Exposition District (which again is local government!) unlimited authority to issue bonds and that these would be publicly guaranteed. It then developed that the stadium would probably not be self-supporting and that public money would be needed to subsidize its operation. At last report, the cost of the stadium had passed $100 million and was still growing—although the stadium itself was not; design difficulties had slowed its construction [4, pp. 178–79].

What had happened was that, in effect, the public had voted to allow the misappropriation of public money. The amounts involved are not very big; after all, the Defense Department can eat up $65 million with the cost overrun on one jet fighter. The point is that the public had been "badly deceived," and that taxes paid by all the people were going to benefit only a few people [4, p. 178]. The stadium, if it is ever completed, will be an impressive structure; unfortunately, it will be as much a symbol of private manipulation of public interests as a monument to sport.

It says something about present-day America that the battle of New Orleans is being fought in cities across the country. The shift of professional football from New York to New Jersey created a big political incident, and so did the related plans for the construction of a stadium. Some cities have fared better. In Seattle, plans for a new stadium went forward under the careful scrutiny of a public board, while in Boston, a new stadium was financed through private commercial means and is doing quite well [4, pp. 104–105]. A scheme similar to that carried out in New Orleans was attempted in Minnesota, but it was uncovered before the vote. Minnesota fans may still have to shiver through their games, but at least their civic pride is intact.

The obvious point is that local government is not so well equipped to handle local problems as many believe. The problems of fragmentation and domination of special interests are merely representative of others that have been engendered by years of neglect and poor management. This happened because citizen-consumers let it happen, those same individuals who are now calling for local control. Volumes have been written on these developments. To explain them, it is necessary to consider public apathy, an increasingly mobile citizenry, structural changes in the economic and social life of the community, and the emphasis on national programs the federal government administers.

The problem is complicated by the differing forces at work on local government. On the one hand, there is an increasing demand for locally supplied services, such as police protection and education. At the same time, many problems are truly national in scope and therefore cannot be handled at the local level. This means that while local government is becoming increasingly important to citizen-consumers, it does not represent any magic formula that can be applied to all problems. Those who favor local government simply because it is local have unfortunately missed that rather obvious point. A two-step process is involved here; the first is to identify the areas for which local government can be effective and the second is to equip such government with the tools to do the job. Assuming that any local government can take on any problem is a good way to ensure frustration and failure.

The pattern of local government is most notable for its variation. Progressive reforms in some areas have shown that local government can serve the individual in his capacity both as a consumer and as a citizen. The need is to expand the reforms so that benefits can be enjoyed by citizen-consumers in all parts of the country. This will not take place until citizen-consumers have organized to press for improvements and to demand that their governments respond to their needs [6, p. 257].

THE BUREAUCRATS AMONG US

The Bureaucratic Hang-up

If there is one outstanding feature of modern life, it is bureaucracy. No discussion of the consumer and public goods would be complete without considering it. While most of us like to think about government in grand terms, global strategies, and national goals, we are much less concerned with such things than we are with the elements of government that touch our day-to-day lives. Citizens may be concerned about foreign policy, but they seldom become as enraged about it as they do when the Department of Motor Vehicles makes a mistake in their automobile registration.

It can be argued that when people speak of making the government *responsive*, as they are increasingly prone to do, they really mean making the bureaucracy responsive. The bureaucracy has the power to make decisions that affect the citizen-consumer most directly. At the most superficial level, it is a problem of perception. Individuals see their own cases as unique, as not conforming to the general rule because of exceptional circumstances. To the bureaucrat, who sees thousands of such cases, the individual's case is no different from others, so it is treated according to established patterns.

A more fundamental problem with bureaucracy, however, goes beyond momentary inconvenience. It concerns bureaucratic intrusion and suggests that such things may impinge on democratic processes. Totalitarian states, like Fascist Spain and the Soviet Union, tend to be highly bureaucratized, while pure democracy, as in the New England town meeting, features direct citizen control. The natural conclusion is that bureaucracy, if not itself un-democratic, is at least a threat to democratic principles [2, p. 103]. In this context, the growing bureaucracy in a country such as the United States is ominous and foreboding. Writing almost two decades ago, Peter Blau noted that "the more a person values equality, the more objectionable is the experience of being subjected to the controlling power of officials" [2, p. 103]. As bureaucracy has grown over the years since Blau's writing, the cause for taking offense has intensified.

Any solution to this problem must surely take into account why the bureaucracy is there in the first place. It is there to provide services. It may be unappealing, but it must be admitted that the bureaucrat is needed, for it is through the bureaucracy that a great deal of public consumption takes place. The legislature can pass enlightened laws and propose progressive programs, but it remains for the bureaucracy to carry them out. Therefore, anyone who rages against the bureaucracy for making society more complex has missed the point. It is the society that has made the bureaucracy more complex. As society has grown, so have the programs needed to deal with its problems. As a result, the bureaucracy needed to administer these programs has grown. To reduce the bureaucracy, it is necessary to reduce the complexity of the society, but that is unlikely since it is impossible to put the country in a time machine, twist a few dials, and return to the simplicity of the good old days.

Thus it is necessary to recognize the bureaucracy for what it is. That recognition includes the realization that bureaucracy can be a way of strengthening democracy and assuring equal treatment for all citizens. It is in this regard that the nation's experience with the Watergate affair has proven instructive. The common element in the various scandals was that individuals felt that they were not bound by routine procedures. The excesses that grew out of this attitude show the need for a fair and impartial bureaucracy that functions without discrimination or favoritism.

It is clear that the citizen's position in the political system parallels the consumer's position in the marketplace. In both roles, individuals need to equip themselves to deal with their present environment. In this case, that means ensuring that the bureaucracy is responsive. The task of the citizen-consumer is to make sure that the bureaucracy functions as an agent of public consumption and that it does so with humanity and efficiency but without bias.

Support Your Local Bureaucrat

Proper functioning of a bureaucracy cannot be achieved easily. Indeed, it cannot be achieved at all unless the general bias against public goods is removed. This bias works against bureaucrats too. An official in a private firm is an *executive*, while someone with a similar position in government is a *bureaucrat*, even though the former may be part of a larger bureaucracy than the latter.* There is no reason to cloak the executive in gray-flannel respectability while portraying the bureaucrat as a mean-spirited individual in eyeshade and sleeve garters.

Public bureaucracies in general are probably neither much better nor much worse than private ones, but they bear a much heavier burden of abuse. Some of it may be warranted, but citizen-consumers cannot expect better services until they are willing to improve the image of the public service. Beyond that, they must be willing to provide the necessary tools. This means modernization and professionalization. It also means more money, which will not sit well with the citizen-taxpayer. But since the citizen-consumer and the citizen-taxpayer are the same person, the need to pay in order to consume quality services is obvious.

Certainly there is room for improvement in public administration. Much of it arises from early neglect, rooted in public misconception. Public

---

* Companies like General Motors and AT&T have more employees and deal with larger amounts of money than most state and local governments in the United States do.

positions have typically been viewed in political as well as economic terms. Thus, through patronage, these jobs became the standard means for politicians to reward the party faithful. Even with the advent of civil service, efficiency too often took a back seat to political considerations.

There is another problem with public bureaucracy that has nothing to do with politics. It is a simple question of size. In the larger cities and states and at the federal level, the bureaucracy has grown so large that it is difficult to operate. While there is pressure for efficient operation, it is seldom sustained. Commissions investigate the problem, their recommendations receive front-page treatment and then, after some minimal efforts, they are forgotten. That is doubly unfortunate because bureaucracies generate their own momentum that creates a pressure for expansion. Anyone familiar with any bureaucracy knows that it is a minisociety with its own status symbols and internal logic. Thus, a clever department head enhances his or her position by expanding the department's staff.

Left unchecked, these tendencies confirm a variation of Parkinson's law, that the amount of work will expand according to the number of people to do it. With more people, the available work is merely divided up into smaller and smaller portions. The bureaucracy then takes on a life of its own and becomes its own reason for being. Citizens, whom the bureaucracy is supposed to be serving, may be looked on as intruders. This problem is real enough, but it needs to be seen for what it is, a technical, organizational question. Too often, discussions of the topic take on emotional overtones that hardly contribute to a solution. How can the bureaucracy most efficiently do the job it is supposed to do? That is the question. Attacks against the bureaucracy are often really directed at the program that is being administered, a confusion that only clouds the picture and makes effective management more difficult.

Citizen control of the bureaucracy presents greater difficulty than the control of elected officials. The latter, at least, must be concerned about the next election. The bureaucrat, however, holds his position by either appointment or a civil-service test. The very professionalization called for above creates a problem. Well-trained professionals may see their responsibility in terms of their specific job, not in terms of the public. This is often a problem with local planning boards, for example, which tend to be preoccupied with technical questions.

A very delicate point arises. It is necessary to insulate the bureaucracy from political pressure and yet at the same time maintain public control and ensure that the bureaucracy is responsive. Balancing these two needs is difficult and requires continual review. The key here is the elected official. While bureaucracies are not responsible to the electorate, elected officials are responsible for the bureaucracy and are therefore vulnerable to pressure.

The public cannot, and probably should not, hope to dominate the day-to-day operations of government. The citizen-consumer's role is to establish the limits within which the bureaucracy will work and the ground rules that will govern its operation. This is very near to the point we reached about effective consumer protection. The important decision for the consumer is to decide in favor of effective protection. Once that decision is made, elected representatives can be presented with an ultimatum: Produce or be voted out. The same is true in this case; the decision must be applied to ensure action.

SOME NEW APPROACHES

The Ombudsman

The traditional methods of citizen control of public goods have concerned us thus far. Recently, efforts have been under way to provide the citizen-consumer with additional instruments of control. These efforts have covered different approaches, most of which are still experimental. They deserve attention as a response to a basic problem. The three examined here are offered to illustrate the direction that such efforts are taking, but they do not exhaust all possibilities.

It is not surprising in these days of imports that one of the best known of these attempts should be from abroad. The idea of the ombudsman comes from Scandinavia and has been widely adopted in Europe. The ombudsman is simply a public advocate, the representative of the public in government. He functions, as one authority noted, to

> provide protection and redress to the individual citizen against abuses by an increasingly remote, yet omnipresent administrative process . . . (and) . . . provide an institution capable of demanding certain standards of conduct and perhaps even of suggesting reorganization. . . . [1, p. 236]

In terms of our previous discussion, the ombudsman becomes an information agent, helping the individual find his way among the maze of organizations that characterize modern government. He also. ensures that citizens receive fair treatment before these various bodies. In a sense then, the function of the ombudsman is to even up the odds and give the citizen a fair chance against government organization.

The common-sense argument for the ombudsman is so compelling that it is not surprising that citizens' groups should be calling for the creation of such a position. The issue is not simple, however, since questions arise about the powers of the ombudsman, his responsibilities and position within the structure of government, and his relation to other governmental groups. There are also questions as to how effective an ombudsman could be, particularly at the federal level. The performance of the various regulatory agencies, which seem continually to overlook their stated purpose of maintaining the public interest, does not portend well for the ombudsman.

Nevertheless, various state and local governments have adopted the ombudsman proposal in one form or another. Though such operations are generally small-scale, they have demonstrated their ability to help citizens in their dealings with government. Even critics of the idea indicate that it may hold considerable merit at those levels [11, pp. 246–55].

It would be a mistake to think of the ombudsman as a magic remedy to the problems that face the citizen-consumer. Such an office can cut the individual's information costs and promote an understanding of how government functions. Responsibility remains with the individual, however; if the ombudsman's office is to be more than a hand-holding operation, the citizen-consumer must be willing to demonstrate the kind of initiative we have from time to time indicated.

Decentralization

Involved is such an overworked word these days, that it is often difficult to tell exactly what it means. It is commonly used, however, in reference to a reform that has gained considerable attention. The logic behind its approach is simple and straightforward. If government programs are actually to serve the people, then the people should be involved in their formulation and administration. By extension, this line of thinking leads to decentralization and to community control of local programs, responsibility being returned to the people in the literal sense. Such proposals have taken two main forms. The first is direct citizen participation in government programs like Model Cities, where local residents are involved in the project from its inception. The second is the administration of existing institutions, such as city schools; in this case, responsibilities are taken from a central administration and vested in groups in various neighborhoods.

These experiments have met massive resistance from established administrative units. Both power and money are involved, making the whole question hypersensitive. City officials do not want to see independent and potentially competitive sources of power springing up within the city. Nor do established organizations want to give up power to smaller units. Predictably, the results of such efforts are confused and confusing. Detached, objective evaluations are difficult to find, but certain shortcomings are evident. Daniel Moynihan, who has worked on the question both in government and in private life, asked why such programs "have had a measure of success, but nothing like that hoped for?" He answers his own question with this disturbing observation:

> It may be we have not been entirely candid with ourselves in this area. Citizen participation . . . is in practice a "bureaucratic ideology," a device whereby public officials induce non-public individuals to act in the way the officials desire. [12, p. 33]

If this is true, then citizens' power is an illusion, and illusions seldom last. If local leaders try to develop programs that they feel are meaningful, differences in perception bring them into conflict with both local and federal officials. These often lead to disillusionment on the part of the citizens and resentment in the community at large.

Decentralization of administration has run into similar problems. In most large cities, the administration of government is so far removed from the individual that there is little identification between the two. Particular areas, representing racial or ethnic groups with their own traditions, typically feel that they are poorly served. The logic of decentralization is to give these people decision-making power over the policies that directly affect them.

There are a host of problems associated with decentralization. This seemingly simple proposal for fragmentation of power may reduce the ability to meet problems in a coordinated fashion. At the extreme, decentralization may destroy the city per se, reducing it to a series of neighborhoods. There should be an optimal mix of centralized and decentralized authority that offers the benefits of both cohesive action and community control. Were there no other elements involved, it could no doubt be found. Other elements are involved, however, complicating the already complicated question. These include racial, social, and economic questions that tend to escalate the level of rhetoric, if not the level of performance. Problems of entrenched power also develop and existing institutions resist any change. One New York official noted that the demand for decentralization has gone beyond merely administration to include policymaking. He continued:

> Skepticism about government processes has gone so far that unelected people—"community leaders"—demand that they be the adjudicators of policy; no Solomon arises to distinguish between the true community leader and the false community leader, so that the process of decision becomes further delayed. [16, p. 31]

Decentralization and community control offer urban dwellers nothing more than the advantages enjoyed by other citizens. Although citizens are free to move if they do not like their local government, this does not apply to the poor and to those who feel a strong attachment to an area. If these groups want more to say in government policy, they must seek it from the government they have. If you reverse this argument, it is possible to maintain that if there were more community control, the flight from the cities might be reduced as individuals found they could attain their goals without moving to the suburbs. America's preoccupation with bigness—the bigger-is-better syndrome—has resulted in the uncritical acceptance of continued growth in urban areas, even though this growth was unplanned and largely unpatterned.

In the nation's largest cities, there is little that can be done about what is in existence; things must be dealt with as they are. The past opportunities that were missed should provide a lesson for the future, however.

TABLE 9.3   Expenditures Per Capita for Selected Categories, by City Size, 1971

Category	City size in thousands *		
	Over 1,000	300–500	50–100
All functions	$569	$271	$189
Education †	107	57	35
Highways	20	21	20
Public welfare	109	6	3
Hospitals †	47	7	6
Police and fire	79	48	38
Sewage and sanitation †	32	28	20
Parks and recreation	13	20	12

Source: Municipal Yearbook, 1973, pp. 98–99.
NOTE: All figures are rounded to the nearest dollar.
* There are 6 cities in the largest class, 21 in the middle, and 231 in the smallest.
† Includes capital outlay.

Many experts feel that a population of about 250,000 is an optimal size for cities. This is large enough for efficient operation, but still small enough to be manageable.

This notion is borne out in Table 9.3, which compares the costs of city services per person in cities of different size. Cities of more than one million spend exactly three times as much per person as cities in the fifty to one-hundred thousand class do, and over twice as much as cities with populations just under half a million. While expenditures on highways are remarkably stable, most other areas show a marked increase. This is most dramatic with welfare costs, which are insignificant in the smaller cities, but account for the largest single expenditure category in the largest cities.* Unfortunately, expenditures for parks and recreation—a quality-of-life category—are about the same in the largest and smallest group, but higher in between.

This suggests that better planning, controlled city growth, and a nationwide population policy are needed to ensure that cities of the future are not merely extensions of those we have. The goal should be more livable cities, where services are delivered efficiently. The periodic breakdown of public services in some of our big cities should underscore this point. The cities we have, however, must be managed. A practical method must be worked out that will involve the people in their own government and yet maintain efficient overall operation. The word *community* in one sense means a group of people with shared experiences and aspirations. It is probable that such a feeling is necessary before the adequate delivery of public services is possible;

* This reflects the fact that the poor are concentrated in the largest cities, which in turn shows the need for a national policy to deal with population movements.

in short, people have to care. If decentralization is needed to develop that feeling, then it should be pursued. The mere fact that improvement is possible should encourage whatever efforts are necessary.

A New Public-Private Mix?

By now it should be clear that when it comes to public consumption, the citizen-consumer is sitting on the horns of a dilemma. He is in an uncomfortable position and it is tempting to say he gets shafted either way. On the one hand (or horn), the citizen-consumer needs public goods. On the other, the very nature of such goods makes individual choices difficult, if not impossible. To attack the root of the problem, it is necessary to ask whether there isn't a better way to provide public goods, one that would account for externalities while still allowing more choice for the individual? There is nothing sacred about the way things are done now. Some goods, like highways and education, are both publicly and privately supplied (toll roads versus freeways; public schools versus private). To a lesser extent, the same thing is true of medical care.

It may be possible to ensure a larger measure of private control over the distribution of public goods. The volunteer army offers a recent example. Under the draft system, anyone selected for service had to serve or face imprisonment. Since defense is a public good, it was assumed that this loss of choice was warranted. With the volunteer army, the individual has a choice. If he joins, it is because service has been made sufficiently attractive for him to choose to do so. The volunteer army is now a reality and while the transition has not been smooth, it has increased personal choice while maintaining national defense.

Another example that is gaining acceptance is the so-called voucher system for education. This approach recognizes that externalities exist in education, but, its proponents argue, the monolithic structure of public education does not really serve the public effectively. Parents and students have little choices as to what type of school they attend. The voucher system would retain public support for education, but paradoxically, do away with public schools [7, pp. 85–107]. It would give parents (or students) vouchers financed out of tax revenues that could be redeemed in educational services only. They could be spent on education at any school of the individual's choosing.

Advocates argue that this plan, by restoring competition to the educational system, would assure those who use the schools a wider choice and better quality. Since public support reaches the schools through the parents, schools that could not deliver adequate services would be driven out of business. A similar system is actually in use at the college level. Many states, even though they maintain their own state universities, provide tuition grants that enable students to attend private colleges or universities. This provides support for private schools and increases students' range of choices.

Opponents of the voucher system maintain that such an approach would produce chaos, promote racial and socioeconomic segregation, and probably spell the end of public support for education. The advent of private "academies" in areas where public schools have been integrated lends strong support to this argument. However, the potential advantages are sufficient to warrant further study of the question with an eye to overcoming possible negative side effects. Fundamental change is always difficult to achieve. In this case, a new private-public mix may not be the answer, but it does provide an alternative, which may work in some cases. If it does nothing more than force us to reexamine the way in which we approach these problems and thereby develop a clearer understanding of public consumption, it will have served a useful purpose.

A Parting Shot

The preceding pages have emphasized the importance of public consumption to the citizen-consumer, pointing to the obvious need for developing a strategy to deal with it. If there were an easy formula for taking care of the problems, there would be a lot less to say about them and decisions could be more conclusive. Unfortunately, no such formula exists, which means that citizen-consumers themselves must look after their own interests.

There is no escaping that point, but it is possible that we have been too pessimistic in assessing the consumer's chances of success. So many elements are involved and so many of them are undergoing significant change that it is difficult at times to see exactly what is happening, let alone what is going to happen. It is possible, for example, that our outlook has underestimated the power of an aware citizenry. It may be that if a few people are concerned enough to point out the problems and publicize them, public reaction will be sufficient to guarantee results. The question is, How deep do these concerns run in the public? In other words, Is consumerism in its application to the public sector a true grass-roots movement or merely a fad?

Time alone will answer that question, but our early analysis suggests a tentative reply. Recall the concept of income elasticity (Chapter 7)—that as incomes change, the demand for particular types of goods changes. Many public goods tend to have a high income elasticity, which means that as incomes rise, demand for them rises at a faster rate. Education is an example; a poor country cannot afford a highly developed educational system, but as income rises, that system is broadened and diversified. In a high-income country, education contains elements of both investment and consumption. That is, some education is vocational training, while some is for the individual's own enjoyment (an idea that may strike some college students as novel). This can be seen currently in the United States with the increased demand for adult education that is both vocational and general.

Education is not the only example. Public recreational facilities furnish another. With higher incomes, they are increasingly in demand. Even traditional services like police and fire protection become more important with high incomes. As the economy becomes still more interdependent, maintaining order becomes important if the different parts of the economy are to function effectively. All of this points to an increased demand for public goods. Put differently, it means a new recognition of the contribution that public goods make to the citizen-consumer's well-being. That is a hopeful thought, for such a recognition is the starting point for effective consumer action in the public sector. If it is possible to be optimistic about that point, then it is possible to be optimistic about solutions.

STUDY QUESTIONS

1.   Some communities try to attract new industry and residents by stressing their low taxes. What does this tell you of the community's thinking about public goods? Do you think such policies are effective? Do you think they are desirable?

2.   Many private and public goods are substitutes for one another. You can swim, for example, in a public or private pool and you could hire a guard or install alarms in lieu of police protection.
   a.   What other examples of this kind of substitution can you name?
   b.   If these goods and services can be supplied privately, why are they supplied publicly?

3.   Public and private goods may also be complements, meaning they are used in conjunction with one another. Automobiles may be private vehicles, but they are used almost exclusively on public highways. Name some other examples of complementarity. What are the implications of this kind of relation?

4.   Explain why the demand for public goods will be greater in communities that contain either high proportions of children or high proportions of elderly people.

5.   For the citizen, what are the alternatives to delegating some political decision making? Are the alternatives either realistic or desirable?

6.   Efforts are being made to revitalize local government at the same time that many local governments are being abolished. School consolidation, for example, is well advanced, and metropolitan government is being advocated (and adopted) in many urban areas. Can these two developments be reconciled? Explain.

7.   One American worker in five is employed by some level of government, while in 1929, the figure was one in ten. Does that mean that public goods are twice as important now as they were in 1929? Are twice as many public goods supplied?

8.   Between 1960 and 1970, employment in the federal government grew by less than 20 percent, while employment in state and local govern-

ment grew by over 67 percent. What does this tell you about the relative growth in demand for services provided at the local level versus those provided at the national level? Discuss. Would you expect this trend to continue?

9.   Discuss the differences between the controls that citizens have over elected officials and over members of the bureaucracy.

10.   The old-style political boss, whose machine ran the city, had ward heelers to look after voters and hear their complaints. Carefully consider the advantages such systems held for citizen-consumers. How does the ombudsman's function differ from these early caretakers of the political system?

11.   Public goods are supported out of tax monies on the assumption that everyone benefits. It is argued, however, that in many cases, the primary benefit goes to middle- and upper-income groups. If that is true, what is the impact of a policy of low tuition at state universities? Contrast the effects of a fee charged at a state park (that can be reached only by automobile) and a fee at an inner-city swimming pool.

SUGGESTED PROJECTS

1.   Does your city or state government have an office of ombudsman or a similar office responsible for helping citizens with problems? (Some universities have ombudsmen.) If so, investigate its operation, the nature of its duties, and so on. If possible, invite the ombudsman or a representative to speak to the class.

2.   How many local governmental bodies are there in your area? Count not just city and county governments, but townships, schools, independent districts, and special authorities. What is the rationale for this sort of division? Do you think the public is well served under such a system?

3.   The chapter began with the assertion that if you asked people to name the things they have consumed, they will not mention public goods. Try it on a random sample. What are the results? What does this suggest about how individuals perceive public goods?

4.   Question 3 under Study Questions suggested that while automobiles are private and highways are public, they are nevertheless complementary goods.

    a.   Calculate the taxes paid per mile a car is driven. This will require estimates of license fees, property taxes, and sales taxes, and also of miles driven and gasoline mileage (needed to calculate gasoline taxes per mile).

    b.   Find out the cost of building and maintaining a mile of highway (the figures should be available through local highway officials and in national studies). How does this compare with the figures obtained in (a)?

c.   What other public costs are attached to automobile use?

d.   Are there externalities involved in highways? Explain.

5.   If there is a model-cities project (or some similar undertaking that features citizen participation) in your area, look into its operation. Has it succeeded in involving citizens in its planning and administration? What sorts of problems have been encountered?

6.   The text did not discuss the specific taxes used to finance public goods; most areas rely primarily on taxes on property, sales, and income.

a.   What are the main revenue sources in your area?

b.   Sales and property taxes tend to be regressive (lower-income groups pay a higher percentage of their income in taxes) while income taxes are more progressive (higher-income groups pay a higher percentage). What is the implication of this fact for the provision of public goods?

c.   Would you say that in your area the cost of public goods is borne equally by all income groups? What about the benefits?

BIBLIOGRAPHY AND SUGGESTED READINGS

1. Abraham, Henry J. "The Need for an Ombudsman in the United States." In *The Ombudsman*, ed. Donald C. Rowat. London: George Allen & Unwin, 1965.

   The author outlines the functions of the ombudsman and builds a case for adopting such an office in the U.S. While some of the statistics are now out of date, this collection of original articles is still one of the most comprehensive treatments of the ombudsman concept available.

2. Blau, Peter M. *Bureaucracy in Modern Society*. New York: Random House, 1956.

   This little book remains a classic. It deals not only with the functions of bureaucracy, but also its place in a democratic society. An excellent introduction to the topic.

3. Buchanan, James M. *The Public Finances*, 3d ed. Homewood, Ill.: Richard D. Irwin, 1970.

   A public finance text that is particularly strong in its treatment of individual satisfaction and public expenditures.

4. Burck, Charles G. "It's Promoters vs. Taxpayers in the Super-Stadium Game." *Fortune*, March 1973, pp. 104–107.

   When the Colosseum was built in ancient Rome, some Romans must have wondered if maybe there was not a better way to spend the money. That is still a valid question, even though pro football has replaced Christians vs. Lions. A good exploration of public benefits vs. private.

5. U.S. Department of Commerce, *County and City Data Book*. Washington, D.C.: U.S. Government Printing Office, 1967.

Statistics and more statistics on American states, counties, and cities. Data on population, income, taxes, expenditures, and other categories.

6. Downs, Anthony. *An Economic Theory of Democracy*. New York: Harper & Row, 1957.

The appropriateness of this classic work can be seen in the problems discussed in the text. Not only is the lucidity of Downs's analysis to his credit, but also that he saw the problem before it had become popularized.

7. Friedman, Milton. *Capitalism and Freedom*. Chicago: University of Chicago Press, 1962.

More from one of America's most imaginative thinkers. Professor Friedman's ideas, including the volunteer army and negative income tax, have had a strong impact on present-day American thought.

8. Galbraith, John Kenneth. *The Affluent Society*. Boston: Houghton Mifflin Co., 1958.

The original treatment of the social imbalance theory, including forceful arguments for more careful attention to public goods.

9. Galbraith, John Kenneth. *The New Industrial State*. Boston: Houghton Mifflin Co., 1967.

Treatment of the differences between perception and reality. A fairly complete summary of the Galbraithian system.

10. Kaplan, Samuel. "The Balkanization of Suburbia." *Harpers*, October 1971, pp. 72–74.

A commuter takes time to reflect on what the proliferation of local governments means to a citizen who is trying to get something done. Well he might.

11. Krislov, Samuel. "A Restrained View." In *The Ombudsman*, ed. Donald C. Rowat. London: George Allen & Unwin, 1965.

Another look at the ombudsman, this time from a less-than-enthusiastic supporter. The author nevertheless sees value in the office.

12. Moynihan, Daniel P. "Toward a National Urban Policy." In *Problems in Political Economy, An Urban Perspective*, ed. David M. Gordon. Lexington, Mass.: D. C. Heath and Co., 1971, p. 33.

One of America's leading experts looks at the problems of the city and how they can be met. Both as an academician and a government official, Professor Moynihan has worked closely with urban problems.

13. North, Douglass, and Miller, Roger. "The Economics of Crime Prevention." In *The Economics of Public Issues*. New York: Harper & Row, 1971.

This reading, like others in the book, shows how economic analysis can be applied to public questions, and also how it is often misapplied. Other topics range from prostitution to major league baseball.

14. Phelps, Edmund S. (ed.). *Private Wants and Public Needs*, rev. ed. New York: W. W. Norton & Co., 1962.

A good collection of readings which, as the title suggests, deals with many of the questions discussed in this text. A good introduction for anyone interested in the subject.

15. Schultz, Charles L. *Setting National Priorities: The 1971 Budget.* Washington, D.C.: Brookings Institution, 1970.

A careful look at the national budget, showing how that massive document reflects national goals.

16. Starr, Roger. "The Decline and Decline of New York." *New York Times Magazine*, November 21, 1971, pp. 31ff.

The executive director of the New York Citizen's Housing and Planning Council looks at the problems of decentralization and how they can be met in a giant city.

10

The Plight
of the Low-Income
Consumer

SPECIAL PROBLEMS OF THE POOR

The Cruelest Jest of All

During the recurring rioting that plagued American cities in the late 1960s, scenes of looting and burning became a nightly feature of the news. While most Americans were appalled, few understood what was really happening and fewer still knew why. Thus, most of those gaping at their television sets would not have appreciated the subtlety in the distinction between robbing and looting made by a young man in Watts: "When you loot a credit store, you are just taking back some of the interest they have been charging you for years . . ." [10, pp. 56–57]. His reasoning was based on conditions confirmed by the National Advisory Commission on Civil Disorders—that consumer-related complaints were a primary source of unrest in the ghetto [11, pp. 139–40]. Once the wave of violence had passed, however, there was a tendency to forget about the causes of the problem. Despite the efforts of people in both public and private life, the situation in the ghetto remained much the same when an uneasy quiet descended on the cities again.

The word *paradox* has been used many times over the preceding pages, and if you are keeping score, here is yet another. While consumer problems are born out of affluence, in the America of the 1970s that affluence is not evenly shared. It would be comforting to say that since low-income groups by definition do not share the nation's affluence, they are at least exempt from the problems that accompany it. Just the opposite is true, and that is the paradox. Low-income groups must face all the problems of consumers, problems brought about by the affluence they do not share. Not only that, but they must bear a particularly heavy burden, for the very fact of their poverty makes them less able to deal with these problems than middle-income consumers.

That is why the problems of low-income consumers deserve special attention. The poor receive few of the benefits and all of the problems of the modern, consumer-oriented society. It is a two-edged sword that cuts them both ways. Setting the problem up this way provides us with our general line of analysis; within this approach, there are two implicit points that should be brought out. The first is that while low-income groups deserve special attention, they do not require a special analysis. Low-income groups can be analyzed just like the general consumer. The difference is that when poverty is taken into account, the results will be different. Our job is to take the various elements of the analysis developed thus far and ask, How does adding poverty into the equation alter the conclusions? The second point follows from the first: *The problem is poverty.* That may seem simplistic, but it is a necessary realization for improvement in the position of the poor as consumers. Treating the consumer-related problems of low-income groups is like treating the symptoms of a disease. The disease is poverty; the symptoms, however unpleasant they may be, are still only symptoms.

That means that no program to deal with the problems of the poor as consumers can hope to be successful if it does not take into account the poverty that is the root of the problem. While this chapter focuses on improving the lot of the poor as consumers, it is important to bear in mind that there can be no final cure until the disease itself is treated. Even if poverty were abolished, consumer problems would remain; there would, however, be no need to single out a special group for special attention.

The Poor—A Profile

Poverty in the midst of affluence has bothered sensitive people for generations. Poverty is never pleasant, but when it is universally shared—as it was on the frontier and is in most underdeveloped countries—its sting is less hurtful. In the United States, however, the contrasts are clearly drawn. Table 10.1 shows that while the number of people living in poverty fell by over one-third between 1959 and 1970, over 12 percent of all Americans still lived below officially designated poverty levels in 1970.* The data also show that while poverty is not a unique problem of minority groups—the white poor still outnumber nonwhite—in percentage terms, the problem is greater for nonwhites. Furthermore, improvement among nonwhites has been less rapid; while the number of whites living in poverty dropped by almost 40 percent between 1959 and 1970, the number of poor nonwhites declined by less than 30 percent. The most striking feature of the family characteristics among the poor is that over half the nonwhite poor are children, a figure that bodes ill for the future.

* Set at $3,970 for an urban family of four in 1970. [4, p. 528]

TABLE 10.1   Persons Below the Poverty Level, Selected Years, 1959–70: With Detailed Characteristics for 1970

Year	Number below poverty level (in millions)			Percentage below poverty level		
	Total	White	Other	Total	White	Other
1959	39.5	28.5	11.0	22.4	18.1	56.2
1965	33.2	22.5	10.7	17.3	13.3	47.1
1969	24.3	16.7	7.6	12.2	9.5	31.1
1970	25.5	17.5	8.0	12.6	9.9	32.1
Head of family	5.2	3.7	1.5	20.3	21.1	18.8
Minors *	10.5	6.2	4.3	41.1	35.4	53.8
Other family	4.8	3.5	1.3	18.9	20.0	16.2
Not related	5.0	·4.1	0.9	19.7	23.5	11.2
1970 as % of 1959	64.6	61.4	72.7	. . . .	. . . .	. . . .

Source: Tables 7.2 and 7.4, Cohen [4, pp. 529–30]
* Children under 18.

These figures might weigh upon the conscience of any American, but from the perspective of consumer economics, they take on added significance. They suggest that a good many poor people are permanently poor. People who have temporarily fallen on hard times may suffer, but they can hold on to the hope that things will get better. Despite the fact that the 1960s were the most prosperous years in American history, most poor people had no such hope. This in turn creates what might be called a psychology of poverty, which itself has important ramifications on the consumer. Since life is unpleasant, there is a desire to escape it through material accumulation. Commenting on this, one observer noted that the problem facing the low-income consumer

> is all the more poignant when it is realized that his pursuit of goods and credit, which in turn makes him so vulnerable to callous exploitation, is in reality what has been called "compensatory consumption," a desire to infuse his existence with dignity denied him elsewhere by accumulating material goods. [10, p. 36]

The poor may be isolated from the majority culture, but they are not insulated from it. They are exposed to all of the same pressures and urges to consume known to other Americans. In an age of instant mass communications, the vision of the good life is constantly before them, being extolled as the model for which to strive. It is not surprising that the poor should want to escape the contrast between that vision and the realities of their own existence. There is no reason to assume that even without these pressures consumption patterns among the poor should be the same as those among other groups. In considering income elasticity, we noted that consumption patterns change with income. Beyond that, it has been stressed that the particulars of individual consumption are a matter of individual tastes [8].

There is no reason to assume that these tastes are the same across the entire population. No one would be surprised to find that a Baptist minister in east Texas has a different consumption pattern from a Unitarian pastor in New York; or that a stockbroker in Sioux Falls lives differently from one in San Francisco. Yet the poor are not usually given the benefit of the doubt. That consumption patterns among the poor typically differ from middle-class norms is somehow taken as evidence of irresponsibility, whereas it is nothing of the kind. Recent experiments with the guaranteed annual income suggest that the poor are as capable of making individual consumption decisions as any other group.

Consumers in general are too often judged against an ideal norm instead of some measure that accounts for the realities of their situation. The marketplace, as it currently exists, is not a conducive environment for consumers, who must therefore overcome the problems in order to be effective. The low-income consumer labors under extra burdens. His plight puts forth a call for understanding, all the more because of the common prejudices that surround its ramifications. Efforts to understand may produce a condecending and patronizing attitude, which is nearly as damaging as judging everyone against a norm. In this analysis, we can be content to let the facts of the situation speak for themselves. There is no better way to get the story straight.

The Crux of the Problem

In the last section we maintained that the everyday problems of consumers fall most heavily on low-income groups. To put it differently, these groups are the least capable, by virtue of their low incomes, of coping with the problems all consumers face. Consumer problems arise from the consumer's lack of leverage in the marketplace. This lack of leverage comes from inadequate information, a failure to understand market mechanism, and the smallness of the individual compared with the market as a whole. The low-income consumer is particularly vulnerable.

Middle-income consumers may be ill equipped to deal with all of the problems of the marketplace, but their dollar votes give them some leverage. Most businesses are responsive to threats of "I'll take my business elsewhere" or "I'll tell my friends about this." The good will that wise businessmen value so highly makes them reasonable in the face of pressure. Consumers who remain dissatisfied can take their business elsewhere. The other tactics—talks with the manager, letters to the company, and the possibility of legal action—are all available as alternatives to the consumer. Such tactics do not always work, and they would not solve all the consumer's problems if they did, but they do offer the chance for consumers to assert themselves in the market.

There is also the question of information itself. A great deal of information is available to the consumer who can seek it out. Experience provides a lot of it. Consumers are also likely to have accumulated residual information, bits of information picked up along the way that become valuable in some later buying situation. Not only are government publications, private services like *Consumer Reports,* and assorted industry information available, but the mobile consumer can move around easily to collect more information. Contrast all of this with the condition of the low-income consumer. We begin with the fact of poverty. This means that the consumer will by definition have less market leverage. It may be a matter of debate as to how well markets respond to economic pressure, but there is no question about the fact that without purchasing power, the consumer cannot exert influence. Low-income consumers are therefore unable to defend themselves through the market mechanism.

The fact of poverty manifests itself in other ways too. It is likely to make low-income consumers less mobile. The poor have fewer private automobiles, and unless they are served by a particularly good public transportation system, the majority of their purchases are limited to stores in their immediate area. This represents a loss of leverage, since area merchants will be aware of these consumers' limitations. The same thing is true of information. There are costs attached to obtaining information, so it follows logically that those with lower incomes will be able to afford less of it. It is also likely that the poor will have less residual information, since the poor make few repetitive purchases, have a narrower range of associations, and not too much market experience.* The rural poor, who in general are quite isolated and have the least experience with the market, are especially vulnerable.

The poor are also generally disadvantaged with regard to public goods, of which education is among the most important. While attempts have been made in recent years to improve education in poor areas, inequality of educational opportunities is still to be deplored. From the consumer's perspective, education is an important source of information and skills necessary for operation in the modern marketplace.

The delivery of other public services too is typically deficient in low-income areas. Services like sanitation, parks, and libraries are often inadequate. The same is true of the quality of law enforcement, not only in police protection, but also in enforcing building codes and other consumer protection legislation. The rural poor are particularly hard hit, in many places receiving hardly any public services.

The same factors that work against low-income consumers in the mar-

---

* The poor, particularly in urban areas, will have some types of information that middle-income consumers lack. The street education that accompanies learning to survive in a ghetto environment may equip the low-income consumer to deal with some types of local consumer problems. The market in general, however, is dominated by the majority culture, so information from a subculture may not apply generally.

ketplace work against them when they seek improved public services. Their lack of political leverage stems from the same factors that reduce their effectiveness in the market. Efforts already made at improved organization, particularly in urban areas, need to be intensified. Prejudice and discrimination complicate the poverty that is at the heart of the problem. Many prejudices work against the poor in general, the idea that they are lazy or deadbeats, for example. Racial discrimination is in this category. It denies opportunities to minority groups, limits their consumption possibilities (in housing, for example), and generally weakens the will of the community to do anything about the problems that face the poor.

Taken together, these factors undermine the position of the poor in the marketplace. The consumer must draw on many resources in confronting the market; the poor, because they lack access to those resources, are systematically disadvantaged. The intensity of their disadvantage is magnified because the hazards that the poor face are greater than those that other consumers experience. Because of their vulnerability, the poor are the special targets of consumer fraud. Senator Magnuson characterizes the ghetto marketplace as a place of "trickery, deceit and fraud." Furthermore, the senator maintains that because sellers have access to legal services and low-income consumers do not, the legal system "has become perverted from a device for protecting the innocent to a means of abetting the dishonest" [10, pp. 35–36].

The problem the poor have in obtaining credit illustrates this point. Since the low-income consumer is classified as a high-risk borrower, he has trouble obtaining loans from the traditional financial institutions like banks, savings and loan associations, and credit unions. This forces him to turn to alternative sources, which often means the credit schemes that local merchants offer. Credit charges in such cases can easily run to many times the cost of the purchase, but since a legally binding contract is involved, there is little recourse for the buyer. Thus, the law is commonly turned against the poor. If they lack access to legal services, there is little they can do to protect themselves. One of the most unfortunate effects is the negative attitude that such developments create towards law enforcement and the legal system.

BEING POOR IS EXPENSIVE

The High Cost of Economy

One of the most inflammatory issues surrounding the low-income consumer is whether or not the poor actually pay higher prices for the things they buy than other consumers do. The ensuing debate has engendered

more than its share of claims, counterclaims, studies, indignation, and confusion. It is necessary to conduct a more measured examination, separating
the parts of the issue and analyzing each in turn.

One aspect that has been inadequately emphasized is fairly straightforward. The poor, by the fact of being poor, are denied many opportunities
to save money that are available to affluent consumers. Buying goods in
bulk, for example, may result in significant savings; poor consumers, however,
seldom have the money needed to cover the initial outlay. Consumers who
take advantage of sale items may also realize savings. This is true of durables,
and also of nondurables like food. The poor can be stopped by high initial
costs or inadequate storage facilities (such as freezers) or both. Limitations
on a consumer's mobility make it impractical to get to a sale, which also
forces the low-income consumer to higher-priced alternatives.

It is in such common, everyday situations as these that the low-income
consumer is hurt. Taken singly, none of them may be especially important,
but together, they represent a potentially significant source of savings that is
denied to the low-income consumer. It is often said that it takes money
to make money, but it is equally true that it takes money to save money.
Notice that in each case, the problem arises from the consumer's poverty.
The normal workings of the system tend to put the poor at a disadvantage.

All of these factors are real enough, indeed costly enough, to the poor
consumer, but they are not what is usually referred to in the poor-pay-more
argument. That argument is more complex and rests on a different set of
assertions. Not surprisingly, it is also much less clear and often more controversial. Thus, it is necessary to examine the question in detail, sort the
issues involved, and attempt a systematic analysis.

Do the Poor Pay More?

The type of consumer fraud we are concerned with here does not
involve the classical fly-by-night operation that bilks the consumer and then
moves on. Rather, it concerns established businesses, which, it is charged,
consistently take advantage of low-income consumers. It is maintained that
may businesses in low-income areas overcharge their customers so that the
poor pay more for similar products than their counterparts in affluent areas.
This controversy has been raging for over a decade. The problem began to
receive serious attention with the publication of David Caplovitz's 1963
book *The Poor Pay More*. Caplovitz's study, carried out in New York City,
suggested that low-income groups are victims of systematic gouging by
ghetto merchants. Not only were prices in ghetto areas higher, but quality
was lower than in middle-income neighborhoods; a variety of other questionable business practices also came to light [2].

The government, moved by increasing debate on the topic, began to
investigate. A congressional subcommittee found, in making a personal
check of a grocery store in Harlem, that

packaged foods were found mismarked, frozen foods were half-thawed and the manager even admitted that after two days on the shelf, packaged meat was taken back to the butcher's block, repackaged, relabeled and redated. [13, p. 16]

The condition of the stores and their products have been a primary source of complaint. In Los Angeles, one ghetto shopper commented that store managers viewed their customers as a "bunch of animals," while a second was even more blunt: "The merchants don't give a damn about Watts. They take their money back to Beverly Hills and never spend a cent fixing up their stores" [16, p. 133]. In the face of such criticism, a more systematic study was instituted. The results were surprising. The Bureau of Labor Statistics in a 1966 study found

no significant differences in prices charged by food stores located in low-income areas versus those charged by stores in higher-income areas. [12, p. 122]

The Federal Trade Commission reported three years later after a survey in Washington, D.C., and San Francisco that there was no evidence that chain store operators "employ discriminatory policies which are designed to exploit low-income customers [6, p. 3]. These findings were hardly consistent with earlier evidence and they certainly did not fit the poor's perception of their own situation. This is essentially an empirical question: Either the poor pay more, or they don't. Yet while the question can be simply stated, the procedures involved are sufficiently complex for conflicting evidence to be expected.

In making cost comparisons between high-income and low-income areas, it is not enough merely to compare the costs for a particular item in the two areas and then assume that all else is equal. On nonstandardized goods, quality must be taken into account. There is also a question about which goods are being consumed in the two areas. The typical market basket of goods for a low-income family will differ from the supply for a middle- or high-income family. Suppose potatoes are cheaper at a market in a low-income area. That is going to be significant if people buy large amounts of potatoes. If on the other hand, some luxury item is more expensive, it won't really matter if people do not actually buy it. It is necessary to know what goods people are consuming before a comparison can be made. This is difficult, because often people are buying different quantities and qualities of different items.

An equally important element to consider is that these purchases are made in *different kinds of stores*. While shoppers in high-income areas have a variety of stores to choose from, those in low-income areas do not. The facts of economic life lead large chain stores to locate in the most profitable areas. The ghetto does not qualify as a profitable area [5]. Thus, the Bureau of Labor Statistics study noted, while prices did not vary significantly if the same type of store is considered, prices are usually higher . . . in the small independent stores which are the most common in the low-income neighborhoods, than in the large independents and chain stores which predominate in the higher-income areas. [12, p. 122]

The FTC. investigation reported similar findings, noting that competition among the chain stores forced price reductions, but since there were few such stores in low-income areas, similar reductions were rare * [6, p. 3].

Summarizing this situation, a report in the *Harvard Business Review* noted that the so-called mom and pop stores predominate in low-income areas. It continued:

> Lacking economies of scale and the advantages of trained management, the "moms and pops" muddle through from day to day and, in the process, contribute to the oppressive atmosphere of such neighborhoods. Their customers generally pay higher prices, receive lower-quality merchandise and shop in shabby, deteriorating facilities. [16, p. 132]

Small stores tend to have higher operating costs than chain stores, which is why the small stores have problems in areas where the two compete. Other elements tend to increase prices in inner-city areas. Buildings are often old, increasing upkeep and insurance costs. Similarly, losses through theft tend to be high [12, pp. 339-41]. The most efficient stores want to locate where costs are low and revenues high. That keeps them out of low-income areas.

Low-income consumers find quality and range of selection lacking. The former is particularly noticeable with meats and produce. Small stores have a tendency to stock small sizes. Per unit, these are expensive, denying the consumer the potential savings of a more economical size.

This discussion has concentrated on food stores because there is more literature on the subject and because everyone has to buy food. However, the same pattern is evident with other types of establishments. Big department stores and discount stores tend to stay away from low-income neighborhoods. For consumer durables, other types of business practices may be as important as price. Credit policies, service, and the quality of the merchandise itself may affect the consumer more than high prices.

Finally, there is the matter of simple gouging through overpricing. While such practices may not be as common as some suspect, they are reported too often to be chance occurrences [10, pp. 37-41]. Even if they take place infrequently, they could still contribute to real suffering on the part of the poor. Strangely enough, the problem might be easier to deal with if it were only a question of exploitation of the poor. If that strikes you

---

* Comparisons between prices in small stores in low- and higher-income areas must be made with care. The latter tend to be either convenience stores or specialty shops, the small grocery having been driven out of such areas. Thus, they are not comparable to small groceries in the inner city.

as a strange assertion, ask yourself, "What's to be done about the problem?" The poor pay more because of the economic complexion of the community. Because of poor profit potential, only small stores with captive markets can survive in low-income neighborhoods. The real problem is that the system has broken down from the poor's point of view. The marketplace works on profits, and where there are no profits, there are no stores. The FTC report concluded:

> In situations where costs are higher in the inner city, they must be covered. Short of a government subsidy of some sort, such higher costs must ultimately be reflected in the prices charged and the services which are offered. [6, p. 6]

While human failings are involved to a degree, the real problem is that from a *social* point of view, the market has failed. It is important to add the word *social*, for in economic terms, the market is operating precisely the way you would expect. It is allocating resources to areas with dollar votes. If those dollar votes were more evenly distributed, the problem would be largely solved. Again, the problem is poverty. The basic way to attack the problem is to go to its source and attack poverty, but that is hardly an operational solution. Past efforts have shown that poverty is stronger than the public's will to deal with it. Even with a change in attitudes, the process would be time-consuming. Thus, while reducing poverty should be maintained as a long-run goal, something more immediate must be done about the problems that millions of people confront in the marketplace everyday.

Unfortunately, it is easier to agree that something needs to be done than to agree on what that *something* is. Various types of government subsidies have been tried. These include low-interest, federally backed loans and subsidized insurance programs for ghetto business people. While these have met with some success, technical and managerial advice is still needed. Such businesses also suffer from a chronic shortage of capital. Most important, the fact that the area is a poor market remains as much of a problem for the ghetto businessman as for any other.

Cooperatives offer another option. Cooperatives offer the possibility for savings as well as better service and more humane treatment. The problem here is similar to the problem facing ghetto businesses as a whole. These ventures require significant capital outlay and specialized managerial talent. Without these ingredients, and they will be difficult for most groups to obtain, the chances for success are not very bright.

One shortcoming of the solutions mentioned thus far is that they treat the problem in isolation, as if it affected only one part of the community. In fact, it is a social problem, which means it has to be considered in terms of the whole community. The solution must be developed on a communitywide basis, not in low-income areas alone. The society may not be able to do very much about poverty in the short run, but it can do something about the impact of poverty. One possibility is providing subsidies, through tax reductions or outright grants, to induce businesses to locate in low-income areas. If the subsidy equated profit levels in low-income stores to those in other areas, the poor would benefit from the access to lower-priced goods. An alternative approach would be to force large stores to locate in poor areas. This would not be possible in all cases, but since public licensing of most types of business operations is required, government has some leverage in the matter.

The public at large would pay in either case. In the first instance, the subsidies would be paid out of tax monies; assuming the tax system is progressive, these would come primarily from high-income consumers. Under the second alternative, stores would have to raise prices throughout the community to make their ghetto operations profitable. Thus, consumers outside the low-income area would pay a subsidy in the form of higher prices.

In a positive vein, additional resources could be directed towards ghetto businesses. The efforts already under way have not been integrated into a comprehensive program. Ongoing financial support is necessary; but perhaps more important, programs are needed to develop managerial skills and provide assistance with management problems.

This discussion has been based on an urban setting, balancing conditions in one part of the city against conditions in another. For the rural poor, however, such adjustments may not be possible. Those living in depressed areas or as tenant farmers, migrant workers, or reservation Indians, are among the most needy. However, their isolation and scattered settlement patterns makes coordinated effort difficult. Furthermore, because they are less in evidence, they may not attract the same attention with their problems as the urban poor. The plight of such people as consumers is not going to be easily cared for. Community and rural development programs may help and cooperatives offer some hope. To help these people effectively will require increased economic opportunities for the rural poor, and also increased options for them as consumers. It is difficult to see how this can be attained without public support.

Neither the alternatives outlined here nor the variations on them that might be developed represent optimal solutions. At best they are temporizing; as interim measures, they could bring some benefits to low-income consumers. However, they cannot properly be termed solutions. That designation must be reserved for the direct attack on the fundamental problems of poverty and segregation, and finally, the social attitudes that allow such conditions to persist.

DISCRIMINATION AND CONSUMPTION

The poor, in addition to their other problems, bear a heavier burden of discrimination than other consumers do. Discrimination is probably best thought of in political, legal, or humanitarian terms, but it does have an economic side that directly affects consumption. Its results are sufficiently important for the subject to warrant a close examination.

Suppose you are looking for an apartment and you find two equally priced units. One is clearly preferable to the other in space, condition, and location. Now suppose that the landlord of the better apartment refuses to rent to you, so you are forced to take the inferior one. What does your choice of apartments—your consumption pattern—say about your own preferences? It says very little because you were not allowed to express your preferences; the choice was dictated to you.

Consumption patterns among the poor reflect a similar lack of choice. Analyzing these patterns as though they are the result of free choices will introduce a significant error, for consumption choices among the poor are artificially limited. The word *artificial* here means that considerations besides taste, price, and income enter into the decision.

The theory of consumer choice is developed around those elements. Given the level of their incomes, consumers are free to buy the combination of goods that brings them the highest level of satisfaction. If discrimination is involved, however, consumers do not enjoy that freedom. So it is that among the poor, observed consumption patterns may say very little about actual preferences. These patterns do show what the poor consumed with the choices they had, but they do not tell how the poor would have spent their money if their choices had not been restricted.

Restricted choice has troublesome ramifications. Housing is a good example. At any time, there exists a given amount of housing, a certain percentage of which will be suitable for low-income groups. Discrimination restricts the supply of housing for the poor by denying them access to units that would otherwise be available. Since the number of poor people seeking housing has not changed, but the available supply has decreased, the price of the remaining accommodations will be driven up.*

Higher prices are the immediate effect of discrimination, but its long-run impact may be even more damaging. Discrimination results in over-crowding in poor neighborhoods and this in turn contributes to a rapid decline in living standards. Carry the process very far and you have all the conditions that have come to be associated with ghettos. Discrimination in this case worsens an already difficult problem.

The impact of discrimination on the poor goes beyond limiting their choices in the marketplace. Job discrimination limits employment opportunities and thus perpetuates poverty. Educational discrimination is even more insidious. If the poor are denied equal access to education, they will be permanently handicapped. Lacking skills, they will not qualify for good-paying jobs that offer an escape from poverty.

Society as a whole also suffers from discrimination. The poor become its

* Which economics students know must always be the case when supply contracts and demand remains the same.

wards instead of being productive members. As a result, the society must bear the high cost of welfare payments and elevated crime rates in low-income neighborhoods. More important, the contribution that low-income individuals could make to society is lost. As a result, the well-being of society is reduced. That is an important point, for while it is fairly obvious that discrimination hurts the person against whom it is directed, the total effect of discrimination is not so clear. Suppose a man who does not like blacks is looking for a job; he has two offers, of which the better one involves working closely with blacks. Clearly, it will cost him to indulge his prejudices, for to do so he would have to accept an inferior position.

The same thing would be true if the man were an employer rather than an employee. The businessman who hires workers on some basis other than productivity places himself at a disadvantage. If a businessman refuses to hire the most qualified applicant because of his race, he will have to be content with a less productive worker. This will raise costs; the employer who does not discriminate will therefore enjoy an advantage [7, pp. [109–10]. One of the best examples of this was the integration of major league baseball. It is hard to imagine, but until after World War II, the majors were for whites only. When the color bar was broken in 1946, owners could not afford to ignore the talents of black players. Those who did, cut themselves off from players of outstanding ability and their teams suffered accordingly.

Professor Gary Becker has shown that discrimination can be analyzed in the same fashion as tariffs [1]. Tariffs increase the cost of imported goods and hence lower the overall level of satisfaction for the economy. Discrimination does the same thing. Employers who discriminate raise their costs and lower their output from a given amount of resources. As a result, the economy is worse off than it might be. If one person discriminates against another, both lose in economic terms. To the person doing the discriminating, that discrimination becomes a product to be consumed. The person with a taste or preference for discrimination pays for it, just as a person a taste for fine wine pays for the best vintages. This formulation explain why discrimination is so difficult to stop.

During Prohibition, it was illegal to consume alcoholic beverages even now there are restrictions on when, where, and by whom the consumed. Yet tastes were such that people were, and are, willing the law in order to drink. Similarly, those with a taste for di may be willing to break the law and face higher costs in or their preferences. That is hardly an encouraging thought who is being discriminated against. It does suggest the ne vigorous enforcement of antidiscrimination laws. Since d commodity, if its price is set high enough, most people sume it.

You may have noticed that there has been no m cost of discrimination. That is by design, for it shows humanitarian to appreciate the costs of discrimina sider themselves hard-headed realists interested only in dollars and cents would do well to consider that fact. When the human factor is introduced, the costs are magnified. Though these costs are more difficult to quantify, they are no less real.

The market is often condemned for being cold and impersonal, yet in this case the problem lies in the fact that personal distinctions made. It is people, not markets, who make distinctions based on race or religion. For the low-income consumer, the elimination of such distinctions would mean expanded choices and hence an improved standard of living. Any treatment of the problems of the poor must deal with that fact.

TOWARDS A PROGRAM OF ACTION

The Need for Special Protection

The poor are among the most vulnerable of all consumers; their need special protection follows. Under the concept of countervailing power, protection becomes a means of offsetting the disadvantages that low-consumers face in the marketplace. There is an obvious need to services available to the poor. Without a knowledge of the law, use it for their own protection. For the same reasons, they legal pressure. Among positive developments are legal aid en formed in many areas, bringing quality legal services he poorest consumers; private law firms are also be-ve to the needs of the poor.

d point is the need for more vigorous enforce-ection legislation. Present legislation covers mer fraud and credit policies to enforce-standards. All consumers are entitled these services to the poor is often d of this protection, the rationale uch protection to be effective, rights. Relations between pose tenants have fallen matically be evicted? not aware of their

be followed, pro-ent court decisions onsibilities. If, for ex-, the tenant may not have important in such cases that ore they get into potentially their leases, they need to know precisely what they are signing, what liabilities they are assuming, and what happens if the terms of the lease are not met by one party or the other. Education and information emerge as forms of protection, giving low-income consumers the ability to protect themselves.

Expanding this point casts protection in a different light. Too often, protection is thought of in *passive* terms. The consumer is being protected from something, so protection is thought of as a reaction to a threat. To be truly effective, protection needs to be *active*, which means equipping consumers to deal with their day-to-day problems in the marketplace. Therefore, affording adequate protection to low-income consumers requires the development of a comprehensive program. While legal services and improved enforcement are an important part of this program, they are not sufficient in themselves. Educational efforts and improved information flow are equally important. A coordinated effort is needed to bring all of these services to low-income consumers, making them all readily available within the community.

Problems of Credit

The broad definition of protection developed above can be expanded still further. In addition to the elements already considered, effective protection requires that mechanisms be established to deal with particularly pressing problems facing low-income consumers. Nowhere is this need more obvious than in relation to credit problems of the poor. Because the poor are not very good credit risks, they have difficulty in obtaining credit from conventional financial institutions. As a result, they are forced to turn either to personal finance companies or to individual merchants for credit. Neither alternative is very appealing for, under the best of circumstances, credit from such sources is expensive.

Because of the added expense, the borrower may find it difficult to meet the payments. A solution requires either more credit (and still more payments), or defaulting on the loan. The latter may be accompanied by garnishment or repossession. In the process, the consumer's prospects for obtaining credit in the future are further diminished. Once this cycle is established, it is difficult to break. The vulnerability of the poor compounds these difficulties. Because they lack alternatives, the poor are easy prey for unscrupulous merchants or finance companies. Contracts may be written in such a way that even the most experienced consumer would have difficulty in figuring them out. Hidden charges such as administrative costs, loan insurance, and prepayment penalties drive the true cost of credit even higher.

Improved education and information would help in this case, but they do not represent the final solution. Better-informed consumers might avoid some of the pitfalls mentioned, but they would still face the fundamental problem of being denied access to credit. No solution is possible without taking that into account.

The basic problem is with the system. Finance companies may be rightfully maligned, but it must be understood that they provide a definite service to the poor. Even if their rates are high, they do at least make credit available. It is in this sense that such companies are often referred to as the "poor person's bank." Until that function is assumed by institutions better suited to the needs of the poor, the problem will remain.

The problems encountered here are similar to those involved in the poor-pay-more argument. Again, the basic problem is poverty itself. In this case, however, institutional arrangements play a more important role. For example, the amount of interest that banks and other financial institutions can charge is set by law. Thus, while they might be willing to lend to the poor if they could charge additional interest to cover the higher risk, they are not free to do so.

It may seem strange that allowing banks to charge more would in any way benefit the poor. The fact that it would shows how much low-income consumers are already paying for credit. Even at higher interest rates, bank credit would still be preferable to alternatives currently available to the poor. In recognition of this fact, the venerable Federal Reserve Board itself lobbied against stricter limits on bank interest charges in late 1973.

To really come to grips with the problem, however, a more positive approach is needed. One obvious possibility is subsidizing loans to the poor. Credit could be granted through conventional sources, with the government paying the difference between actual interest charges and the true cost of the loan. Some programs like this are currently under way. The Federal Housing Authority supports programs to ensure the flow of mortgage credit to low-income persons—FHA 235.

Despite some obvious benefits, there are a variety of problems attached to this approach. The most important is its cost. If it were truly effective, an interest subsidy would be expensive. Furthermore, the administrative costs would be significant, particularly if each loan request were to be individually reviewed. Some interest subsidy might be desirable, but to rely on it as the sole means for increasing credit for the poor seems unwise.

A more promising approach is to insure loans to low-income consumers. The loan could be provided through conventional financial institutions; it could be provided at a more favorable interest rate because the guarantee would reduce the risk to the lender. If the borrower repaid the loan on schedule, no additional costs would be involved. Only when the borrower defaulted would the insurance become a factor. Such a program would not have to be totally supported out of public monies. Bank deposits, for example, are currently insured through the Federal Deposit Insurance Corporation, a publicly administered insurance scheme to which most banks contribute. A similar arrangement could be made to insure loans to the poor, with part of the money coming from the government and part from the banks themselves. The cost to any one bank would be insignificant and the risk would be spread over more banks.

It is important to emphasize the need for financial counseling as a complement to any program of this sort. The questions involved in the use of credit are complex, and consumers typically have trouble mastering all of them. Thus, it is not sufficient merely to make credit more available to low-income groups. To make that credit more effective, it is necessary to provide assistance in its use.

A thorough survey of the credit needs of the poor would also be useful. The greatest need among the poor may be credit to cover relatively small expenditures. If so, available funds could be stretched to help more people. That is merely a supposition, however, for the true dimensions of the problem are not known. More research is necessary to find out what actual needs are and to provide a basis for devising a program to meet those needs.

The problem as a whole can be traced to the market mechanism. The market may respond to pressure imperfectly, but it does respond. Those who lack the resources necessary to apply such pressure are simply bypassed by the market. In that sense, they are nonpersons. The question is whether a society can allow the existence of nonpersons and the institutions that create them.

Consumer Organization and the Poor

The thrust of this discussion concerns programs to help low-income consumers. The poor have recognized that a comprehensive program may not be forthcoming for some time. In light of this, they are organizing to meet their own problems. Somewhat surprisingly, perhaps, consumer organizations have made more headway among the poor than among consumers overall. That may seem surprising because the poor face the same kind of disadvantages when it comes to organization—namely, a lack of leverage— that they face in other areas. However, the lack of a specific goal, which is such a problem for most consumer organizations, is minimized in the case of the poor. The poor face a wide range of problems, but in most cases these are immediate and obvious. This provides direction and focus and simplifies organization.

The consumer organizations among the poor have taken different forms. Some have fostered boycotts or rent strikes in response to specific grievances. Others have lobbied for improved public services, such as transportation and law enforcement. Educational efforts have also been undertaken. Some groups have promoted local business development or the formation of cooperatives. Local conditions have determined the particular nature of the response.

Soon after the Office of Economic Opportunity was formed in the mid-1960s, it supported the development of neighborhood consumer groups. Their success in generating community support showed that they were fulfilling a real need. Unfortunately, many of these organizations endured stormy existences, which in many cases limited their effectiveness and contributed to their early demise. Their main problems centered around antagonism with the community at large. The community power structure took offense at their activities, and the groups came to be looked on as troublemakers. As funding for OEO was reduced and the office was dismantled, support for such efforts was phased out. While some groups continued to operate, the level of their activities was reduced.

There is a footnote to this story. Much of the money that had been channeled through OEO was diverted to state and local governments in the form of federal revenue sharing. Local officials, once they gained control of the money, could hardly be expected to continue to support programs of which they didn't approve. This raises serious questions about which level of government is actually most responsive to local needs.

To the extent that local governments reflect the local power structure, it must be concluded that such groups have a vested interest in the status quo. In some cities, citizens' groups have been formed to oversee the spending of revenue-sharing funds. Such groups may be necessary to ensure that federal monies are not diverted away from community action programs.

Not all consumer action groups met such an unhappy fate. Some have expanded their operations and effectiveness. One successful group is Philadelphia's Consumers Education and Protective Association (CEPA). This association works among the poor to promote consumer education, the investigation of complaints, and legal reform. The group has also supported more direct action with boycotts. The abuses that CEPA and groups like it have uncovered testify to the needs of low-income consumers [10, pp. 46–52]. Such testimony is hardly necessary. The needs of low-income consumers should be obvious. Even so, efforts to deal with the problem have thus far done little more than scratch the surface. There has been an unwillingness to come to grips with the problems of the poor as consumers just as there has been a reluctance to deal with the problem of poverty per se.

The most immediate need, then, is not for a particular program, but for a change in attitude. Until the public recognizes these problems and commits itself to dealing with them, little improvement can be expected. No one can predict when that recognition will come. It takes no particular insight to conclude that if it does not come, even more serious problems lie ahead. These will affect not only the poor but all consumers, and could shake the foundations of the consumer society itself.

STUDY QUESTIONS

1. In Chapter 7 it was argued that individual consumers have more leverage in small neighborhood stores. This is the type of store that low-income consumers most commonly shop in. Does the argument apply in this case? Explain.

2.   What parallels can you draw between the problems faced by college students living near a large university and those faced by low-income consumers? Show how the problems in each case arise from similar factors.

3.   Many college students have incomes below the poverty level and thus could be officially classified as poor. Even though they have similar incomes and face similar problems, what is the basic difference between college students and low-income consumers as discussed in the text?

4.   Why should low-income consumers in smaller cities be relatively better better off than consumers with similar incomes in larger cities?

5.   Efforts to build low-income housing outside of low-income neighborhoods have been resisted in many communities. If such projects are carried through, however, they help reduce the problems of the poor as consumers. Explain why that is so.

6.   In almost any city, low-income neighborhoods feature boarded-up stores and empty commercial buildings. Does this provide any insights into the problems of poor consumers? What does it suggest about possible solutions to those problems?

7.   The elderly, even those who are not poor, face many of the same problems as low-income consumers. Explain. What are the differences between the two groups as consumers?

8.   Problems that the rural poor face receive less attention than problems of urban poverty. Which group is better off as consumers, do you think? Explain.

9.   "If the poor had any pride, they wouldn't live as they do; they could at least find decent housing." Comment.

10.   Explain how the enforcement of antidiscrimination legislation can be considered a form of consumer protection.

11.   The discussion in Chapter 4 indicated that the smaller the down payment and the longer the payment period, the higher the total interest charge on a loan. What is the relevance of that fact to the low-income consumer?

12.   Would a loan-guarantee program such as that discussed in the text have a significant impact on interest charges paid by other borrowers?

SUGGESTED PROJECTS

The obvious project in this chapter deals with the poor-pay-more controversy. That is a considerable undertaking, however, and classes may want something less complex. Thus a number of alternatives are offered that deal with the question but avoid the technical difficulties involved in a full-scale investigation.

1.   Several assertions were made in this chapter about low-income consumers, including such things as their lack of mobility and their limited choice of stores. These can be checked by using United States census data. Large cities are broken up into census tracts; data such as income, automobile registration, and commercial establishments is given for each tract. Review these data for your city or some nearby city. What patterns emerge? Incidentally, census data are valuable as a research tool; students with an interest in these questions should become familiar with such statistics.

2.   Impressions can sometimes be misleading, but they do provide a basis for judgment. Spend some time browsing through stores in a low-income shopping area. Do you consider it a favorable environment? Make notes on the quality of merchandise offered, including produce and meats in groceries. Do you think quality varies from that available in other parts of town? Discuss.

3.   Those interested in a more systematic study may actually want to make a survey of prices in various parts of town. This must be done with care; it is also important to be discreet, since merchants (and sometimes consumers) are sensitive about questions on pricing.

In undertaking such a survey, there are two important points to keep in mind:

—Be sure that comparisons are made between comparable products and comparable types of stores.

—Be sure that you pick products that are actually being purchased.

The first point relates to the discussion in the text concerning the differences between large stores and small stores, product sizes, quality, and so on. The second concerns expenditure patterns of different income groups. Expensive cuts of meat, for example, are not commonly consumed in low-income areas. Similarly, comparisons of price on a large-console television-stereo combination would be misleading.

The Department of Agriculture publishes suggested grocery lists for different income levels; these might be used as a basis for comparing food prices. For other items, select products that you could reasonably expect residents of the area to consume.

It is probably best to make the survey relatively short. This might provide less information, but it will be easier to conduct and probably give you truer information. In interpreting the results, discuss possible sources of error or biases.

For additional information, check citations 2, 5, 6, and 12 in the Bibliography. Also, see Appendix.

4.   The credit problems facing low-income consumers were discussed at length in the text. Conduct a survey to see how interest charges vary in your area. Check conventional financial institutions, personal finance companies, and individual merchants. Be sure to include all costs of credit, not just the interest rate.

5.   If there is a legal aid society or similar group in your area, invite a representative to speak to the class on the legal problems of the poor.

6.   What sorts of programs are under way in your area to help low-income consumers? Survey private efforts, as well as those undertaken by state, local, or federal governments. Evaluate their effectiveness of these activities.

BIBLIOGRAPHY AND SUGGESTED READINGS

1. Becker, Gary. *The Economics of Discrimination,* 2d ed. Chicago: University of Chicago Press, 1971.

   The classic economic analysis of discrimination since the first publishing in 1957. The analytical going is a bit heavy at times, but even the novice can get something from this penetrating work. It is also valuable in illustrating the imaginative use of economic theory. For an introductory analysis, see [14].

2. Caplovitz, David. *The Poor Pay More.* New York: Free Press, 1963.

   The original inquiry into the problem. While Professor Caplovitz's methodology has been questioned, he may be credited with focusing public attention on this serious problem.

3. Cargill, Thomas F. "Credit Unions and the Low-Income Consumer." *Journal of Consumer Affairs,* Summer 1973, pp. 69–76.

   A study of OEO's efforts to expand the flow of credit to the poor via credit unions. Results suggest that credit unions can play a positive role in this regard.

4. Cohen, Wilbur F. "A Program to Abolish Poverty." In *Human Behavior in Economic Affairs,* ed. Burkhard Strumpel, et al. San Francisco: Jossey-Bass, 1972, pp. 523–48.

   A good treatise on the problems of poverty and how they can be met. Contains a good statistical summary.

5. Dixon, Donald F., and McLaughlin, Daniel J. "Do the Inner-City Poor Pay More for Food?" Temple University and the Academy of Food Marketing, 1968.

   A survey of food prices in Philadelphia, which suggests that while the poor do pay more, it is because they are forced to shop at high-priced, inefficient stores.

6. *Economic Report on Food Chain Selling Practices in the District of Columbia and San Francisco.* Government Operations Committee, U.S. House of Representatives, 91st Congress. Washington, D.C.: U.S. Government Printing Office, 1969.

    Another study of food prices, which again suggests that the problem centers on the types of stores available.

7. Friedman, Milton. *Capitalism and Freedom.* Chicago: University of Chicago Press, 1962. Especially Chap. 7.

    Not surprisingly, Professor Friedman sees discrimination in terms of market forces and therefore has little sympathy for legal restrictions. Required reading for anyone interested in the topic.

8. Friedman, Milton. *Study of Consumer Expenditures.* Vol. 18. Bureau of Labor Statistics–Wharton School. Philadelphia: University of Pennsylvania Press, 1957.

    An important study of consumer spending carried out in the 1950s. Evidence suggests that savings and expenditure patterns among blacks in segregated areas differs from patterns for whites of similar income.

9. Legal Aid Society of Polk County, Iowa.

    Legal Aid brings legal services to the poor and investigates problems facing the poor. In Iowa, the society successfully prosecuted a landmark case expanding the rights of tenants.

10. Magnuson, Warren, and Carper, Jean. *The Dark Side of the Marketplace,* 2d ed., Englewood Cliffs, N. J.: Prentice-Hall, 1972.

    A must for those interested in finding out about the fraud and deception practiced on the poor.

11. *National Advisory Commission on Civil Disorders: Reports.* Washington, D.C.: U.S. Government Printing Office, 1968.

    A review of the causes of the civil disturbances of the 1960s, including the part of ghetto merchants and their excesses.

12. National Commission on Food Marketing. *Special Studies in Food Marketing,* Technical Studies, nos. 7 and 10.

    Additional evidence on variations in food prices.

13. "Paying More for Being Poor." *Time,* December 1, 1967, p. 16.

    A report on congressional investigations of prices in the ghetto.

14. Samuelson, Paul. "Economics of Discrimination, Race and Sex." Chapter 39 in *Economics,* 9th ed. New York: McGraw-Hill Book Co., 1973.

    An introduction to the analysis of discrimination by a leading American economist. Those familiar with earlier editions of Professor Samuelson's text will not recall this chapter. Its inclusion reflects growing interest in these problems.

15. Smith, James D. "Birth Control and Economic Well-Being." In *Human Behavior in Economic Affairs,* ed. Burkhard, Strumpel, et al. San Francisco: Jossey-Bass, 1972, pp. 501–22.

A look at family size and income level, including needs of families of different sizes. Valuable for estimates of income need for different families.

16. Sturdivant, Frederick D. "Better Deal for Ghetto Shoppers." *Harvard Business Review*, March–April 1968, pp. 30–39.

A good summary of the problems of ghetto shoppers. Emphasis is on the efficiency of marketing in the ghetto.

17. Tuckman, Howard P. *The Economics of the Rich.* New York: Random House, 1973.

A recent study, which includes valuable information on distribution of income and wealth.

II

The Future of
the Consumer Society:
Waiting for the
Apocalypse

A FLAWED UTOPIA

"Emptiness, emptiness . . . all is empty," says the Speaker in *Ecclesiastes*, "What does man gain from all his labor and toil under the sun?" [I, iii]. The answer that the ancient Hebrews gave to that question is not known; certainly more and more people today find such questions bothersome and unsettling. That fact alone should give us reason to pause. Only a few years ago it would have been sufficient to answer that man's "labor and toil" had brought the unparalleled accumulation of material wealth—but no more.

The quote from *Ecclesiastes* was written over 2,500 years ago. While such questions are not new, the perspective from which we view them is. In earlier times, when most people lived at or near subsistence, the goal of satisfying material wants seemed sufficient. Now, most people in most Western economies can not only satisfy their daily needs but enjoy refinements that even their grandparents hardly dared dream about. That is a considerable achievement, but despite all this abundance, people have increasingly come to wonder if they are really any better off. What has really changed, then, is our idea of *better off* or *well-being*. These concepts have always been tied to the accumulation of material goods, the more affluent person being better off.* Now well-being is interpreted much more broadly.

---

* Statements like "Money can't buy happiness" are favored by people who have neither. Health may be the significant ·exception to the equation of materialism and well-being.

Wealth still plays a part, but it is now only one aspect of the definition rather than the definition itself.

It is not surprising that these changes should be most noticeable in the affluent United States. They are reflected in a variety of subtle ways, of which attitudes towards job satisfaction offer one illustration. People who have been out of work for some time will not be too particular about the kind of jobs they get; if they express any preference, it will probably be for a job that offers steady income. Yet in a survey of heads of households in the United States, George Katona found that only 34 percent gave job security the highest priority; almost the same number, 35 percent, ranked job satisfaction highest. By contrast, in Germany 70 percent put job security first and only 10 percent gave top priority to satisfaction [9, pp. 126–27].

You may recognize in this discussion the recurrence of several themes we have touched on before. With affluence, consumption itself becomes complex and its very definition changes. Consumers become less concerned with the goods itself and more mindful of the combination of characteristics it possesses. By extension, then, the consumer's perception of consumption as a whole changes with rising incomes. To many people, these changes have been unsettling. Professor Galbraith noted that until recently, success was defined in rather narrow, economic terms. He states that now, however,

> few will admit publicly to believing that the accumulation of wealth is the only measure of virtue. We have now a much more incoherent set of goals. . . . All of this, of course, has an aspect of chaos for people who were reared to believe in the simpler tests of economic performance. [6, p. 72]

Consumers today have realized the dreams of centuries, only to discover that those dreams were too small. The standards of measurement have been changed so that yesterday's utopia becomes today's stark reality. When the goal seemed to be within reach, it slipped away. Just as increased production is no longer a universally accepted goal for the economy as a whole, the additional accumulation of material goods is not accepted as the goal by all consumers. While fate has never dealt kindly with utopians, it is because their vision of the good life was dismissed as an impossible dream. Most utopian thinkers envisioned a world in which an individual's material needs would be fulfilled but subordinated to a sense of community, religious conviction, or love of humanity. In retrospect, that may seem like a vain hope. Yet in recognizing materialism itself as an inadequate goal, the utopians proved particularly discerning. To date, only the material aspects of their dream have been attained, and the results are decidedly non-utopian.

Consideration of the consumer's problems ultimately turns out to be an analysis of a flawed utopia. That may seem like a contradiction in terms, but it provides a useful point of view. The varied elements that intertwine in this analysis, while they ultimately converge, often seem to be moving in different directions. Analysis involves so many factors and they operate at so many different levels that it is difficult to bring them all into focus at the same time. Like so many of the problems encountered up to this point, there is no easy answer in this case. In facing this situation before, we tried to take the problem apart and look at its various components. That procedure did not always provide definitive conclusions, but it did allow us to make some sense out of what otherwise would have been a bewilderingly complex issue. That seems like the most profitable approach in this case too, but caution is required, because the way the different parts fit together is especially important. Understanding them in isolation is insufficient; it is necessary to understand how they interrelate.

To do that requires the recognition that the problems of the consumer society sprang from a variety of sources. Some of the problems can be traced to specialization, which makes greater affluence possible and isolates the consumer. Greater affluence, in turn works changes on the consumer; it changes both the pattern and the character of consumption. At the same time, various outside forces are working on the consumer. These include not only changing attitudes but technological constraints as well.

Working together, these forces have tarnished the cherished goal of affluence. Our purpose now is to see precisely how they have done it. In tracing the different elements and identifying the contribution each makes to the overall picture, we can reasonably assume that despite all the changes that have taken place, consumers' fundamental goals have not changed. That is, consumers would rather be better off than worse off. If people still prefer to be better off, but feel that they aren't, then the problem must lie with the definition of "better off." We suggested that earlier, when it was indicated that it is no longer possible to equate well-being with material accumulation. The problem now is to find out precisely what is meant by the phrase.

THE REALITIES OF THE CONSUMER SOCIETY

Hassled, Harried, and Humbugged

The most obvious drawback to the consumer society, with all its splendid affluence, is that it is a lot of bother. The accumulation of material goods itself creates problems, and the more sophisticated the goods, the greater the problems. This is the most basic aspect of the question; it has nothing to do with lofty notions of the meaning of life or the ultimate consequences of consumption. Rather, it concerns the simple fact that the more you have, the more you have to go wrong.

Let us take a mundane example, a lawn mower. The term *power* applied to lawn mower is a misnomer; all lawn mowers are powered, it is just that some are powered by people, while others are powered by machinery. The latter can make the job of cutting grass a lot easier, but at a price.

Power lawn mowers are not just more expensive to buy than hand mowers; they are more expensive to maintain. Gas, spark plugs, tune-ups, starters, and a lot of other things are necessary to maintain what looks like a relatively simple machine. People with hand mowers do not share these problems. They may have sore backs, but they are spared the frustration that goes with owning a power mower. If they want to (or more realistically, have to) mow the lawn, they can simply go out and do it. As long as they can keep themselves moving, there is no problem with keeping the mower moving.

Power mowers are not the only examples of devices that are supposed to simplify life but often end up making it more complex. Vacation homes are fine, but they mean two water heaters to worry about, two lawns to mow, and two roofs to leak. Similarly, color television is more of a problem than black-and-white; television more of a problem than radio; radio more of a problem than books, and so on. You can supply additions to the list yourself. In the extreme, this argument leads to the enslavement of individuals to their material belongings. Most people probably do not feel enslaved, but they are certainly more than a little aggravated. Our lifestyles have grown so complex and so dependent on so many things that the chance of any one thing's going wrong is greatly increased. Since things are so interrelated, when something goes wrong, everything else is affected.

It might seem that the increase in leisure time would offer some escape from these problems. Unfortunately, these same principles apply to leisure, or what passes for leisure. As Staffan Linder pointed out so well in *The Harried Leisure Class* [10], more people victimize themselves than are victimized when it comes to leisure. With increased affluence, leisure time becomes increasingly valuable. Because of its value, the natural tendency is to try to use it fully. That in turn leads to the feverish pursuit of leisure-time activities, a pursuit that is ultimately exhausting. Even people who manage to avoid such pitfalls cannot escape altogether. People who have been quietly enjoying tennis for years discover that its sudden growth in popularity means they cannot find a court. Those who simply enjoy walking in the woods now must be concerned with being run down by a maniac on an off-the-trail motorcycle. If Robert Frost were still alive, he would find it difficult to stop by the woods on a snowy evening without having his horse frightened away by a snowmobile. Quiet pleasures may be the best, but they are increasingly difficult to come by.

Some people do manage to avoid these problems. The very rich have others to worry about them, but the typical consumer, while affluent, is not rich. A few consumers are very wise, or perhaps merely lucky, but most of us do not fit under either of those headings. The result is that more and more consumers are questioning mass consumption not because they find it boring or distasteful, but simply because it is too much trouble. It is not a question of alienation or disaffection; it is rather a matter of the effort involved. These factors affect (or afflict) some consumers more than others. Most consumers, however, find themselves confronting these problems at some time or another. The drive for simplicity and the return to so-called natural pleasures reflects the fact that they provide the easiest path. All of this is difficult to face for people who have been raised in a society that glorifies material things, but more and more people are coming to accept the need for change.

Deep Down It's Shallow

While most people find that life in the consumer society is hectic, they are still trying to cope with its difficulties. Some, however, have carried their questioning a step further; they look at mass consumption and wonder what it has gotten us. If one believes the images that Madison Avenue flashes across the television screen, the paramount achievement of all of this is a clean bathroom bowl. The modern consumer, as portrayed in advertisements, seems to be concerned with little else. It is no wonder that real consumers have begun to question whether it has all been worth it. People find that increased consumption does not necessarily bring increased satisfaction. Particular wants may be satisfied, but life itself is not satisfying. As George Katona has noted: "*Excessive* materialism is not a necessary consequence of increased well-being or of striving for further well-being" [9, p. 200, emphasis added].

Additional words from *Ecclesiastes* are worth considering:

> What reward has a man for all his labor, his scheming and his toil here under the sun? All his life long his business is pain and vexation to him; even at night his mind knows no rest. This too is emptiness. [II, xxiii]

Though thousands of years separate George Katona and the Speaker in *Ecclesiastes*, they are both making the same point. The accumulation of material goods does not in itself guarantee a full and satisfying life. Indeed, its "pain and vexation" may detract from that goal. Professor Galbraith was saying something similar when he observed that in any definition of well-being,

> intellectual purpose has some role, new modes of life have some role and artistic purpose has some role. The sense of whether one is living a reflective and tranquil existence has begun to take on some meaning. [6, p. 72]

"A reflective and tranquil existence"—that single phrase sums up the changes that affluence has worked on the consumer. Would anyone have thought of asking a person in a 1930s breadline if his life was tranquil? It is highly unlikely. When people face serious economic dislocation, they are concerned with where their next meal is coming from. Reflection and introspection are luxuries that cannot be afforded until immediate needs have been fulfilled. These new goals may be incompatible with the old. A hassled consumer has little time for reflection. The continual pressures of modern life that beset the individual make tranquillity at once more attractive and more difficult to attain. That frustration and even hostility should result is not difficult to understand.

It is easy to see why today's radical thinkers have played on this theme, stressing alienation [7]. Paul Baran speaks of the "lethal fragmentation of the human personality under capitalism," and pleads for individuals to be considered as human beings, not as consumers [1, p. xvii]. In this text, the words *individual* and *consumer* have been used interchangeably, yet it is easy to lose sight of the fact that consumers are people and that the *consumer society* is *human society*. Growing concern with the reaction to the problems of affluence has been duly recorded by the media, thus focusing attention on some of the most intense manifestations. The counterculture receives close attention and life in the commune is well documented. However, the extremes affect only a tiny part of the population and are less significant than more subtle changes that are evident in the behavior of large numbers of people.

We have examined some of these in the text. While the vocational aims of students are often unclear, such uncertainty does not bother the students as much as it does their parents. It is increasingly common for students to break up their education with a year off to travel or to just work a while. Groups like the Peace Corps have been stripped of their earlier glamour, but they still have a strong appeal. Nor are these changes limited to students and youth. As Katona noted, workers are increasingly concerned with job satisfaction. Young executives are turning down promotions because it would require them to move, even though they know such actions slow their climb up the corporate ladder. In recognition of these trends, large firms are reexamining their personnel policies. Some now question the value of shifting people around just for the sake of a move. Others offer time off for public-service activities.

Since it is difficult to obtain a true perspective on these changes, it is easy to exaggerate their importance. Every era has its dropouts. American history tells the story of many utopian communities, like Brook Farm and New Harmony, and also religious splinter groups, like the Shakers. Recently, the years between the two world wars had their lost generation and featured Mencken's stinging satire on American life. In the past, however, such reactions were limited to fringe groups or elites. Now they are making an appearance in the American mainstream. That appearance coincides with a much broader reaction against modern, technological society. Rationalism and scientific inquiry, which have been the basis for most modern thought, face a growing challenge. There is a new emphasis on the senses, on feeling as opposed to knowing. Introspection and intuition have taken on new status, and so have mysticism, the supernatural, and exotic religious forms.

These reactions taken together show a dissatisfaction with modern life and all its complexity, and by extension the consumer society, itself an outgrowth of centuries of scientific invention and innovation. Mass consumption is such an integral part of the society as a whole that it is very difficult to analyze it as a separate question. The problems of consumption are the problems of modern society.

A House Divided

The points discussed thus far have been internal, growing out of the character of the mass-consumption society itself. One aspect, poverty in the midst of affluence, cannot be viewed as internal only. While it is an outgrowth of affluence, poverty acts, or has the potential to act, as an external constraint on consumption patterns. The last chapter dealt with the details of the problem. Now we need to look at the question in the broader context and see where poverty fits in the overall pattern of the consumer society. It is also necessary to look at poverty in the international context, which means reversing the sequence and considering the problems affluence creates in the midst of poverty.

It is obvious that most of the problems of affluence we have touched on do not apply to the poor. It is doubtful if many low-income consumers feel overburdened with material goods; similarly, few of them are bored with consumption or find it unfulfilling. Individuals are not very likely to worry about the real value of a third car or a second house if they are not sure about their next meal. While most consumers struggle with affluence, the poor must deal with a more immediate concern, scarcity. Such an unstable situation, if it endures, threatens the whole society. That the situation contains the roots of violence was well demonstrated in the 1960s; but violence is not the most serious threat. An affluent society that learns to live with poverty develops a callous disregard for its own problems; that sort of blindness must ultimately be self-defeating. If a society cannot respond to poverty, it can hardly be expected to respond to other, more subtle problems it faces.

A willingness to accept poverty can therefore be interpreted as a sign of social decay. It can only mean that the society has become self-seeking and self-indulgent. Those are hardly attributes associated with a vital, problem-solving people. Such a society is headed towards self-destruction. It is in that sense that poverty acts as an ultimate constraint on mass consumption. Even so, this is only a partial effect. The problems of affluence and poverty exist among countries as well as within countries. The world is divided into "haves" and "have nots," and most countries belong in the latter category. Areas like Western Europe, North America, and Japan are the exceptions. From a world view, the proportions are turned around and the problem is affluence in the midst of poverty [12].

Until recently, most Americans did not look at this situation in terms of its implications for mass consumption. However, like all affluent countries, America depends on resources drawn from low-income countries.

American affluence depends not only on Arab oil, but Bolivian tin, Zambian copper, Brazilian coffee, and Canadian timber.* Americans tended to take this for granted, even when it became clear that we were consuming a disproportionate share of the world's resources. Even though the United States has only about 6 percent of the world's population, over one-third of the world's resources is needed to keep its mass-consumption society going. The Arab oil boycott of 1973–74 graphically illustrated American vulnerability, at the same time representing only the tip of the iceberg. Similar efforts on other products may not produce boycotts but could contribute to rising prices and possible shortages.

Part of the problem lies in the perspective of consumers in the industrial countries. Because of their affluence, they tend to look on world resources as their own preserve, finding it difficult to comprehend the situation of people in less developed countries. Tourists, for example, fly halfway around the world to view game in East Africa without giving it a second thought. Yet within that area, competition exists between the game animals and the domestic herds of local inhabitants. Bitterness arises over claims that the latter suffer for the sake of rich tourists. This perception gap needs to be closed, as it poses a real threat to world economic stability. That threat clouds the future of both mass consumption in the industrial countries and the newly won increases in the standard of living in less developed countries. A difficult reassessment is necessary, but the pain will be much greater if the matter is ignored until it has reached crisis proportions.

The New Imperative

Resource availability deserves close attention. There are limited supplies of mineral resources and conventional energy sources, which raises the point whether affluent consumers can really afford the lifestyle they have developed. The final constraint on the mass-consumption society may be that it is too expensive. Excesses will have a twofold consequence. The first aspect is that critical resources may be exhausted. Even if they are not, there is the broader issue of how rising demands of mass consumption affect the environment. Increased production is required to meet these demands, and that places increased stress upon the environment.

Pollution is not new, but it was only after prosperity became well established that the problem became a main concern. The first concern of a poor economy is generating income; that the environment is damaged in the process is of secondary importance. To most people, a full stomach is more important than clean air and certainly more important than vague threats of future calamities. Thus, while affluent economies cannot afford to ignore the environment, less affluent ones cannot afford to consider it.

* Canada, of course, is a rich, industrial country, but it is a principal supplier of raw materials to the United States. The Canadians have become increasingly uncomfortable in this role and have taken steps to preserve their resources for their own use.

The public at first discounted environmental concern as extremism, and some of the gloomier predictions probably were. However, the seriousness of the problem soon became apparent as smog alerts were declared in large cities and floods caused by denuding of the countryside became more severe; specific problems, such as oil spills, were also recognized as serious threats. Environmental limitations began to loom as a plausible constraint on future growth. Even when those limitations were not immediate, people came to realize that their well-being was endangered because of environmental decay. Life in a city full of smog, noise, and congestion is not much fun. With this recognition, the environment came to be viewed as a part of consumption itself. Increases in one type of consumption—traditional goods and services—were endangering another, the environment.

All of this was taking place at a time when the average American assumed that there would always be enough of everything. Environmental decay might have suggested possible future difficulties, but it was not until 1972–73 that the word *shortages* sprang back in to the American vocabulary with dramatic suddenness. Food and fuel shortages began to appear. Meat prices soared, and there were times when no meat was to be had at any price. Other shortages followed, ranging from raisins to wood products, chemicals to plastics. Judged by an absolute standard, these problems were not severe, but they came as the first breezes hinting of an impending storm. From that standpoint, they were ominous indeed. It was over energy that the storm finally broke. With the Arab oil boycott of 1973–74, prices rose as supplies fell, and serious dislocations resulted. Unemployment rose as some industries could not meet their energy requirements and others, like automobiles, could not sell their output. Fuel oil was rationed, gas stations closed, and rationing of gasoline seemed probable as the lines at the gas pumps grew longer.

It may be that at some future date, these developments will be counted as blessings. Though they were bitter medicine, the rash of shortages provided dramatic proof of the problem. It should now be clear that the mass-consumption society can operate only at a very high level of resource use. It should be equally clear that consumption patterns must be reevaluated in that light to see if they are still viable. While all of this *should be* clear, some people tended to treat the problem as a momentary inconvenience. Once the immediate problems were past, they seemed to want to forget about them. The problem, however, will not go away. The shortages observed thus far are merely symptoms of a deeper problem, and to ignore them is as dangerous as ignoring the early symptoms of a serious illness.

It is possible to pick almost any area of American life and find examples of resource waste. Buildings are constructed so as to require year-round climate control, with no possibility of even opening the windows. Products are elaborately packaged in expensive containers. The ubiquitous aerosol can has become the symbol of this waste. Though pressurized containers are expensive and not very efficient, they are convenient, which explains why products as diverse as paint, deodorant, cheese, and frosting are packaged that way. It is in transportation, however, that the problem is most glaring. The American transportation system has grown up almost wholly around the private automobile. Few large cities have adequate public transportation systems, and this lack is still encouraged by government policy. The federal government is much freer with financing for highways than it is with monies for developing alternatives. To make all this worse, the big, heavy cars that are characteristic of United States production and consumption require substantial resources to produce and great amounts of fuel to keep them running.

Since we have been so wasteful, there are at least significant opportunities for improvement. Many people, however, have serious doubts as to whether or not curtailing waste would be sufficient. They maintain that even if we economize much more than we have shown any inclination to do in the past, the problems would still be overwhelming. Serious crises are predicted for as early as the 1980s, and certainly by the end of the century. Recent experience suggests that such projections should be taken seriously. The resource constraint is not a matter of personal choice. Consumers almost certainly will be forced to alter their consumption patterns. Such an alteration, if it is severe, could cause serious social strains. To avoid that unhappy possibility and to ensure that required adjustments are made as equitably as possible, it is necessary to begin now. That doesn't mean that everything has to be changed, but it does mean that everything has to be reevaluated according to a strict standard.

TOWARDS A RECONCILIATION

An Obvious Conclusion

We have outlined the main elements involved in the future path of the mass-consumption society. Despite the diversity of the forces at work, there is a common factor that unifies them. In every case, conditions have changed so that old assumptions are being called into question. It was always assumed that increased consumption would increase well-being, but increasing numbers of people find consumption either a bore or a bother. It was assumed that the problem of poverty would either take care of itself or at least exist quietly, yet neither has happened. It was assumed that resources would always be available and that the earth would regenerate itself, though neither seems to be true. Any society works on a set of premises or assumptions that give it a sense of continuity and stability. When these are shaken, repercussions are felt in every aspect of life. It should not be surprising then that these changes have shaken the life of the modern consumer. These are not superficial changes; there is nothing cosmetic about them. They represent a fundamental alteration in the approach to consumption, with affluence acting as the agent of change.

This is clearly a time of transition. That much is certain. Unfortunately, during any such period, the precise character of change is uncertain. Different forces are pulling in different directions at different speeds and until they work themselves out, the final result will be unclear. Therefore, it is dangerous, even reckless, to predict the precise path of future events. That should be sufficient warning against overgeneralizations and prepackaged conclusions. While the caution should be taken to heart, there is still something that can be said about the most probable course of future developments from the pattern of cumulative trends. That is hardly a sweeping claim, but it is all that anyone could justify at this point.

The Future—Prospects and Patterns

The surest clue that significant change is under way is the present questioning of the assumptions that have guided modern economic development. Unless people feel that conditions have changed, they will not feel the need to change the basic principles on which they operate. The need that increasing numbers of people now feel for such a change indicates that the consumer society has moved into a new phase.

In Western countries, particularly English-speaking ones, consumption has traditionally been viewed as a private affair based on choices of individuals. This intensely personal aspect of consumption may now be giving way to a new sense of community based on a recognition of interdependence among consumers. Individuals have come to realize that their own well-being is tied to the well-being of the community as a whole. Patterns of development differ among the affluent economies. The idea that individuals maximize their welfare by private market choices never took hold in Europe to the degree that it did in Great Britain and the United States. A sense of paternalism was retained in Europe that protected the consumer from many of the vagaries of the market. This sense was also reflected in attitudes towards change, which Europeans tended to resist, but Americans embraced.* Much of this resistance has broken down with recent economic advances in Europe; George Katona found, however, that in terms of attitudes and expectations, the European countries are still more "traditional," while the United States is more "dynamic" [9].

There is a paradox in the differentiation, which the Europeans, who have long suffered under such distinctions, are quick to point out. What has all this dynamism gotten the United States? It has generated the series of problems discussed above; the United States was the first to develop a mass-consumption society and therefore the first to face its problems. The Europeans can now afford to be smug and suggest that their more plodding approach may in the long run turn out to be superior. Related to future developments, however, is an important point that Katona has found; despite

* Katona quotes the European commentator and politician J. J. Servan-Schreiber, who said that Europeans "continue to suffer progress rather than pursue it." [9, p. 201]

the problems in the United States, American consumers are much more optimistic about the future than Europeans are [9, pp. 41–59]. Significantly, the differences are not restricted to older people. The differences are actually greater among younger people [9, p. 201].

That suggests that Americans have not given up on the consumer society despite their problems. It also suggests that those who predict dramatic change or expect the American consumer to make an about-face are bound to be disappointed. Change can be significant without being abrupt. Just as a building can be completely remodeled without altering its basic structure, the consumer society can undergo fundamental change without being dismantled and replaced. These realizations provide a framework for analyzing current developments as well as a good hint for future direction. You will recall that each of the four points discussed under the realities of the consumer society pointed to a depressed level of consumption in the future. Interpreted within the traditional framework, this would represent a significant movement away from mass consumption. The key phrase is "traditional framework," which implies the consumption of goods and services in the classic sense. However, with affluence, this traditional view is too narrow. Affluence changes the character of consumption, changes what is being consumed. In the context of Professor Lancaster's redefinition of consumption, the particular set of characteristics that people consume changes with rising incomes.

We related Professor Lancaster's argument that "goods are not goods" to such qualities as status and convenience. However, simplicity is also a characteristic, and so are a sense of contentment and peace of mind. Even Professor Galbraith's "tranquil existence" reflects a specific set of characteristics attributable to a particular consumption pattern. With affluence, people can afford to consume more goods with those particular characteristics. It may happen that the consumption of such goods will interfere with the consumption of other goods. At one level it is simply a question of deciding which is more important. People who value tranquillity will simplify their lives accordingly. The consumption of tranquillity, however, requires time, which is an increasingly scarce commodity. It is again a question of work versus leisure. People will choose the latter when it brings them more satisfaction than the consumption of actual goods and services.

Those who are devoted to the work ethic see an immense danger in that possibility. They conjure up images of a nation full of indolent people idly consuming leisure. Ambition, innovation, and progress become things of the past and the economy stagnates; the grasshoppers triumph over the ants. If you think about it for a minute, you should see that the fear of this danger is unrealistic. People are not about to turn their backs on materialism; they are too fond of it. Neither are they going to give up work, which makes possible consumption of all kinds. What they are doing, however, is taking a hard look at both. Materialism remains important, but it is a means, not an end. The end or goal is satisfaction, which requires more than just material goods. It requires, among other things, the time to enjoy material goods.

Leisure time now becomes a factor. There is much to be said for just sitting and thinking, but few of us would enjoy filling all our spare moments with such activity. Rather, people are beginning to view leisure in a properly creative sense. It offers the opportunity not just for relaxation, but also for individuals to develop their full range of talents. This is shown in growth of adult education programs and of interest in the arts and the highly individualized hobbies and crafts now available. Unfortunately, all of this got stuck with the name "doing your own thing," but at least people now realize that they have a thing to do. In a sense, that realization gives people the chance to become more human. If affluence means anything more than a clean bathroom bowl, it must mean that people have the opportunity to develop their own humanity. Those who worry about the overall level of economic activity should see that such pursuits generate economic activity for others; it is just that the composition of such activity has changed.

A similar pattern may be detected about work. As more and more Americans express a preference for jobs that are in some way satisfying, work is becoming more than merely a way to earn money. It is becoming a form of consumption itself. People are increasingly unwilling to segment their lives into *work* and *living*. They are looking for employment that offers them some sense of fulfillment, showing again a broad view of well-being. Workers are turning to jobs that may pay less but offer personal satisfaction. In the same view, employers are finding that to make their jobs attractive, they must emphasize such opportunities. When these opportunities are minimal, problems develop. Assembly-line jobs, for example, may be well paid, but they are largely boring and repetitious. Workers develop the so-called blue-collar blues, with corresponding increases in absenteeism and labor turnover and decreases in performance. To counteract this, some large firms have successfully experimented with efforts to break up the assembly line. Workers are responsible for producing an entire unit, with appropriate rewards for quality work.

All of this points to a large-scale redefinition of consumption. The reinterpretation of consumption has actually been under way for some time, although people may not have been aware of it. Pets, particularly dogs, offer an example of goods that are still being *consumed* as before, but for quite different reasons. The American Kennel Club retains a classification of "Working Dogs," which illustrates the change. At one time, all dogs were working dogs; if they did not work, they were not kept. Now, except for a few farm animals and creatures kept by their masters for security, dogs are consumption items.

A similar change is evident with children, if you will allow the comparison. When society was primarily rural and agricultural, children were an important source of labor; they also were a sort of social security for their parents. Few children today perform either of those functions; they represent instead a very expensive form of consumption. A 1972 estimate indicated that it could cost a family up to $200,000 to raise two children and put them through college [8]. This includes income lost by the mother who stays home with her children, a figure that will obviously vary. It still helps explain why more young couples are limiting their families; they cannot afford not to. More properly, they prefer to vary their consumption rather than taking it all in the form of children.

What is happening, then, is that people are consuming more, not less, but they are also consuming differently. They are much more sophisticated in their consumption. There is no reason to assume that these trends will not continue into the future. The opposite can be expected—there is every reason to suspect that the trends will become more pronounced. Abba Lerner had something like this in mind when he looked into the future and suggested:

> Perhaps the only possibility of a state of plenty lies not in the increase of goods, but in the reduction of wants. If a culture of simple living on Gandhian lines should be universalized, it might indeed be possible to provide fully for the requirements of all. [11, p. 266]

On the face of it, that might not seem very probable. Despite the interest in Eastern religions, it is unlikely that most people are going to begin living like Indian ascetics. If, however, you substitute "redirection" for "reduction" and interpret "Gandhian lines" to mean a concern with the quality of life, then the possibility seems much less remote.

Despite present trends, some might argue that things will not work out this way. They can point to examples of self-indulgent consumption that suggest a much less promising future. There is really no final answer. Clearly, however, it is not a question of the continuation of the consumer society in its traditional form versus the sort of transition discussed here. If the trends identified here do not assert themselves and gain the ascendancy, the mass-consumption society is in serious trouble. If mass consumption cannot adjust to both the needs of individuals and the realities of world resources, then it is surely doomed. Those who lack a taste for apocalyptic visions will see that there is really no alternative. It is not an *either-or* matter, but rather *if-then*. If the adjustments that are already under way continue, then the prospects for the future are encouraging indeed; if not, there is little reason for optimism.

Here again, perspective is important. It is easy to get carried away with dreams of bright or dismal tomorrows. The typical consumer, however, does not think about such things very much. Most of us are small thinkers most of the time. Even college professors, who have more time for such reflections than most people, are preoccupied with mundane questions of tenure, raises, or how to pay for braces on the children's teeth. This is probably a good thing. As people quietly go about the business of living their own lives, they may unobtrusively come to many of the same conclusions outlined here. As they do, the accumulation of small, subtle changes will produce a significant alteration in modern society. That may be the ultimate significance of the consumer revolt. "It is," to close with Professor Galbraith's words, "a revolution not in economic forms, but in values" [6, pp. 71–72].

STUDY QUESTIONS

1.   One of the great themes of American history has been the democratization of areas that were previously the reserve of elites. Thus, art and literature broadened their appeal to serve a mass audience. The widespread concern with the quality and significance of life represents a continuation of this trend. Can you give any other examples of this process? What is the significance of such developments for the consumer society?

2.   Occupational fields like journalism, the law, and teaching, which offer flexibility and some freedom from routine, are becoming increasingly popular. Explain this development in terms of this chapter. What changes will this bring about in other types of employment?

3.   In Chapter 1, recent reactions to materialism were described as *conspicuous nonconsumption*. That is not entirely accurate. Why?

4.   In *Porgy and Bess*, Porgy sings, "I've got plenty of nothing, and nothing's plenty for me." Would most people agree with that? If nothing is not plenty, what is?

5.   People who are unemployed typically expend a great deal of effort searching for jobs that will reduce the leisure time they have. If they are successful, they will then spend equal amounts of effort to eke out a bit more leisure. Does this sort of behavior make any sense? Explain.

6.   One worker to another on Monday morning: "I'm glad to get back to work so I can recover from the weekend." Comment.

7.   A century ago, workers were pressing for a 60-hour work week and a 12-hour workday.
   a.   Can you compare what leisure meant to workers then with what it means to today's workers?
   b.   There has been an obvious explosion of leisure time in the last 100 years. Why, then, should leisure remain such a scarce commodity?

8.   In mid-1974, the Japanese finance minister said that Japan would have to lower its growth rate to avoid increased criticism for depleting world resources. In what way is that a historic comment? Could it have been made a generation ago? Discuss.

9.   The world of the future, as science fiction portrays it, features a computerized life of leisure. What would be the value of leisure under such conditions? Would work—any work—be valued differently from the way it is now valued?

10.   New consumption forms, like traditional ones, may contain internal contradictions. Thus, the peace and quiet of a remote cabin hideaway may be highly valued, but if everyone sought such a refuge, the countryside would be overrun. Is there any way around this kind of problem? Discuss.

11.   The coming years are not going to be easy ones for consumers. What sorts of people are going to find the adjustment most difficult? Is there any way these difficulties can be eased?

12.   Do you think changes in consumption patterns will make public goods more or less important? Explain. Will changes in the composition of private consumption also call for new forms of public consumption? Discuss.

BIBLIOGRAPHY AND SUGGESTED READINGS

1. Baran, Paul. "A Marxist View of Consumer Sovereignty." In *The Political Economy of Growth*. New York: Monthly Review Press, 1957.

   Marxism, like most other ideologies, has its own utopian vision. Baran looks to a world free of the dehumanizing influences of capitalism.

2. Boulding, Kenneth E. "Human Betterment and the Quality of Life." In *Human Behavior in Economic Affairs*, Burkhard Strumpel et al. (ed.). San Francisco: Jossey-Bass, 1972, pp. 455–70.

   A leading economist and social scientist looks at human betterment in a broad perspective. Professor Boulding takes a careful look at the question in terms of a dynamic system, finding that things may go "from bad to better, or from bad to worse."

3. *Ecclesiastes*, in *The New English Bible*. New York: Oxford University Press, 1971.

   One of the most thoughtful, and many feel most beautiful, books in the Old Testament. Regardless of how one feels about religion, the significant and timely questions it raises are worth pondering.

4. Galbraith, John Kenneth. *The Affluent Society*. Boston: Houghton Mifflin Co., 1958.

   In the context of this chapter, it is clear that Professor Galbraith understood the process of affluence before most people were aware of it. A good starting point for anyone interested in the topic.

5. Galbraith, John Kenneth. *Economics and the Public Purpose*. Boston: Houghton Mifflin Co., 1973.

   In this, his newest, book Professor Galbraith continues the line of thought developed in his earlier work. As the title implies, he is not convinced that the public interest and the interest of the economy as currently organized are the same.

6. Galbraith, John Kenneth. As interviewed in *Forces*, no. 22, 1973, pp. 71–75.

7. Gintis, Herbert. "Consumer Behavior and the Concept of Sovereignty: Explanations of Social Decay." *American Economic Review, Papers and Proceedings* 62 (May 1972): 267–78.

A radical economist and the alienated consumer.

8. "The High Cost of Kids." *Newsweek,* January 10, 1972, p. 36.

A report on the ever increasing cost of raising children. Estimates were prepared by the Commission on Population Growth and the Future.

9. Katona, George, Strumpel, B., and Zahn, D. *Aspirations and Affluence.* New York: McGraw-Hill Book Co., 1971.

An excellent comparative study of trends in consumption patterns and consumer expectations in Europe and the United States. One of the best available sources on the subject.

10. Linder, Staffan B. *The Harried Leisure Class.* New York: Columbia University Press, 1970.

An excellent analysis of what it means to be affluent. Again, this is a classic on the subject of the consumer's problem in the high-pressure, mass-consumption society.

11. Lerner, Abba P. "The Politics and Economics of Consumer Sovereignty." *American Economic Review, Papers and Proceedings* 62 (May 1972): 258–66.

12. Myrdal, Gunnar. *An International Economy.* New York: Harper & Row, 1969.

A sympathetic treatment of the problems of underdeveloped countries by the noted Swedish economist. Professor Myrdal has continually emphasized the policy implications of international income variations.

13. Scitovsky, Tibor. "Arts in the Affluent Society: What's Wrong with the Arts Is What's Wrong with Society." *American Economic Review, Papers and Proceedings,* May 1972, pp. 62–77.

An interesting look at the arts and affluence by a leading economist. Contains comparisons of support for the arts in Europe and the United States.

14. Zahn, Ernest. "The Consumer Society: Unstinted Praise and Growing Criticism." In *Human Behavior in Economic Affairs,* Burkhard Strumpel, et al. (ed.). San Francisco: Jossey-Bass, 1972, pp. 433–51.

A highly relevant paper in terms of this chapter. Especially strong in tracing intellectual attitudes towards the consumer society in the postwar years. As good a summary of the question as there is available.

Appendix

As mentioned in the Preface, the projects included at the end of the chapters are based on the idea of the marketplace as a laboratory. All students are consumers, and the projects are intended to relate their daily problems to the material covered in the text. In this relation, the projects show theory in action and stress applying concepts to real-world conditions.

If one includes controlled conditions in the definition of a laboratory, the market does not serve very well. So many different forces are at work in the marketplace that they are difficult to isolate. The variation leads to all the methodological problems with which researchers in the social sciences are so painfully familiar. The projects in this book will provoke problems. Many of them involve sampling or surveys, subjects that in themselves provide sufficient material for several courses. In using these projects myself, I have found two successful approaches. The size and complexion of the class must determine the proper response.

The first is to meet the problems head on, dealing with them as one would in a scientific, professional paper. This requires concentrating on a few projects and developing them in depth. It also assumes either that students have a background in sampling and testing techniques or that they are willing to do a great deal of extra work. This approach is more difficult in a large class, but under the right conditions and with the right students, it can be rewarding.

Most of us, however, work most of the time under conditions that are not ideal and with students who are not expert at these procedures. These facts of life argue for an alternative approach. The alternative requires a flexible attitude, beginning with the recognition that the projects are not going to provide definitive results or break new scientific sod. Such was not the intention for the projects anyway. The efforts can nonetheless uncover interesting trends and provide significant insights, without meeting all the requirements that might be set for a Ph.D. dissertation.

The projects are, above all, a learning tool. They are meant to involve the students, give them experience in the field, and provide a basis for discussion. Being overly rigorous may actually detract from these goals. That is not an invitation to be sloppy and careless; it means the projects should be evaluated in terms of what they are intended to do. The results cannot be treated as definitive and must be interpreted with care. But they can provide a basis for discussion and be a means either to underscore key points or to draw out new ones. In most cases, the projects are best viewed as preliminary investigations. As such, they can be most valuable.

Perhaps what is more important, they can also be enjoyable. My experience has been that students respond very well to these challenges. Most seem to welcome the opportunity to take their education beyond the classroom and into the real world. As they do, they show remarkable initiative and imagination. Carrying out the projects may be as valuable as the results obtained. The students, in wrestling with designing questions and conducting surveys, gain a significant appreciation of both the issues and problems involved. For many, it may be their first real research experience, and while not many will win their wings, most will enjoy trying.

Several practical hints are worth passing along. When possible, it is useful to sample different groups. These can include groups of students, neighbors, or randomly selected individuals. It is not necessary to worry overmuch about being truly scientific, but it is worth trying to get a representative survey. How questions are designed is very important. Simple straightforward questions are the best. In most cases, however, it is also useful if people will just discuss the question in general terms. Impressions collected in this way can be most valuable. It goes without saying that tact is required in personal contacts. That is equally true of the price surveys and comparative-price projects. Merchants are often not humored by such efforts. There is nothing wrong, however, with simply going in and asking about prices as any customer would. That is probably the best approach to take.

Problems are not likely to be significant, except in the case of the comparison of prices in low-income and other areas suggested in Chapter 9. Not only are the methodological problems more significant in this case, but in many areas the issue has become hypersensitive. Thus, considerable discretion may be required; the instructor can decide what approach to make, according to local conditions.

The projects included in the text are merely illustrative. Individual instructors can think up their own projects according to local opportunities and the interests of the class. Students can also contribute their ideas. There is no shortage of possibilities. No projects were included for Chapters 2 and 11, but some opportunities exist and instructors may wish to devise their own.

The manner in which the projects are used depends on the individual instructor. I have found it useful for students to carry out the project, report it to the class, and lead the discussion that follows. In this way, it is possible to build the class session around the projects. That takes time and creates certain organizational problems, but it is worth the effort. With big classes, that procedure may not be practical. It might then be advisable to make the projects optional, have reports on only selected projects, or have the projects written up but not reported to the class. The projects could even be a basis for discussion without actually being carried out.

Our clarification has concentrated on projects that involve surveys or actually going out into the marketplace. Some projects concern other aspects, either library research or reviews of local laws and institutions. These present fewer methodological and practical problems, but are no less useful.

Suggested projects in some of the last chapters of the book mention using resource persons from the community in the class. There is an obvious danger here; those who have yawned their ways through such talks are well aware of it. For that reason, prior contact is advisable. However, if such persons are carefully chosen and presented, they can make a valuable contribution to the class. There are increasing numbers of competent, well-trained, and dedicated people serving in the consumer area. Their experiences and perspectives can be most useful. In most cases, they are only too willing to have the opportunity to air their views.

It may be that once the project approach itself has been accepted, the details are not particularly important. Most instructors can work them out for themselves according to the specific conditions. The idea of using the market as a laboratory is important, however. It expands the scope of the course and provides a unique opportunity to integrate classroom material with experience. Some instructors might want to cooperate with a local consumer protection group. Others might want to develop a unified theme throughout the semester. All will find, as I have found, that projects can give the course personality and can focus classroom activities.

Index

Date Due
